Seamanship

FLAG MEANINGS (SINGLE LETTER SIGNALS)

signify very urgent or important … common use.
May be made by any … * see note 1)

A I have a DIVER D… well clear at slow …

*B I am taking in or di… … or carrying DANGEROUS GOODS

C YES (affirmative.)

*D KEEP CLEAR of me I am MANOEUVRING WITH DIFFICULTY

*E I am ALTERING my course TO STARBOARD

F I am DISABLED, COMMUNICATE with me

G I REQUIRE A PILOT (when made by fishing vessels operating on the fishing grounds - "I am hauling nets".)

*H I HAVE A PILOT on board

*I I am ALTERING my course TO PORT

J I am ON FIRE with DANGEROUS CARGO on board, KEEP WELL CLEAR

K I WISH TO COMMUNICATE with you

L You should STOP your vessel INSTANTLY

M MY VESSEL IS STOPPED and making no way through the water

N NO (Negative.)

O MAN OVERBOARD

… - all persons … port on board - vessel is ABOUT to PROCEED TO SEA
At sea - fishing vessels - "My nets are fast to an obstruction"

Q My vessel is HEALTHY and I REQUEST FREE PRATIQUE

*S My ENGINES are GOING ASTERN

*T KEEP CLEAR of me ; I am engaged in PAIR TRAWLING

U YOU ARE RUNNING INTO DANGER

V I REQUIRE ASSISTANCE

W I REQUIRE MEDICAL ASSISTANCE

X STOP carrying out YOUR INTENTIONS and WATCH FOR MY SIGNALS

Y I AM DRAGGING MY ANCHOR

Z I REQUIRE A TUG (made by fishing vessels on the fishing grounds - "I am shooting nets"

NOTES
1 * When made by sound these signals must comply with the requirements of the International Regulations for Preventing Collisions at Sea, Rules 15 & 28.
2 Signals 'K' and 'S' have special meanings as landing signals for smallboats in distress (International Convention for the Safety of Life at Sea 1960)

Seamanship

Seamanship

Robin Knox-Johnston

Hodder & Stoughton
LONDON SYDNEY AUCKLAND TORONTO

British Library Cataloguing in Publication Data

Knox-Johnston, Robin
  Seamanship.
  1. Sailing   2. Seamanship
  I. Title
  623.88'223   GV811

  ISBN 0-340-37995-2

FOR BERTIE MILLER
who taught me the basics of seamanship

CONTENTS

INTRODUCTION

The essence of a good seaman is a member of the crew who can, in accordance with the old definition, 'hand, reef and steer'; in other words one who knows what he's doing about the boat, and does it enthusiastically whilst anticipating what he might need to do next.

Seamanship is the knowledge and skill required to be a good seaman, which enables the efficient and practical management of a boat, both at sea and in port.

In its widest sense, the subject includes everything involved in the safe voyaging of a boat from its departure port to its intended destination. But in this book I have largely ignored navigation, knowledge of Maritime Law, sail trimming and engineering as these aspects are more than adequately covered by specialist books on their individual subjects.

Seamanship, in the sense that I mean it, is a dynamic art, constantly adapting to new ideas and materials. In the golden age of sail, when the only form of sea transport was by sailing ships, seamen were quick to adapt and adopt new ideas, and the same applies today. The seaman of even a hundred years ago would have envied us flexible steel wire rope, man-made fibres and sailcloth, stainless steel, and so on, but he had learned how to use his inferior materials remarkably efficiently. Many of these old techniques are still in use, and most of our modern ways of doing things are developments of well tried and trusted methods.

I have included most of the current methods used to carry out the seaman's task, together with examples of some of the older methods, many of which have fallen from use aboard today's boats. The knowledge of how these older evolutions were worked often helps one find a solution to a modern problem.

From making the right knot, to predicting the weather correctly, it all becomes easier with practice. The more you learn, the more knowledge you can bring to the solution of a problem; and there is nothing quite as satisfying as knowing that you have done a job properly and in a seamanlike manner. This will provide the enthusiasm to tackle the next job and make your seamanship fun – which is what it ought to be.

Parts of a Yacht

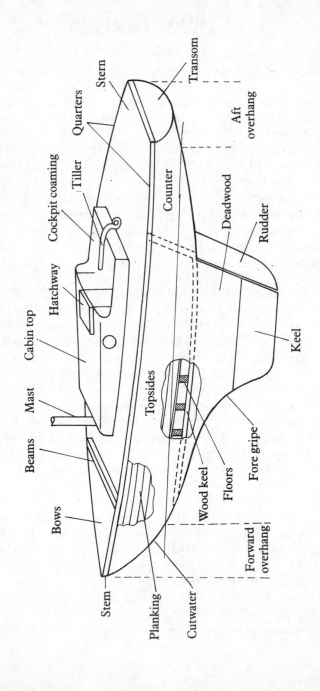

1 BOAT HANDLING

STEERING

Compass Every sailor should be familiar with the layout of the compass card and how it is divided. The modern method of division into 360° is easy to follow. The revolution commences with zero on north, with east being at 90°, south at 180°, west at 270° and back to north again at 360°. The older system of points and quarter points required the helmsman to memorise 128 different quarter points. In this system, the card was divided into 32 points, and each of these points subdivided into quarter points.

To steer a course by compass, the lubber line, that is the mark inside the forward end of the compass in line with the boat's head, is brought round by swinging the boat, until it is on the desired point on the compass. A newcomer to sailing invariably has difficulty at first in grasping the concept that you take the lubber line round to the desired compass course and not the other way round. It is sometimes hard to visualise that the small compass card is the fixed object which always points in the same direction, because the boat seems so much more solid, but a novice helmsman will find things a lot easier if he can think of the compass in this way. An inexperienced helmsman must be expected to relapse from time to time, and go 'chasing the lubber line', trying to take the compass point to the lubber line instead of the other way round, and should always be put on watch with someone with steering experience.

Magnetic compasses, of course, point towards the north *magnetic* pole, and this is not necessarily the True north geographical pole. Furthermore, the north magnetic pole moves about very slowly. To add to our miseries, the lines of force between the south and north magnetic poles do not run in straight lines and so the difference between the magnetic and true norths varies all over the globe. However, the effect on the compass, known as variation, is shown on navigation charts.

There is no way of correcting the compass for variation, and so the course must be adjusted to take it into account. The rule is to subtract westerly variation from the compass course to find the true course, and add easterly variation. A simple method of remembering how to correct the error is:

Variation West – Compass Best
Variation East – Compass Least

Thus, if the variation at a particular place in the world is 15° west, the compass course will be greater than the true course, i.e. for a true course of 275°, the course to steer would be 290°. If the variation were 15° east, the compass course to steer for a true course of 275° would be 260°.

The other error of the compass with which the helmsman should be familiar is due to the magnetic variances caused by the metal in the boat and is known as deviation. This can be compensated for by means of corrector magnets, and is usually carried out by a specialised compass adjuster when a boat is commissioned or after a major refit or long lay-up. The compass adjuster will produce a deviation card once the compass has been corrected and swung to find out the deviation on each major heading, and this card will show the final small errors left on each heading which are due to the boat's magnetic influence. The deviation is applied as a correction to the compass course in exactly the same manner as the variation.

Example:
Course required 275° True. Variation 15°W, Deviation 3°E
275° + 15° Variation − 3° Deviation = 287° Compass Course

Course required 165° True. Variation 8°E, Deviation 2°E
165° − 8° Variation − 2° Deviation = 155° Compass Course

Course required 050° True. Variation 7°E, Deviation 3°W
050° − 7° Variation + 3° Deviation = 46° Compass Course.

The true course corrected for variation only is known as the magnetic course. The true course corrected for variation and deviation is known as the compass course.

The navigator should always give the helmsman the course to steer as a compass course, but a helmsman should aim to understand how the compass course is arrived at.

Because the compass will align itself with the magnetic lines of force passing through its position, it follows that anything with magnetic properties placed close to the compass will alter these lines of force and thus cause the compass to become inaccurate. The helmsman should make sure that there is nothing magnetic about his person, such as a knife, and that magnetic objects are not placed close to the compass by accident. It is all too easy for beer cans to end up next to the compass during Happy Hour and these can cause quite large swings in the compass. The effect of a magnetic object upon the compass decreases by the cube of its distance from the compass. Thus a beer can one foot away from the compass is the equivalent of three beer cans two feet away.

Although it is unusual for helm orders to be used on a small boat, a knowledge of them and their meaning can be useful, particularly in difficult navigation conditions where the navigator or skipper might be in the bows of the boat and wishes to give a change of course to the helmsman.

Steering orders Nearly everyone has heard of 'Hard a-port' or 'Hard a-starboard', meaning, turn the tiller or wheel so that the rudder comes over to its stops on the port or starboard side respectively, but this is almost always an emergency order, and causes a violent change of course. If less rudder angle is required, the order would be perhaps, 'Port or starboard 10', meaning to put the rudder over to 10° from amidships. On receiving this order the helmsman repeats the order, turns the wheel or tiller to give the required rudder angle, and then reports '10 of port wheel on.' It is up to whoever is conning the boat to tell the helmsman when to bring the helm back or increase the angle, by giving an order such as 'Port 15' or 'amidships'. All such instructions are repeated, and the report is made when the instruction has been carried out to avoid a misunderstanding.

Other common instructions are 'Ease the helm', meaning to reduce the amount of rudder angle. If the order 'Port 15' had been given, followed by 'Ease the helm', the helmsman would reduce the angle to about half.

'Steady' is used when the helm is over and the boat comes onto a desired course. The helmsman notes the compass course, or an object ahead at the moment the order is given and then steadies the boat on that heading. The person giving instructions should always try to let the helmsman ease the helm before giving the order 'Steady' as otherwise the helmsman will have to apply a lot of helm the other way to bring the boat on course.

'How's your head?' is a question to the helmsman asking not how is his hangover from a previous night's run ashore, but to call out what heading the boat is on at that particular moment.

'Steer . . .' is the instruction to steer a new course, and will normally be given after 'Steady' and 'How's your head?', when the navigator wants to adjust the new course.

The helmsman should always report if the boat loses steerage. This means that the boat has stopped and is no longer responding to the action of the rudder.

Finally, when handing over the helm to someone else, the helmsman should clearly tell him the course and the new helmsman should repeat it. This avoids confusion, and the wrong course being steered accidentally. He should also make sure that his successor is steering the proper course before going below. The course that has been handed over should be told to the watch leader, who should satisfy himself that the new helmsman is steering this course.

Helmanship This art can only be mastered by practice. The objective is to keep the boat on a straight course with minimal use of the rudder, and this is only achieved when the helmsman has the feel of the boat, and can anticipate the effects of wind, sea and swell.

Some people find it easy to steer on a fixed point of the compass, others will steer a steadier course if they are allowed to steer between two points such as, for example, 350° and 360°, because they anticipate the swings better. An experienced helmsman should be able to hold any course given to him, but it is worth experimenting with an inexperienced helmsman to see which method gives the best performance.

The most common fault is to use too much helm to bring the boat back on course. This often leads to over-correction of the swing, and the helm has to be swung the other way again. A good helmsman should aim to apply just sufficient helm to bring the boat back on course and no more. This skill does not come overnight and calls for plenty of practice. In time though, a person can anticipate when the boat is going to start to yaw off course, just from the feel, and apply corrective helm in advance.

Holding a steady course is most difficult in a following sea, because the boat will be pushed around by the seas, and most compasses will swing about as the boat pitches and rolls. A helmsman will attempt to try and hold a compass course, but the compass will be misleading him because of its swings. In these circumstances, try to find something on the horizon, or at night a star, to steer for. Even if, by day, there is no land in sight, use waves or clouds as a heading reference, glancing at the compass when the boat is steady to check the heading.

On a sailing boat, steering a particular course is likely to be less important than sailing to a certain apparent wind angle. The compass course will vary with changes of wind speed and direction. In this case, one of the easiest ways to steer is to get the boat onto the required heading and then note the compass heading. The compass becomes a reference for the course, and by glancing in turn from the wind angle indicator to the compass, a good course can be sailed, and the helmsman will notice any changes that occur in wind force or direction.

If boat speed is the criterion rather than a particular course, the helmsman will have to concentrate on holding the correct wind angle. In light weather the apparent wind can play tricks. The instruments at the masthead may be well damped, and react slowly or jerkily to changes of wind direction. In these circumstances it is easy to steer round to keep the apparent wind angle at its correct angle on the display and then suddenly find the boat has gone about. The secret is to find out from where the true wind is coming, using the smoke from a cigarette or something similar as a guide (if the boat is moving, the smoke will show the apparent wind). Then choose a suitable course and steer by the compass ignoring the wind indicator, which will fluctuate quite a lot, but the boat will be kept moving, and tacks, which cause it to stop, will be avoided. It is necessary to check the apparent wind direction at frequent intervals, but, once the boat is moving, the apparent wind should increase and then the instruments will be more reliable.

Every time the rudder is moved from amidships it is creating drag, so the less it has to be moved the faster the boat will go. On a flat sea, steering a steady course without having to use much rudder is quite simple, but the moment the boat starts to pitch in a head sea, or yaw in a following sea, the rudder is going to have to be used to correct the course. The skill comes in using the minimum amount of rudder necessary to hold the course, and anticipation of the boat's movements to avoid yawing.

When tacking, gybing or making any alteration of the course, apply only as much helm as is required to bring the boat round in a wide arc. This keeps the way on the boat and, particularly when tacking, means that the boat should still have headway on as the sails are sheeted in. All too often in the excitement of the moment, a helmsman will put on full helm when half would do. This slows the boat right down, and loses distance. Each boat will require a different amount of helm to bring her into the wind, and this will change with the wind strength and the set of the sails. If the boat is to be raced, it is well worth spending some time out practising, so that the minimum 'braking' effect is achieved on each tack.

As a corollary to this, of course, if you wish to take way off the boat when not under power, such as when coming alongside, work the rudder from side to side to slow down the boat.

There is a tendency for helmsmen to think that because they have the boat on its ear and making a lot of noise, they are sailing fast. This is particularly the case when on a broad reach, where the temptation is to harden up to increase the apparent wind, and then bear away using the increased wind and speed. The boat will certainly cover more miles this way, but the track of the boat is a zig zag, and more miles are needed to cover the same distance towards the destination. It does not seem to be as fast to steer a steady course, but in fact, at the end of the day the boat that steers a steady course will be closer to its destination than the one that has whizzed around at high speed. Some helmsmen, particularly young Turks, find this hard to believe, and the only way to prove it to them is by being able to pinpoint positions at the beginning and end of their tricks on the helm.

The helmsman should glance regularly to windward to look for squalls and luff up, or bear away when necessary. The indication of a squall is a very light rippling of the sea's surface. Often this will cover only a small area and will quickly pass, but whilst the squall is there, the increased wind can help the boat to go faster. Dark clouds, or in certain parts of the world, any cloud, can indicate that there is more wind coming beneath or around the cloud.

Weather and lee helm   Weather helm occurs when it is found necessary to hold the tiller up to weather to hold a steady course. Lee helm is the opposite: the tiller has to be held to leeward to hold a steady course.

Some people like a little weather helm on a boat as, if the helm is left for any reason, the boat will luff up. However, any helm, weather or lee, is an indication that the boat is unbalanced, and it should be remembered that whenever the rudder is turned, it is causing resistance to the boat's forward movement and if it has to be held slightly one way or another to hold a steady course, the boat will be losing speed.

The usual reason for weather helm is that the centre of effort from the sails is too far aft. As weather or lee helm is caused by an unbalance somewhere, a good method of checking it is by trying to reef the mainsail to get rid of weather helm. One reef in the mainsail should remove weather helm. Equally for checking out lee helm, reef the headsail, or set a smaller one, and this should remove lee helm. The drastic solution is to move the mast heel forward, but usually weather helm can be reduced by raking the mast forward. If raking the mast forward does not ease the problem, or the boat still has over-heavy weather helm, consult a naval architect, or if the boat is new, take the problem back to the builders.

If the boat has lee helm, try raking the mast aft to deal with the problem. Do bear in mind that the helm feel will change as you reef sails and with the weight of wind. So whatever serves to remove either unbalance with full plain sail set will not necessarily do the same in different conditions.

Before taking any drastic action by moving the mast however, all the other possible causes of helm unbalance should be examined. By changing the distribution of weights about the boat, the trim of the hull can be changed, and this will change the centre of lateral resistance. Moving the centre of lateral resistance forward, by trimming a boat down at the bow, or trimming her by the head, has the same effect as moving the mast aft and vice versa.

MANOEUVRING UNDER SAIL

Manoeuvring a boat under sail is one of the most satisfying aspects of seamanship. No two boats behave in exactly the same way, and varying the amount of sail set will alter the handling characteristics of any boat, so the only way to find out how a particular boat behaves is to go out and try her. The behaviour will probably vary depending upon the sea state. It might be well balanced on a flat sea with a certain suit of sails, but become unbalanced and behave quite differently once she gets into a seaway.

There are two basic points to bear in mind when manoeuvring under sail. The first is that when the boat is brought head to wind she will lose way and stop. The distance she will travel before she stops will depend upon the speed she was travelling, the wind strength and the weight of the boat. She is stopped by the combination of losing the driving force from her sails and the wind against the front of the mast and rigging. A heavy boat will carry her way longer than a light boat, and will eventually stop further along into the wind. The second point is that the mast and rigging will act as sails to a certain extent so that even when the sails have been taken down, if the boat is heading down wind she will receive enough impetus from the wind in the mast and rigging to give her way, and the only method to stop her is by bringing her head round into the wind. When the wind is on the beam, some boats will move sideways whilst others will tend to crawl ahead.

A sloop will tend to come up into the wind if under mainsail alone, or if she is carrying more main than headsail, and tend to pay off downwind when under headsail alone or when carrying more headsail than mainsail. The boat can be sailed under either sail alone, but will require more attention at the helm. The objective should be to try and achieve a balance between the sails that requires the least amount of rudder bias and use of the helm.

A ketch is likely to be very different. Usually they handle very easily under head sail and mizzen, but can balance under main and staysail in some cases. The disadvantages of the ketch rig are that when close hauled, the flow of air off the mainsail often interferes with the mizzen, and when sailing downwind, the mizzen blankets the mainsail. However the advantage of this rig is that, in comparison with a sloop of the same hull size, the sails are smaller and make handling simpler. Balancing a ketch is best achieved by setting the boat on the desired course and then adjusting the sheets.

Getting underway   In most cases it will be sensible to use the boat's engine to clear a berth, mooring or anchorage, as in these crowded conditions the boat should be as manoeuvrable as possible to avoid inconveniencing others.

However when there is plenty of space and it is safe to do so, a sailing boat should be sailed out, as it is good practice for the skipper and crew and concentrates the mind wonderfully (on the boat's manoeuvrability).

Leaving from a mooring   The method used to get underway will depend upon the prevailing conditions, the amount of manoeuvring room available, and the direction in which one intends to go when underway. A boat on a mooring or at anchor will usually lie to wind *and* tidal stream, and if both these forces are moving in the same direction, the mooring will be right ahead. In these circumstances, hoist the mainsail and leave the sheets loose. Next decide on which tack you want to start. Assuming it to be the starboard tack, hoist the jib and let it flap, but have the sheet ready to haul in on the starboard side. Haul in on the buoy mooring on the starboard side and take it off the cleat. Throw the rudder to port, sheet home the jib on the starboard sheet so that it is aback, and when the weight comes on the mooring line throw it clear. Once the boat has paid off to port, the jib can be tacked and the mainsail sheeted in, and the boat is now sailing. Both sheets can be adjusted as required for the chosen course.

If wind and current are in opposite directions, matters are somewhat simpler because there is a choice of forces. When the stream is stronger than the wind it will be possible to hoist the jib, leave the sheets slack whilst the buoy is let go, and then take the weight on the sheets, remembering to steer clear of the buoy. If the wind is the stronger force, the boat will lie to the wind, but the weight on the mooring line should be less. Hoist the mainsail, and the jib, and set the jib aback to turn the head round. Let go from the buoy and sheet home as required. If the

Sailing Off a Mooring

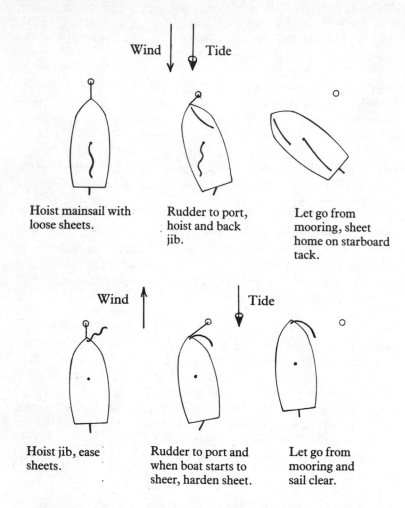

Hoist mainsail with loose sheets.

Rudder to port, hoist and back jib.

Let go from mooring, sheet home on starboard tack.

Hoist jib, ease sheets.

Rudder to port and when boat starts to sheer, harden sheet.

Let go from mooring and sail clear.

wind and tidal stream are strong make sure that the boat will not be driven onto the buoy by the wind the moment you let go. Usually however, the weight of the wind on the boat will drive you clear.

When the wind is on the beam, hoist the headsail and leave it to flap with the sheets free until the mooring is cast off, then push the boat out and sheet in. You can hoist the mainsail as soon as there is room to come head to wind.

If the wind is from astern, the current is probably coming strongly from the bow. The mainsail may not like being hoisted with the wind filling it, so set the headsail and let fly the sheets. Give the boat a sheer with the rudder, let go the buoy, and sheet in the jib.

One of the great joys with a catamaran is that the boat can be sailed straight off down wind over a buoy so that it passes between the hulls. The jib is hoisted, partially sheeted so that the boat starts to move ahead, then the buoy is let go and the jib sheeted to give more power.

Leaving an anchorage   Carry out the same procedure as for leaving a buoy, but haul up on the anchor until it is up and down first. In calm conditions the anchor can be hauled right up and stowed before setting sail, but when there is a wind in the anchorage, leave it just holding until the sails are hoisted and ready to be trimmed. Once the sails have started to work, heave up as quickly as possible. If there is room, the anchor can be sailed out; that is, the boat's way can be used to pull the anchor clear of the bottom. The worst situation is when the anchor continues to hold and pulls the boat round into the wind again just as you were hoping the boat would sail out. The only safe thing to do in these circumstances is to let the sheets fly on the sails and start all over again.

Be wary when sailing out of an anchorage downwind, as the pull of the water on the anchor makes it very hard to heave inboard, and it can veer about as it nears the surface and damage the hull. On one occasion, when I was leaving an anchorage downwind in a large catamaran, a squall pushed the speed up to over ten knots, and the 75 lb CQR anchor broke surface 30 feet back from the bows and started to sheer from side to side threatening each hull in turn. It took all hands bar one, and a degree of desperation to get the anchor in quickly.

Leaving from a pontoon   When leaving an alongside berth under sail, if the wind is blowing off the quay or pontoon, set the sails, leaving the sheets slack, and once all is ready let go and sheet home. If the wind is blowing onto the quay it is best to motor clear, or put out an anchor and warp off the quay before setting sail. This is because, although in theory the boat would sail straight off at an angle to the quay, in practice, before the boat gathers headway, she will tend to be pushed against the quay and damage her topsides.

If there is a current from ahead, this can be a help. Hoist the sails, leaving the sheets slack; cast off all lines except the aft spring, which should be made ready to slip. Push out the boat's head, sheet in and slip the aft spring as she gathers way. If the current is coming from astern, it is best to warp the boat around before starting to hoist sail at all.

If the wind is from right ahead, set the sails, back the jib, and sheet in the main. The boat should drift clear, then the jib can be sheeted in. When the wind is from aft, use the jib only until the boat has sailed clear of the quay.

A moment's thought before taking action is very rewarding, and always ensure that your crew are throughly briefed as to what they have to do and what your intentions are before starting.

Bringing up to a mooring   Observe the angle at which any other boats on moorings are lying. This will tell you how the boat will lie once she is secured, and also give you an indication as to the relative strengths of wind and current. Unless the wind is very light, or there is a strong current flowing in the opposite direction to the wind, in which case one can sail downwind onto the buoy under headsail, it is best to come up onto a buoy from a point down wind. This requires accurate judgement of the amount of way the boat will have once she is rounded up into the wind. It is necessary to pick this point on the water where the boat should be put head to wind and then sail to it. The foredeck crew needs to be ready with a boathook and a short mooring line which is already secured to the boat at one end. As soon as the buoy can be reached, put this mooring line through the ring and either knot it quickly on the ring or pennant, or bring it back on board and make it fast. The boat is then temporarily secured, and the sails can be got out of the way.

The worst situation is to bring the boat's head into the wind and then find that she loses way short of the buoy. In this case, the sails will have to be used to sail off and come back in for another go. It does not matter so much if you overshoot a little so that the boat loses way when the buoy is abeam, as the boat will drop back onto the buoy in due course.

On a boat with a high freeboard, where putting a line through

Manoeuvring Onto a Buoy

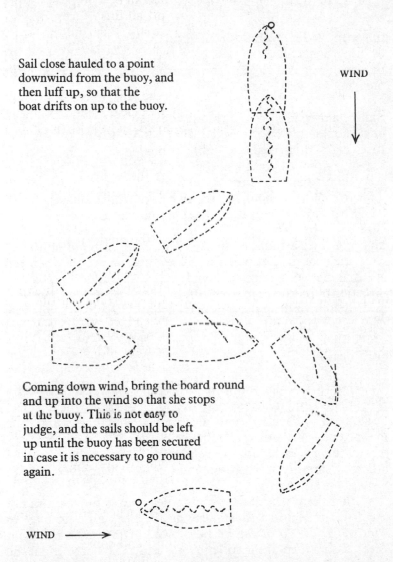

Sail close hauled to a point
downwind from the buoy, and
then luff up, so that the
boat drifts on up to the buoy.

WIND

Coming down wind, bring the board round
and up into the wind so that she stops
at the buoy. This is not easy to
judge, and the sails should be left
up until the buoy has been secured
in case it is necessary to go round
again.

WIND ⟶

the buoy's mooring ring is difficult from the deck, it pays to
drop the dinghy when close to the mooring, and let one of the
crew row to the buoy, make the dinghy fast, and then standby to
take the boat's mooring line which can be thrown to him from

the foredeck. The procedure is to approach the buoy, luff up so that the boat stops, lower the dinghy and send it clear of the boat, and then sail round and come back in towards the buoy.

Always have the anchor ready before sailing onto a buoy so that you can let go and stop the boat drifting towards the shore or other boats once the sails have been dropped, but never let the anchor go too close to the mooring itself as it may foul the mooring's ground chain.

Sailing alongside   Sailing alongside a pontoon, pier or another boat should only be attempted when conditions are favourable. In general this means a light to moderate wind, which is blowing along the berth so that the boat can be luffed up and stopped in position. If these conditions do not exist, it is much safer to motor in and avoid the risk of causing damage to your own boat or others; or if the boat has no motor, one can sail as close to the berth as is possible, let go the anchor and then throw mooring lines ashore, or send them ashore in the dinghy and warp the boat in. The worst possible situation occurs when you are making your approach and the wind suddenly changes direction or increases in strength. In this case you must get clear immediately or drop the sails and anchor. Usually this will only happen where the berth is close to buildings which create a sudden wind shift, or at anchorages with high mountains or cliffs nearby.

Heaving-to   When you want to stop the boat, but only for a short period and it is not worth dropping the sails, the boat can be stopped by backing some of the sails so that they counter the forward power of others. Probably everyone has seen paintings of square rig vessels with the sails on the foremast aback and the others apparently still setting, and this was the method used to heave-to in square rig.

With a sloop, the easiest way to heave-to is to tack and not sheet in the leeward sheet, leaving the headsail held over to windward. The boat can be held by adjustments on the main sheet, easing it out if she still moves ahead, and sheeting in if she gathers sternway.

The sheeting positions for a ketch will depend upon the relative size of the sails. Normally, with the headsail aback, the main eased and the mizzen sheeted in, a ketch will heave-to.

Trimarans will heave-to the same way as monohulls, except that they are likely to gather sternway rather easily and it may be necessary to put a little tension on the main sheet to counter this. Catamarans, particularly when the mast is stepped well back, will almost definitely gather sternway, and if the mainsail sheet is taken in, they are likely to come head to wind, but may still have stern board. In this case put the helm over so that the stern of the weather side is swung up into the wind. The boat will eventually stop and start moving ahead, but by leaving the rudders over she will luff up again, and the whole process is repeated with the boat moving slowly ahead and astern.

A boat which is hove-to will tend to drift to leeward, the amount depending upon the strength of the wind and the boat's grip in the water.

MANOEUVRING UNDER POWER

In these days of almost universal auxiliary powered racers and cruisers, most boats use their engines at the beginning and end of a voyage. In crowded fairways and marinas it is not only a great deal safer and therefore more seamanlike; it is considerate.

A boat's handling characteristics under power are almost as individual as when sailing, and the skipper of a new yacht should spend some time learning how she behaves. In calm conditions, the most important factor is going to be the transverse thrust of the propeller, and this will particularly apply when going astern. A propeller blade is designed to bite into the water and 'carve' its way through, imparting a forward or backward thrust as it does so. However it also has a sideways effect.

The sideways or transverse effect will be to one side above the shaft and the opposite below. Although it appears that these two forces should cancel each other, this is not quite the case because the water is slightly more dense lower down and also, being further from the surface, less liable to disturbance. The result is that the lower part of the propeller grips the water better, and the transverse thrust is slightly greater.

Manoeuvring Alongside, Single Screw – Right-handed Propeller

Port side alongside

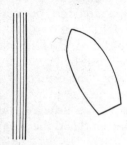
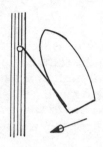
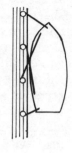

Approach berth slowly, fenders and back spring ready.	Back spring made fast, engine slow astern, the paddlewheel effect pulls the stern in to port, and the spring stops the boat moving astern.	In position, made fast.

Starboard side alongside

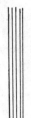
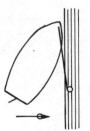
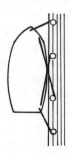
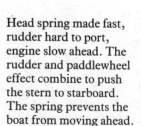

Approach berth slowly, fenders and head spring ready.	Head spring made fast, rudder hard to port, engine slow ahead. The rudder and paddlewheel effect combine to push the stern to starboard. The spring prevents the boat from moving ahead.	In position, made fast.

Manoeuvring Alongside, Single Screw --
Left-handed Propeller

Starboard side alongside

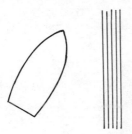 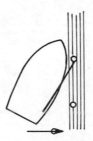 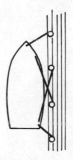

Approach berth slowly, fenders and back spring ready.

Back spring made fast, engine slow astern, the paddlewheel effect pulls the stern in to starboard, the spring stops the boat moving astern.

In position, made fast.

Port side alongside

  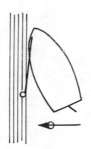 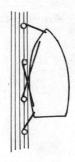

.Approach berth slowly, fenders and head spring ready.

Head spring made fast, rudder hard to starboard, engine slow ahead.
The rudder and paddlewheel effect combine to push the boat's stern to port, and the spring prevents the boat from moving.

In position, made fast.

Manoeuvring Onto a Berth

Strong tide parallel to berth

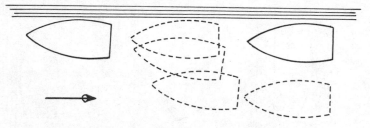

Come in towards the berth slowly stemming the tide, and parallel to the berth. When level with the berth, slow the speed so that the boat is only making sufficient headway to stem the tide and hold itself level with the berth. Put the helm over so that the boat slowly crabs into the berth. Keep the engine running until at least the headline is ashore and made fast.

Wind off the berth

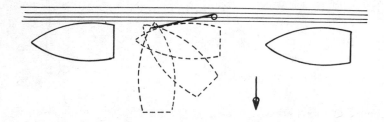

Come in head to wind, and put out a headline to stop the boat drifting off. Put out the head spring, and then put the helm over and go ahead on the engine. The boat should spring into the berth. The above diagram assumes a right-handed propeller.

Manoeuvring Off a Berth

Springing out of a berth

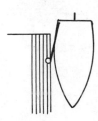

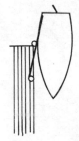

Have fender ready to keep boat off the corner of the berth. Single up to back spring, and ease back spring until the boat is halfway out of the berth.

When boat is halfway out of berth, secure back spring, and put the helm over to starboard.

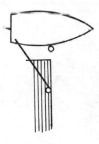

As the boat motors slowly astern, the back spring will pull the stern around.

Once the boat is round, put the helm to port, and let go the spring. Motor slowly ahead.

Manoeuvring Off a Berth

Using the tide

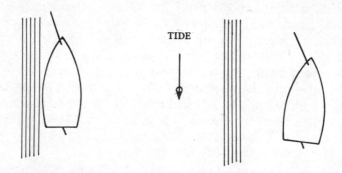

When the boat is berthed head to the tide, lead out a headline as far as possible, and make it into a slipline. Let go all other lines, and put the rudder to starboard. The tide will force the boat off the berth. This is the same method as used to get a ship's boat clear of the side when the ship is still moving ahead.

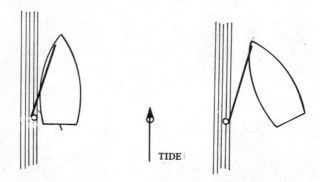

When the boat is berthed stern to the tide, single up to a slip head spring, and put the rudder to starboard. The boat will swing clear of the berth. If the boat needs a start, put the rudder to port, and go slow ahead on the engine.

Propellers come either left- or right-handed. Looking at the propeller from astern, if when going ahead it turns clockwise the propeller is known as right-handed. If it turns anticlockwise it is left-handed.

With a right-handed propeller, on its lower sweep when going ahead, the blade tends to 'paddle' the boat's stern to starboard. When going ahead under power therefore, the bow will tend to drift off to port. The opposite is the case with a left-handed blade, and the bow tends to drift to starboard.

Because propellers are designed to push a boat ahead, their shape is not usually as efficient astern, with the result that the 'paddling' effect is greater and the transverse thrust more pronounced. Thus when a boat with a right-handed blade is going astern, the stern is pushed to port.

This has a considerable bearing on how a boat should be manoeuvred. If a boat with a right-handed propeller is lying alongside a marina berth, starboard side to, when she goes astern she will tend to come to port and draw the stern from the pontoon. If the same boat is coming back into the same berth, when she puts her engine astern her stern will tend to draw away, and make mooring more difficult. If, however, she was coming into a berth port side to, and was coming in at a slight angle to the berth, when the engine was put astern, it would draw the stern into the pontoon, making mooring easier.

The transverse thrust also has an effect upon a boat's ability to turn in a circle. If the boat has a right-handed propeller, and therefore the bow tends to drift to port when going ahead, the boat will have a smaller turning circle if she turns round to port rather than to starboard. This would be called turning short round.

When manoeuvring in a tight corner, the boat can be turned in a very small space by using transverse thrust. Turn the *opposite* way to the smallest turning circle going ahead. The reason is that the transverse thrust has a greater effect when the engine is going astern. Thus if the boat has a right-handed propeller the sequence is as follows: rudder hard a-starboard – engine ahead. The moment the boat gathers headway, engine stop and then astern, helm amidships. The moment the boat has sternboard, engine ahead, rudder hard a-starboard. Repeat until the boat is turned.

If the boat has the rudder in the wash of the propeller, the

Turning Circle – Left-handed Propeller

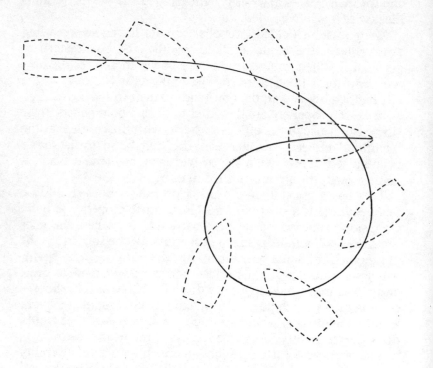

Boats pivot around a point about one third of their length
from the bow, and their momentum causes them to slide on
in their previous direction.

The paddlewheel effect helps to turn a boat with a
left-handed propeller more quickly if she turns to starboard,
and a boat with a right-handed propeller more quickly if she
turns to port. The boat's turning diameter is therefore
smaller when using the paddlewheel effect.

The turning circle, from full ahead and the helm hard over in
either direction, should be known by the seaman, as should
the advance of the boat – the distance she would continue in
her previous course whilst manoeuvring.

wash is diverted better when the rudder is hard over, and the boat turns more quickly. A brief burst of full ahead on the engine, with the rudder hard over, gives a tremendous sideways kick.

Once there is a slight wind, the manoeuvrability of the boat will begin to be dominated by her windage and her underwater resistance. This varies from boat to boat, but to give an example, an old fashioned gaff ketch with bowsprit with more draft aft than forward, will, when beam on to the wind, tend to have her bow pay off down wind. A modern sloop, with central keel, may lie almost steadily beam on, others will tend to round up into the wind.

The only real way to be certain of a boat's handling characteristics is to go out and practise manoeuvring. The experience will make you a safer navigator and increase your knowledge of boat handling generally.

Twin screw   Many power cruisers today have twin screws, which makes manoeuvring simpler, but the comments in the previous section regarding transverse thrust are just as applicable. It is usual for twin screw boats to have the port propeller left-handed and the starboard right-handed. Since the propellers revolve in opposite directions, when both are going ahead or astern at the same speed the paddlewheel effect is cancelled out.

**Transverse Thrust or Paddlewheel Effect:
Twin Screw**

Port propeller,
left-handed.   Starboard propeller,
                      right-handed.

Transverse Thrust or Paddlewheel Effect

Screw race, right-handed propeller – going ahead

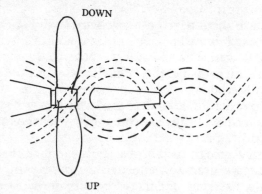

DOWN

UP

The angle of the blades sets up a transverse effect as well as the fore and aft effect. As the propeller churns the water nearer the surface, it is the movement of the lower blade that has the greater effect.

RIGHT-HANDED – going ahead   LEFT-HANDED – going ahead

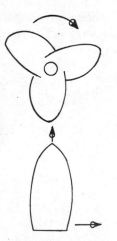   

Stern cants to starboard when going ahead. It will cant to port more briskly when going astern.

Stern cants to port when going ahead. It will cant to starboard more briskly when going astern.

The reason why the port propeller is usually left-handed and the starboard right-handed is that when it is necessary to turn the boat short round, i.e. in a confined space, the paddlewheel effect assists the turn. Looking at the diagram, if the boat is to be turned to starboard, the port propeller will revolve as shown, and the starboard propeller, being put astern, will revolve anti-clockwise as well. The paddlewheel effect will therefore be the same with both propellers, and will paddle the stern to port and the bow to starboard.

It is much easier to manoeuvre a twin-screw boat in a confined space just by the use of the engines alone, and with the rudder or rudders amidships. To avoid damaging the gearboxes however, always move the gear lever from ahead to astern slowly, allowing the gears to rest briefly in neutral in between.

The Williamson turn   When it is necessary to bring a powered boat back on to her original track but in the opposite direction, as when a crew member has fallen overside, the Williamson turn is used.

Put the helm hard over so that the boat swings towards the side on which the crew member fell over, until the boat's head is 70° round from the original course. Then put the helm hard over the other way and steady up when the boat is on the reciprocal of the original course. This should bring the boat back to a person or object that has fallen overside.

The ability of the boat to come back on the exact reciprocal course is dependent upon a number of factors, such as the rudder angle, the trim of the boat, the wind direction and strength. However it is fairly accurate, and one or two practice turns will soon enable the helmsman to know what minor corrections to apply.

Local effects
Shallow water effect   When a boat comes into shallow water, the flow of water to the propeller is restricted and this will reduce the boat's speed. In addition, the mean draft of the boat will be increased, more so as the boat goes faster. Power boats should slow down as they approach shallow water so as not to risk bottoming, or damaging their propellers.

Sailing boats will find that they experience more drag as they get into shallow water.

The Williamson Turn

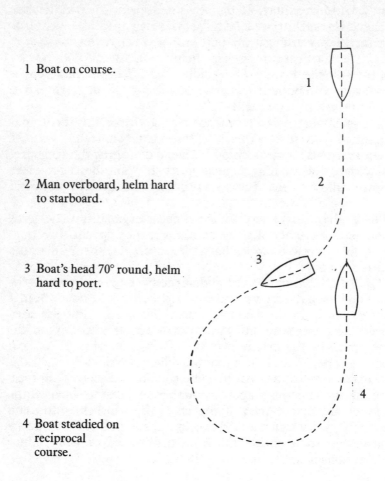

1 Boat on course.

2 Man overboard, helm hard
  to starboard.

3 Boat's head 70° round, helm
  hard to port.

4 Boat steadied on
  reciprocal
  course.

Channel effect The pressure created by the movement of the
hull through a narrow channel will tend to keep a boat in the
middle of the channel, with the result that less helm will be
required. As a boat approaches the bank, the pressure will build
up and tend to push it away. When the channel bends, the boat
may require very little helm and in some cases, opposite helm
may be required to prevent the boat swinging too much.

Quay effect If the engines are put ahead on a boat alongside a quay, water will be sucked aft, and the boat will tend to be drawn into the quay. If the engines are put astern, water is pushed forward between the boat and the quay, and will force the boat away from the quay.

PROPELLERS

Also known as screws, propellers are measured by their diameter and their pitch, the pitch being the distance the propeller would move the boat ahead if it was revolving in a solid rather than water and there was thus no slip.

Thus a 16 × 20 propeller is one in which the diameter is 16 inches and the pitch is 20 inches.

Slip of a propeller Slip is the difference between the actual speed of the boat and the speed that the engine revolutions would give with the propeller if it were revolving in a solid. It is caused by the water yielding to the blades of the screw as it forces the boat ahead. Slip will increase if the hull is dirty or the wind and seas are ahead.

Fuel consumption to speed ratio The builders of a boat should always provide an indication of the boat's fuel consumption at a certain speed, but these figures may not be very accurate, and it is sensible to work out new figures based upon the log, weather conditions and state of the hull.

The most accurate method is to fill the fuel tank to the brim, and when the voyage is over, refill the tank to the same point, and note from the fuel pump the exact quantity of fuel used.

On long voyages, the knowledge of the boat's fuel consumption is vital, and there is a very approximate formula for calculating the change in fuel consumption for a change in speed.

$$\frac{\text{New Consumption}}{\text{Old Consumption}} = \frac{\text{New Speed}^3}{\text{Old Speed}^3}$$

This formula works quite well up to the maximum hull speed of a boat, but beyond that point, the fuel consumption will increase dramatically.

Hull speeds   The simple and approximate formula for calculating the maximum hull speed of a displacement hull is:

$$\sqrt{\text{Waterline Length}} \times 1.4$$

The figure of 1.4 is arbitrary, and will be greater for light fine hulls and less for heavy cruising hulls.

TOWING

There is a lot more to towing properly and safely than meets the eye, both from the towing and the towed boat's point of view. Like all good seamanship, good towing is a matter of preparation. Unfortunately an emergency tow does not usually provide much time for preparation, so it is worth going over the boat, and the equipment on board, to make sure that the necessary equipment and strong points for towing and being towed are available.

On the towed boat, a strong point forward such as a king post or anchor winch is the best point to attach the tow line, but if nothing suitable exists, the line can be taken to the mast provided precautions are taken against chafing the mast coat. Avoid taking the line to deck cleats as these are seldom strong enough. In theory the tow line ought to be taken to a senhouse slip at each end so that it can be let go quickly in an emergency, but as few boats carry a slip on board, an axe or heavy sharp knife should be kept handy whilst under tow.

When towing, a boat should ideally have a towing point between midships and two thirds of its length from the bow. This enables the towing boat to manoeuvre. On most yachts this is not possible because there are obstructions in the way with the result that a towing yacht usually has difficulty in manoeuvring, and can find its course being dictated by the tow line. One method to reduce this is to put the towline onto a bridle led

Towing

Towing astern

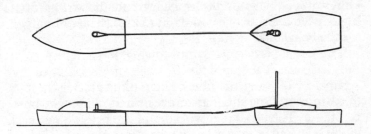

This allows the towing boat to pivot around the towing bollard. For long-distance tows, the towing hawser should be lengthened and weighted, or the towed boat's anchor cable used as part of the hawser to provide spring.

Towing astern with a bridle

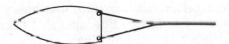

The towing boat will not be able to manoeuvre as readily with a bridle, and the turning circle will be much larger.

Towing alongside

Place fenders between the boats, and get the lines really tight. Should only be used in sheltered waters.

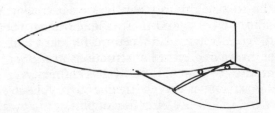

from each quarter. A single line led to one point right aft will, unless the towed boat is very much smaller than the towing boat, make manoeuvring almost impossible as the boat will be pulled aft to one side the whole time. To straighten the boat, either the engine must be stopped to take the weight off the tow line, or the line must be eased out to take the weight off enough for the boat to swing round.

There is not often an obvious towing point aft on a yacht, and the deck cleats are unlikely to be strong enough to take the strains, so the best method of rigging the bridle is to take it forward round the superstructure or mast and make both ends fast there. Then lead the two sides of the bridle down each side of the boat and use the aft mooring cleats as a guide only. Make sure that the bridle is protected wherever it comes into contact with a hard point, and also ensure that it cannot snarl on anything.

Few boats carry a special towing hawser, but most carry some heavy line capable of taking the strain of the boat surging. This might be the kedge anchor warp, or a long mooring warp, but any good length of rope, or ropes joined together, that can take the surging weight of the boat will suffice. At sea a long tow line makes the task simpler; about ten times the boat's length is ideal. If it is necessary to knot lines together to achieve this length, use a carrick bend to join the lines.

Generally the towed boat supplies the tow line, hence the need to have a line on board capable of towing the boat.

There are three basic types of towing, the medium to long distance tow in open waters, the short-distance tow in sheltered water, and the tow in confined waters. All three have different requirements and therefore different methods are used.

Open waters   Where both the towed and towing boats are likely to be affected by sea or swell waves, the boats need to be sufficiently far apart to avoid any risk of collision. In fact, the boats should be from eight to ten boat's lengths apart. The greatest strain on the boats and the tow line occurs when the boats are on different waves and the tow line snaps taut. This can be avoided by having either a long heavy tow line, or by putting weight into the towline. The line does not have to be tight for towing; so long as there is even a slight forward pull, the towed boat will follow the direction of pull.

A safe method of taking a tow

Take the strain on the towing cable at an angle, and not in
direct line with the towed boat. This reduces the rate at
which the strain comes onto the tow line, and the towing boat
is less likely to be sprung back on the tow, as, being slightly
sideways on, it has more resistance.

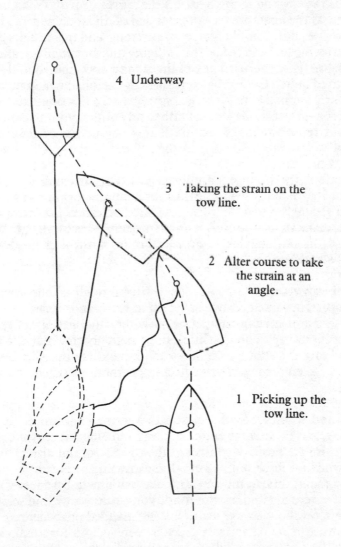

4 Underway

3 Taking the strain on the
tow line.

2 Alter course to take
the strain at an
angle.

1 Picking up the
tow line.

The standard method is to use up to 30 metres of the towed boat's anchor chain for towing; a greater length can be used, in fact the more chain used, the less the likelihood of the tow line parting. At the towing end, this chain should be secured to a strong line which can be easily fastened on the towing boat, and be able to be cut free if necessary. The weight of the chain which causes the towline to sag beneath the waves provides a natural spring. If the boats are on different waves, the towline straightens a little, but is unlikely to come up taut, and this lessens the strain on the line and the boats. If there is no anchor chain, and a plain line is to be used throughout, the tow line should be weighted down. Car rubber tyres are quite effective, and in fact one good method of providing a 'spring' in the tow line is to split the line and attach the ends to either side of the tyre. Add more tyres if more weight is required. If no tyres are available, a heavy weight suspended from the middle of the tow line will have some effect.

Chafe is the worst enemy when towing, particularly as the two boats are likely to yaw. Make sure that the tow line or cable is led through a good fairlead and the fairlead is packed with some material to reduce chafe. If a rope is being used, the fairlead should be packed with leather or cloth, if chain, then wood should be used.

Sheltered waters   On a flat sea it will be possible to tow for a short distance using only a strong line between the two boats. The speed of towing should be such that the line is not taut when underway. The tow line can be kept shorter than for an open sea tow, about 2–3 times the boat's length. The lines should be led through fairleads, and precautions taken against chafe.

Confined waters   In the confined waters of a harbour or a marina, it is usually far better to tow from alongside. Not only does this give positive control of the towed boat, it also allows the two boats to be stopped and manoeuvred as necessary.

In modern craft, and in particular with twin screw towing boats, it does not matter which side you go alongside, but with a single screw boat, it is usual with a left-handed propeller to put the towing boat on the starboard side of the towed boat, and vice versa. This is because when going ahead, the towed boat will drag and tend to pull the towing boat's bow over towards itself. The transverse thrust of the towing boat helps to correct this and makes it easier to steer in a straight line. When using a twin screw boat, use the inside engine for power and the outside one to help steer.

The towing boat should be well secured on the quarter of the towed boat in such a way that its stern overlaps the stern of the towed boat. Fenders should be placed between the two boats and then the headline, backspring, stern line and aft spring should be set up as tight as possible, so that the boats cannot surge against each other as the engines go ahead or astern.

A useful method if towing alongside is not practicable is to pass the tow line round a bollard in the bows of the tow boat. This enables the towing boat to manoeuvre as it likes, the only inconvenience being that the crew of the tow boat has to duck every time the towline swings across the boat. This method would apply to any small boat that has no mast, and is much more efficient than towing from one of the quarters of the tow boat.

Passing a tow When it is obvious that a boat is calling for a tow, close in if possible, and establish contact, and then plan. If both boats have VHF this is the obvious method of communication to use. Once the plan has been agreed, stand clear and prepare the boat for towing by setting up the bridle and clearing obstructions from the deck. On the stopped boat, the tow line should be flaked out, and attached to the anchor cable or its strong point, and if the anchor cable is to be used, this should be flaked on deck and secured to the strong point. Both boats should have heaving lines and messengers ready.

The towing boat should prepare the shape required to be shown under the International regulations for preventing collisions at sea, or should prepare the white lights required under the same regulations.

The boats should not close each other until everything is ready on both boats.

In calm conditions it is a comparatively simple matter to motor close to the stopped boat and throw a line. In this case if the towing boat makes less leeway than the stopped boat, the towing boat should approach from windward. If it makes more leeway, she should approach from down wind. If they have about the same leeway, but conditions mean that if the boats rolled in opposite directions their masts might hit each other, the answer is to make an approach from ahead or astern.

When the weather is rough the boats will not want to get too close to each other, and may even be out of heaving line range. As very few yachts carry a line-throwing pistol, alternative methods have to be used. One good method is to float a line across attached to a fender. This works if both boats have less leeway than the fender. If they do not, the line can be thrown over to windward and paid out and it will slowly move clear of the boat. The line can also be attached to a sea anchor which is then picked up by the towing boat, a messenger of stronger line should be bent on and hauled across. The tow line can then be passed over and secured on board the towing vessel. When the tow line is secured, the towing boat should slowly turn so that it lies ahead of the stopped boat and then very carefully go ahead so that the full tow line and cable can be paid out without putting strain on the tow line. Once the weight comes onto the line, very gently take the strain under power and check that everything is holding. If all is well, increase speed slowly with frequent checks, until a comfortable towing speed is reached.

If the tow is taking place in shallow water, or the stopped boat is anchored in shallow water or close to a lee shore, the tow should be commenced with a short line only and the stopped boat can keep its anchor ready to let go if things go wrong. Once both boats are well clear, and have sea room, the speed can be slowed to allow the anchor cable to be connected up to the tow line.

On tow Frequent contact should be made whilst the boats are on tow to ensure that all is well at both ends. A constant check must be made on the towlines, particularly at the fairleads, and if necessary the line eased or taken in to 'freshen the nip', i.e. allow a different part of the line to be chafed.

On the towed boat, the helmsman should follow in the wake of the towing boat, and if the helm has to be left, the wheel or tiller should be lashed amidships. When alterations of course are necessary, the boat should be steered round. On the towing boat, the towline should be watched continuously to make sure it is not jumping clear of the water, as if it is, the speed is too great, and the threat of damage increased. If sudden alterations of course are necessary, warning should be given either by hand signals, on the VHF or with the fog horn.

Slipping the tow In an emergency, the towing boat may find that it is being endangered by having a boat in tow and in this case the tow will have to be slipped. It should then stand by the stopped boat until conditions improve or to take off the crew if it becomes necessary. The stopped boat should haul in the complete tow line, and if in sufficiently shallow water, should let go the anchor. It should then prepare everything for a new tow.

It is the towing boat that should slip and not the towed boat, as the tow line hanging over the stern could get entangled around the propellers or restrict manoeuvrability.

When the destination, or more crowded water, is being approached it will be necessary to shorten the tow. Speed should be reduced slowly until the slack can be hauled up on the towed boat. The tow line should be reduced to about 2 to 3 boats' lengths, or at least so that the length of anchor cable in the tow line can be brought in board and re-shackled to the anchor which should be made ready for use. The towing boat may not be able to take the tow into port in which case the towed boat will need to anchor until other arrangements can be made.

HEAVY WEATHER

Heaving-to When the prevailing weather conditions reach the point where it is no longer safe or comfortable to continue sailing, the time has come to heave-to. This means taking the way off the boat and allowing her to lie as comfortably as possible. It should only be done if there is plenty of sea room around you. If you are close to land when the conditions deteriorate, it is best to head for the nearest port or shelter. If there is no obvious shelter, you will have to head out to sea away from the land unless, of course, the wind is offshore. But even then, if the wind direction changes you could find yourself in trouble.

Heading out to sea in bad weather may seem the illogical

thing to do, but it gets the boat away from the most obvious danger of being driven ashore, and the waves are more likely to be spread out and more even. The sea always heaps up as the water shallows which explains the short unpleasant waves near a beach.

When a boat is hove-to she will always drift to leeward – downwind. The speed of drift depends upon the proportion of boat in the water as opposed to the proportion exposed to the wind. Some boats will drift quite quickly. I have experienced 72 miles of drift when hove-to for 24 hours; some will drift much more slowly. One has to make a judgement as to the possible duration of the gale, and one's distance from land before making the decision to heave-to, but always leave a good margin of safety.

Often when people talk about how a boat should be hove-to in very rough weather, they are referring to accounts they have read, or personal experience of one or two boats. Advice received this way should be listened to, the information noted, but not necessarily followed. Boats come in so many different hull shapes, keel shapes, and rigs that no two boats can be expected to behave in the same way. Even identical boats from the same production line can behave differently in bad weather; the variation in the stores carried and their stowage positions can alone alter a boat's behaviour. Bear in mind that the size of the sea is relative to the size of the boat. A ten foot high wave can knock a twenty-four-footer flat, but will only roll a seventy-footer. Similarly a twenty-four-footer will have to heave-to in conditions that allow a larger boat to keep sailing. The objective should be to find out the limits for your boat, and what makes her feel comfortable in any particular conditions. By noting other people's experience in a vessel similar to your own in heavy weather you will probably get a pretty good idea of how your boat likes to be treated, but this will only be an indication of what should be done – a form of rough tuning. You may hit upon the ideal arrangement first time, but it is unlikely, and it is worth experimenting to find out what really suits the boat.

The first point to remember is never lie across the waves so the side of the boat offers the wave maximum resistance. Apart from the crew discomfort caused by a heavily rolling boat, a large wave or a vertical one will sooner or later smash into the side and roll the boat over, or cause considerable damage.

Laying a boat beam on to a big sea is always a risky business, and if you have been holding a boat nearly head to a sea, but decide to run off down sea instead, you should always wait for a series of slightly smaller waves to come along and then bear away as quickly as possible before the next large ones appear.

Heaving-to means bringing the boat to a stop. The simplest method of doing this is to go about, without adjusting the headsail sheets. However, if she will not go about (in heavy seas it is often difficult) then haul the headsail to windward, or if the boat has more than one headsail, the foresail. The mainsail is still driving the boat into the wind but the headsail being aback stops her. Most boats, provided the headsail is not too large, will tend to drive slowly forward, but the speed will be insignificant. Once the boat has been hove-to, it is possible to reef or change sails.

In modern boats, it is not always necessary to heave-to to get sails off, or reef, but experience will tell you what suits you best.

The question now is how to lie best in the prevailing conditions, and there are several basic methods to choose from.

Hove-to under sail   Some boats will lie very comfortably with the headsail aback, and the main sheeted in just sufficiently to balance it. In strong winds, the headsail would be the storm jib, and the mainsail would be fully reefed or the trysail set. In a ketch, try the storm jib and reefed main, or reefed mizzen or possibly the smallest staysail and reefed main or trysail.

Certain boats will lie very comfortably under just a fully reefed mainsail or trysail, but usually this only applies to boats with a lot of wind resistance forward such as a bowsprit.

Hove-to under bare poles (lying a-hull)   All sail is taken down and securely stowed. Some boats will lie quite comfortably just off head or stern to wind and sea with no sail up, and if your boat is one of these, you are fortunate.

You will have to experiment as to how to leave the rudder; some boats like it lashed amidships, some prefer it lashed hard over one way or another. The main point to remember is that the rudder must be lashed in the preferred position. If the rudder is left loose, and the boat is driven backwards by a wave, the rudder will be thrown one way or another, and can easily break its bearings. If the rudder is lashed, the force on it will be great, but nothing like as great as if it crashes up against its stops.

Lying to a sea anchor　Personally I hate sea anchors. The only time I ever used one the tripping line became totally tangled with the hawser. It took a long time and aching muscles to haul the thing back on board, and two days to sort out the resulting 'snake's honeymoon'. However, they will greatly reduce your drift if set properly. The secret is to pay out two or three fathoms more tripping line than the length of the hawser, and to pay out the tripping line from a point on the boat well away from the hawser. The boat will lie quite firmly to a sea anchor streamed from the bow or stern, but the strains on the hawser

Sea Anchor

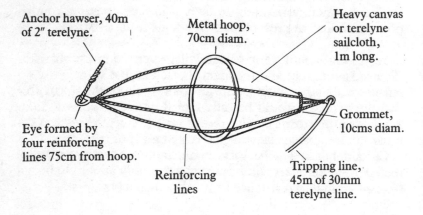

Anchor hawser, 40m of 2″ terelyne.

Metal hoop, 70cm diam.

Heavy canvas or terelyne sailcloth, 1m long.

Eye formed by four reinforcing lines 75cm from hoop.

Grommet, 10cms diam.

Reinforcing lines

Tripping line, 45m of 30mm terelyne line.

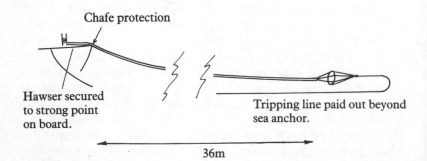

Chafe protection

Hawser secured to strong point on board.

Tripping line paid out beyond sea anchor.

36m

are considerable and it should be checked for chafe at the fairlead at frequent intervals.

If a large wave strikes the boat when it is lying to a sea anchor, the boat will not have the 'give' she would have if lying a-hull or hove-to under sail.

It is possible to control the rate of drift using a sea anchor by the simple expedient of pulling on the tripping line. This collapses the sea anchor and will allow the boat to drift at a faster rate. This method is used to control a boat going into a beach through surf, or through a harbour entrance when there is a large sea running. The sea anchor is allowed to grip as a wave comes up to the boat, which keeps the boat end on to the wave and prevents broaching, and then the anchor is tripped in the trough to allow the boat to be moved in toward the beach or harbour.

A type of sea anchor in use in the USA by both fishermen and yachtsmen is a parachute, an ordinary second hand parachute or similar arrangement. The parachute is attached to about ten times the boat's length of warp and streamed out from the bow of the boat. Once the parachute opens, it provides a very positive sea anchor. On multihulls a bridle about four times the boat's length should be connected to firm holding points on either side of the boat and connected to the warp. Multihulls have laid to 50 knots plus of wind with a parachute as a sea anchor, and because the anchor is so positive, the boat does not tend to lurch backwards and possibly damage the rudders.

The only difficulty with a parachute as a sea anchor is recovering it afterwards. A good trip line is essential. Fasten 30 feet of light line to the top of the parachute, and lead it to a buoy, then attach the trip line to the buoy. This will help to keep the trip line clear of the main warp.

Some recent tests have shown that in a heavy sea, a sea anchor can be tipped over by the circular motion of the water within a wave. This is less likely to happen if there is a constant pull on the sea anchor. In some cases though, the sea anchor can be turned almost inside out, and the cone become entangled in the reinforcing lines. One quite successful solution to this problem is to put lashings or netting around the reinforcing lines.

The use of oil with a sea anchor To prevent waves breaking over the boat when lying to a sea anchor, oil can be spread over the water. Only a good vegetable, fish or animal oil should be used, and it needs to be allowed to seep out over the water. The best way of doing this is by means of an oil bag, made from canvas. The bag should be made from two pieces of canvas about 12 × 9 inches, and stuffed with oakum. Pour the oil into the bag and draw the mouth closed. Either attach the bag to the sea anchor, or pay it out on another line so that it lies upwind and up sea of the boat. The oil will slowly spread over the surface of the sea, taking longer to do this in colder climates.

Drogues   The common drogue is a sea anchor, or a smaller version of the same design, used for steadying a boat or slowing her down. A small version is used with liferafts or with safety dan buoys as a sea anchor.

A drogue, put out astern of a power boat, will steady the boat, and prevent her from yawing in bad sea conditions. They are supplied to, and used by the Royal National Lifeboat Institution for this purpose.

Streaming warps   At sea, where there is plenty of room, and it is desired to keep the stern to the seas, but not slow down completely as would happen with a sea anchor, an effective method of 'braking' is to stream warps over the stern. The most effective brake is a bight, where both ends of the warp are made fast on board, and the loop of the rope in between is allowed to drag out astern. The bight gives extra drag, but this drag can be reduced by shortening in on one of the ends. I used this system in the Southern Ocean with great effect, and the bight kept the stern into the waves at all times, removing the danger of rushing

Streaming Warps

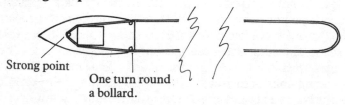

Strong point

One turn round
a bollard.

100-200m, depending on
weight of rope and weather
conditions.

down the front of a wave and broaching. Any ropes streamed
out behind will provide a drag, and they also have a dampening
effect upon the waves astern.

The amount of warp required to hold the stern into the wind
and waves depends upon the wind strength and boat, but as an
example, I found that a total length of 600 feet of 2-inch
circumference (⅝ inch or 16 mm diameter) rope streamed as a
bight (so that the bight itself was 300 feet astern of the boat),
would comfortably hold a ten-ton Norwegian sterned boat's
stern into the wind.

Warps should not usually be streamed from the bow as the
boat can still surge astern and this puts a very great strain on the
rudder and can break it.

Heaving-to in multihulls Handling a multihull in really
rough seas calls for alertness. The only basic rule is never to
allow the boat to come beam onto the seas. If this happens the
wave can lift up the weather side of the boat and a sharp blow,
such as from a breaking wave crest, can tip the boat right over.
It is best to lie aslant on the waves, bow to if possible, but if the
wind rises above force 10, then put the quarter to the waves and
semi run off, leaving just enough headsail to give steerage way.
If the boat is run straight down the waves, she will tend to rush
down the front of a wave, and in a short sea she can bury the bow
into the back of the wave in front. At high speed this will cause
damage at best and a pitch pole at worst. Lying to a sea anchor is
all right up to a certain point, but if winds above force 10 are
expected it is probably unwise as the size of wave to be expected
in those conditions could smash a boat held by a sea anchor; the
boat will need to 'give' to the waves.

I survived a force 12 in the Gulf Stream about 200 miles south
of Cape Hatteras in a 70-foot catamaran by putting the quarter
to the waves and leaving up about 40 square feet of headsail.
The waves were particularly steep, about 50 to 60 feet high, but
only when one directly caught the boat's stern or beam did I feel
in real danger.

Opinions vary as to what to do with the boards. Personally I
leave the weather board half down and take the lee board right
up. This reduces the tendency of the boat to trip over its lee hull
and capsize. Too much board down can put an enormous strain
on the board boxes.

Roller furling headsails   If a roller furling headsail system is fitted to the boat, and both the mainsail and the headsail are reefed, the centre of effort of the boat will move forward, and the wind will tend to blow off the bow of the boat. This is fine if you intend to run with the wind on the quarter. If however you wish to head into the wind, it will be necessary to furl the headsail completely, and set a staysail whose centre of effort is nearer to the mast. An additional consideration is that in heavy weather, the roller furling gear will be put under more load than it should, and could possibly fail, whereas a staysail, particularly one made of a strong cloth and hanked to its stay, puts much less strain on the rig.

Setting more sail   The most difficult decision to make when in heavy weather is exactly when it is safe to set more sail again. The wind speed dropping might mean a temporary lull or it might mean a general easing in conditions. It would be wrong to set more sail just because the wind has started to ease, as the waves will still be large and pushing the boat could damage her. On average it takes between four and eight hours for the waves to ease, and the first sign that they have started the diminishing process is that the crests start to break back down the back of the wave rather than rolling forward.

2   DECK SEAMANSHIP

It used to be said of the seaman that he was a jack of all trades but master of none. Owing to the wide variety of knowledge required to run a boat, there is indeed considerable truth in this statement. Some of this knowledge does not fall under any obvious heading like boat manoeuvring or knots, but consists of knowledge and skills without which no seaman is fully competent about the deck. This chapter deals with some of those general skills.

BELAYING A ROPE

A rope should be belayed, or made fast, in such a manner that it will not let go accidentally, but also so that it can be let go quickly, easily and under control.

Always start by belaying a rope with a round turn, whether the holding point be a cleat, bollard, ring bolt, or any other object. This gives an immediate hold if there is any strain on a rope, and also allows further turns, or a knot, to be applied or let go more easily and safely. After taking a round turn on a ring bolt, the rope should be secured by two half hitches. On a cleat or bollard a number of figure-of-eight turns should be taken before finishing with another round turn, or a locking turn.

Some sailors argue that sheets should never be cleated up fully, and that only sufficient turns should be taken to take the weight, the end of the sheet being held constantly by a crewman. This is sensible in a racing dinghy or on a fully crewed ocean racing yacht, but not very practical when cruising or sailing short-handed. Even so, when the sheet is belayed it should never be over-cleated, as you may have to release it in a hurry.

Ropes should always be belayed to a strong holding point, that has no sharp corners to damage the rope. Cleats should be

Turning Up a Rope on a Bollard

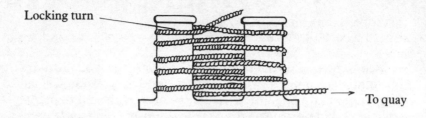

Locking turn

To quay

as large as necessary to avoid the rope jamming beneath the horns, and should always be through-bolted to a strong backing plate. Having belayed a rope, always coil up the end neatly, so that it can be let go without snagging.

Belaying a Rope Round a Cleat

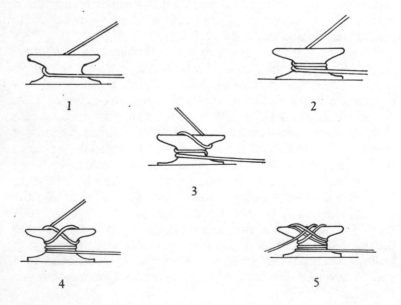

STOPPERS

A stopper is any means of holding a warp, sheet, halyard or guy temporarily whilst its lead or cleating point is being changed, or when it is necessary to take the weight on a rope whilst removing a riding turn on a winch.

The old fashioned stopper is a short rope strop made fast to a secure point, and attached by means of half hitches to the rope to be belayed. It should be led as near as possible in line with the strain on the rope. The stopper rope should be of a smaller size than the rope it is to hold, but strong enough to take the strain. Always ease the strain gently onto the stopper and make sure someone is holding its tail all the time the strain is being held. Once the main rope has been re-led, take the weight, and only untie the stopper when all weight on it has been removed.

Stoppers can also be put on wires, but the stopper should be of chain with a rope tail. The method is exactly the same as for a rope stopper.

Stopper on sheet to enable winch to be changed

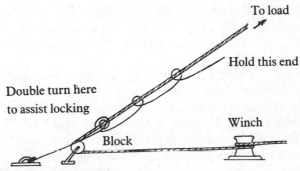

To load

Hold this end

Double turn here
to assist locking

Winch

Block

Eyebolt or other secure point

JAMMERS

The modern type of stopper is the jammer which operates on a cam lever and works by compressing the rope between a fixed base plate and the serrated edge of the cam. The greater the strain on the rope, the tighter the cam is jammed onto the rope. These stoppers are fixed in place, and must be carefully lined up so that they fall exactly in the natural line taken by the rope to its winch. To release the stopper, the weight must be taken on a winch and then the cam lever can be swung free. The advantage of this sort of stopper is that it allows ropes that are not being used to be left under tension and frees the winch for other purposes. However, be wary that the teeth on the jammer are not too sharp as they can cut into the rope. Never leave any rope bearing a load on a jammer; it should be held on a winch or a cleat.

COILING ROPE

Rope should never be left in a heap on deck. Apart from this being untidy, the rope will tangle and kink, and then will not run out quickly through a block or lead. Left lying, a rope can become entangled with other ropes or deck fittings, or trip up the crew. It can also slip overside and possibly become entangled with the propeller. Left on deck, a rope gets wet, and picks up dirt which can damage the fibres, particularly with man-made fibre rope.

Right-handed rope should always be coiled clockwise. Left-handed rope should always be coiled anti-clockwise. Braided rope should be coiled in figure-of-eights. Once coiled, rope should be hung up clear of the deck, and not left lying around on deck or in lockers. If a rope has been properly coiled and hung up, it should not tangle when being uncoiled.

When coiling a rope onto a drum or spool, one person should revolve the drum, and another feed the rope onto the drum so that the turns lie tightly together. When taking a rope off a drum, hang the drum on a swivel and pull the rope off the drum. If the rope is just thrown off the drum, it will build up turns and be more likely to kink.

If a rope becomes full of turns, one easy method of clearing them is to pay the rope out overside when the boat is moving, taking care that the rope flows clear of the propellers. The turns will unravel themselves after a time, and the rope can then be hauled back onboard, coiled, and hung up to dry.

COILING WIRE ROPE

It is very rare to find wire that is not laid up right-handed, so it is generally safe to assume that a wire should be coiled up clockwise. If there are turns in the wire allow the wire to coil the way it wants. It will form a coil turn that flips beneath itself, known as a French turn. After putting in a French turn, carry on coiling up as before, unless further turns are in the wire in which case further French turns may be required. Once a wire has been coiled up, put three or four lashings around the coil to hold it in place.

Avoid pulling on a wire rope which has tight turns in it. The turns will tend to pull even tighter, and will eventually kink the wire permanently. The only really effective method of removing turns from a wire rope is to lay the wire out for its full length, and then roll the turns out towards the nearest end of the wire.

SWEATING A ROPE

This is a method of gaining extra tension on a rope that has been pulled tight, where there is no tackle or winch available; for example, a halyard coming down a mast to a cleat just above deck level.

Take a loop round the cleat and hold the tail in the left hand. Then heave the main part of the halyard away from the mast with the right hand. Swing your weight in towards the mast and downwards, at the same time taking up the slack on the halyard created by this movement with the left hand. Provided the tension is always held with the left hand, it should not slip. If two people are available, one can heave the halyard out from the mast and the other hold the tail around the cleat, and heave in the slack.

Any rope can be sweated like this provided there is a good cleat to take a turn around.

HEAVING LINES

All boats should carry a heaving line, and it is a requirement of most race safety regulations that a buoyant heaving line of at least 15 metres (50 feet) in length be carried in an accessible place. It is used as a messenger, between two boats or a boat and a quay, when it is desired to pass a heavy tow line or mooring warp. The lightweight buoyant heaving line also acts as an item of safety equipment, and can be thrown towards a person in the water or a liferaft.

Commercial heaving lines are usually made up from ratline, but nowadays most yacht heaving lines are made from 5/16 inch (8 mm) diameter polypropylene line. To make up a heaving line, make a monkey's fist (see Chapter 5) at one end of the chosen length of line, placing a small weight in the middle of the knot; golf balls are an ideal size and weight.

To use a heaving line, make up a small coil of the line, which includes the weighted end, of perhaps eight turns, then make up another slightly larger coil. Make the other end fast onto a stanchion or other convenient holding point on the boat. Then take the smaller coil in your throwing hand, and the other coil in the other hand, and throw both coils at the target. It is essential to ensure that there are no turns in the line, as if there are it will tangle and fail to reach the target. Like everything else involved in good seamanship, practice improves performance.

When throwing a heaving line, try to throw it close to the receiver, but slightly to one side, as the impact of the knot in the end can be painful.

SWINGING THE LEAD

A lead line consists of a suitably shaped lead weight attached to a light line, which is marked at intervals to show the depth of water when the weight touches the bottom. Swinging the lead line to obtain a sounding requires practice, and it is best learned when the boat is at anchor or moving slowly in uncrowded waters. Keep other people clear as, to start with, the lead may become out of control and land anywhere.

Carefully uncoil the line and make sure it has no turns. Then make a small coil of about six or seven loops of the lead line and follow this with a larger coil. Secure the inboard end of the lead line to an eyebolt or something similar on deck.

If right-handed, stand at the position of maximum beam of the boat on the starboard side forward. It is going to be necessary to lean out overside, so secure yourself to the boat with a safety harness in such a way that you can lean out against the harness. Take the lead line about eight feet from the lead in the right hand, and allow the lead to hang down. It should be clear of the water. Take the rest of the coil in the left hand. Then start to swing the lead fore and aft, making sure that the lead is swinging parallel to the ship's fore and aft line. When the swing is felt to be under control, increase it until the lead is coming up almost horizontal at each end of the swing and then let go when it is going forward and horizontal on the next swing. As the line is let go with the right hand, throw out the line in the left hand, so that the lead can fly forward unrestrained. Once the lead hits the water, allow it to fall to the bottom unrestrained, but with the line passing over the hand so that you can feel when the lead stops falling. Quickly gather up any slack and observe the point on the lead line at the water's surface as the line becomes vertical. Then call out the depth to the helmsman or skipper and haul the leadline inboard and coil it carefully for another throw.

Normally underarm swings are sufficient to get the lead well forward when a small boat is underway, and gives the leadsman time to allow the lead to reach the bottom before it passes beneath him. However, in a fast-moving boat or deeper water, the lead will need to be heaved further forward so that there is more time for it to reach the bottom. The full overarm swing will give the lead greater momentum, but it requires more skill and practice. Start by swinging the lead as before, but when the lead has reached the horizontal point on each swing, put extra force into the next swing forward and take the lead round in a full circle. Usually three overarm swings will be sufficient, then let go when the lead is coming up to the horizontal on its forward sweep.

If the boat has a high freeboard, it will be possible to lengthen the amount of line between the lead and the leadsman; however, start with a short length, and then gradually allow more line to slip out through the right hand once the swings have gathered momentum.

Arming the lead   When the nature of the bottom is needed to confirm a position, the lead line is armed so that it can bring back a small sample of the sea bottom. In the bottom of the lead is a small cavity into which is pressed a mixture of tallow and white lead. When the lead strikes the sea bottom, some particles will adhere to the mixture, and can be brought to the surface for examination.

Markings on a lead line   The standard hand lead line is 25 fathoms of three-stranded dressed hemp of half inch (12 mm) diameter; however nowadays, a polyester braidline would be more convenient. Always wet and stretch hemp before putting the marks on the line.

There are twenty divisions on a lead line at one fathom intervals, nine 'marks' and eleven 'deeps'. (This leaves 5 fathoms of unmarked line at the top end.) The marks are as follows:

    2   Fathoms – A piece of leather with two tails
    3   Fathoms – A piece of leather with three tails
    5   Fathoms – A piece of white linen
    7   Fathoms – A piece of red bunting
    10 Fathoms – A piece of leather with a hole in it
    13 Fathoms – A piece of blue serge
    15 Fathoms – A piece of white linen
    17 Fathoms – A piece of red bunting
    20 Fathoms – A cord with two knots

The deeps are at 1, 4, 6, 8, 9, 11, 12, 14, 16, 18 and 19 fathoms.

They are sometimes indicated with a small piece of marline, but may be left unmarked, and the leadsman will judge them. Notice that all the marks use different colours and materials, so that it is possible to feel the depth at night.

On a yacht, a 20 fathom lead line may be too long and a 20 metre line more convenient (allow 25 metres total length). If so, the marks should be put on at metre intervals instead of fathoms. A standard hand lead weighs between 7 and 8 pounds, but a 3–4 pound weight will suffice for a smaller yacht.

THE LOG

The log is an accurate system used for telling the boat's speed and distance covered. Speed at sea is measured in knots (nautical miles per hour). The nautical mile is the average distance on the earth's surface subtended by one minute of latitude. This is about 6080 feet, but is generally taken as 6000 feet, 2000 yards, 1000 fathoms or 10 cables.

The earliest form of log was a triangular piece of wood on the end of a line which was thrown overside so that the wood stayed stationary in the water and the line was paid out from the ship. By measuring the amount of line paid out in a fixed time, say 30 seconds, the speed could be calculated.

The calculation is quite simple. If the boat is making a speed of one nautical mile per hour, it will cover 6000 ÷ 60 minutes = 100 feet per minute. Thus in 30 seconds, 50 feet of line will be paid out. If the boat is making a speed of 12 nautical miles per hour, 600 feet of line would pay out in 30 seconds. In practice, if these units were being used, a knot was put in the line every fifty feet, and so it was only necessary to count the number of knots that paid out in 30 seconds to know the speed. Hence the term knot as a unit of a vessel's speed. Distance was calculated by taking the average of the hourly readings.

If a shorter line is all that is available, cut down on the time selected for measurement, and shorten the distance between the knots accordingly. Thus, place the knots 25 feet apart if 15 seconds is being used, or 16 feet 8 inches apart if 10 seconds is the time chosen.

Trailing Log   The trailing log was a successful method of providing an accurate and continuous record of the distance covered. It consists of a rotator with slanted fins attached, which when dragged behind a boat at the end of a braided line will be rotated once as it passes through a fixed distance of water. A small clock instrument is attached to the other end of the line on the boat which counts the number of revolutions and is calibrated to convert it to distance travelled.

To stream a trailing log, clip the tow line on to the clock and pay out the line as a bight until the rotator is in the hand. Then throw the rotator well clear into the water. This avoids the rotator becoming tangled in its tow line and also, by putting the rotator out last, the line does not get wound up before it is clipped on to the clock.

To hand the log, start pulling the tow line inboard and then unclip it from the clock. Pay out the clip end of the line on the other side of the boat as fast as the line is hauled in. This keeps the two ends clear of each other and, if the line is passed inboard of a stanchion, gives you a better chance of grabbing the line again if it slips from your hand. Hold the rotator until all the turns have been removed from the line and then haul in again and coil up the line.

Trailing logs are very accurate, but they are more trouble to set up than the modern hull-fitted impeller with electronic read-outs for speed and distance covered. They are difficult to read when the clock face becomes wet, particularly at night. Another disadvantage lies in the line trailing astern, and the occasional liking for rotators shown by sharks and dolphins.

LIFELINES

The guardrails and stanchions on most small craft are not strong enough to take the weight of a crewman being thrown across the deck, and they give a false sense of security. If bad weather is expected secure lifelines should be rigged along the vessel, either to provide handholds or a strong point on which to fasten a safety harness.

The lifeline should be a specially made wire or strong rope. It should lead as nearly as possible down the centre-line of the boat, so that a crew member at the full stretch of his safety harness can reach the guardrails, but cannot fall overboard whilst still attached; being dragged alongside the boat in the water is extremely dangerous.

Obvious places to secure the lifeline are the mast and stem-head forward and something strong, like a winch, aft. It should be secured at intervals of not more than ten feet. Set the lifeline up as taut as possible so that it cannot move about and snag fittings on deck.

A simple method of setting up a rope lifeline is to secure the end to one firm point and lead the line towards the other chosen secure point. About 2 or 3 feet from that point, put a marline spike hitch in the line and then take the line through or round the second secure point and back and through the loop of the marline spike hitch. Then pull tight. This gives a mechanical advantage of about two to one, and allows the line to be made taut. Once the line is taut, grip the line as it comes through the loop of the marline spike hitch so that it cannot slip and knot it with a couple of half hitches.

SENDING A MAN ALOFT

Inspections, repairs or breakages to the mast or rigging can be easily made using the boat's equipment by sending one of the crew aloft in a bosun's chair.

The traditional bosun's chair is made from a stout plank of wood, about 2 feet to 2 feet 6 inches, by 8 to 10 inches. The wood should be at least one inch thick. Four holes, one inch in diameter, are drilled about one inch inside each corner. Then take about 4½ metres (15 feet) of new 16–20 mm (⅝–¹³⁄₁₆ inch) diameter rope, preferably terylene, and lead it up through one hole and down the hole on the same side but opposite end of the plank. Lead it diagonally across the bottom of the plank to the opposite end, up through the vacant hole, and then back down through the vacant hole the other end. Now short end splice the two ends of the rope together beneath the plank, and seize them together where they cross over. Hang the chair by the resulting two rope loops above the plank from a hook, with a weight on the plank to stretch the rope out. Finally, take a large galvanised eye, and seize the two ropes together at the apex over the eye. This will provide an obvious fastening point for hoisting and prevent wear on the ropes. If there are any signs of wear on the ropes on a bosun's chair at any time, the rope should be renewed immediately.

The modern bosun's chair is custom made out of heavy sailcloth, and has webbing straps sewn into it leading to a ring which provides the fastening point. Never buy one that does not have a wooden seat sewn into it, as without this seat the chair becomes very uncomfortable in use after a short time. Chairs of this modern type, some of which have straps to retain the chair round the thighs, are – if properly made – much safer to use than the traditional chair, but they should be inspected regularly for signs of chafe or wear, and taken to a sailmaker for repair if you are not confident of your own ability.

In an emergency, when it is necessary to go aloft but there is no chair on board, a bowline on a bight may be used. Double-up six to ten feet of 16 mm (⅝ inch) diameter rope, and make a bowline over the doubled-up part. The line is doubled because the two thicknesses of rope are easier to sit on. When the end of the bight is pulled through to complete the knot, make sure that there is sufficient length in the bight so that it can be passed under the arms of a person sitting in the bowline. This provides support for the back of the user and a greater degree of safety.

When choosing how to send someone aloft, you must take into account what has to be done and where. If it is to work before the mast, then any masthead halyard for the genoas or spinnakers will do. If it is to work behind the mast, then the main halyard is best. If the mainsail is set, then the spinnaker halyard will have to be used. If the work is at the masthead, remember that the spinnaker halyard is usually passed through a masthead swivel block secured to a crane and this will keep the person slightly clear of the mast. A genoa halyard usually goes through a sheave into the mast, and this will restrict the person's freedom of movement when he is at the top.

Never send anyone aloft on a damaged halyard, or a halyard that is insufficiently strong to bear the person's weight and the jerks that inevitably occur. If none of the halyards are strong enough, then either the mast must come down, or find a crane and send the person aloft in a bosun's chair on the crane hook.

When securing the bosun's chair to the halyard, never rely upon a snap shackle alone. Clip the shackle onto the chair, but then back it up with a lashing of rope from above the swivel on the snap shackle and round the securing ring or rope of the chair. If the halyard does not have a shackle in the end, it may be hitched onto the chair. A good locking knot should be used. A bowline is usually all right, but I have known one come loose on new rope. Secure the end of the bowline with a couple of hitches, or use a round turn and two half hitches to start with. Always check the knot, with the weight on it at deck level, before sending anyone aloft.

When the person is in the chair, and the knot tested, take turns on the most convenient and powerful winch. Put as many turns as possible on the winch drum – a minimum of five – and make sure that a responsible person is tailing, that is, pulling the rope as it comes off the winch. Nowadays many yachts have self-tailing winches, in which case the winchman should always watch the tail of the rope and should stop winching and hold the tail if he wants to pause for breath, or look aloft. Care must be taken to avoid riding turns on the drum. If they do occur, stop winding the winch, and tell the person in the chair what has happened so that he can grasp a shroud for safety. Then gently surge the line on the winch until the riding turn has been cleared. The most usual causes of riding turns are a bad lead, or the person in the chair pulling himself up with his arms and momentarily taking his weight.

Once the person aloft has reached the desired height, belay the tail of the rope on a cleat, or back onto the standing part of the halyard. This should now not be tampered with without informing the man aloft. The bosun's chair should, if the work to be done will take any length of time, be tied to some convenient point aloft to hold it in place.

When someone is aloft, one person on deck should be watching him continuously, and ensuring that no-one else touches the winch. In order that the person in the chair can be heard in an emergency, keep shouting on deck to a minimum.

When the time comes to lower the person in the chair, carefully take the rope off the cleat or undo the knot, ensuring that the tail is held firmly at all times; then reduce the number of turns on the winch to five if the winch drum is smooth, or four if it is roughened. Holding the tail of the rope in one hand, ease the turns around the winch with the other. Whilst lowering the man, watch the winch *not* the person aloft. Try to ease out the line smoothly, as if it is jerked the descent becomes uncomfortable for the person in the chair and the risk of the rope running away around the drum increases. The person in the chair should try to hold onto something firm, for example a shroud or stay, and push himself clear of obstructions such as spreaders as he descends.

If the boat is pitching or rolling, the chair becomes a pendulum from the masthead as soon as it leaves the deck; preventing swings or jerks is then exceedingly difficult. If the chair is jerked away from the mast, it will swing back again with considerable force which can cause injury. When sending someone up the mast at sea, therefore, shackle a spare halyard to a point close to the foot of the mast, haul it as taut as possible on a winch, and tie it off. Then put the bow of a shackle from the bosun's chair around this halyard. The chair cannot now swing far from the mast, and the person in it can use the mast as some support as he goes aloft.

The golden rule when working aloft is to take your time; do not allow yourself to be distracted, and always double check everything that you do.

TAKING EQUIPMENT ALOFT

If work involving equipment, nuts and bolts or screws, is necessary, the most convenient method of taking these up the mast is in a bucket suspended within arm's reach of the chair. In a seaway, however, the bucket can swing about and tip out its contents, so a canvas bag closed by a zip or velcro is better.

Any tools, or heavy items that are to be taken above the deck should be tied to the chair by lanyards so that whatever happens, they will not fall down onto the deck causing injury or damage, nor necessitate either using another halyard to send them back aloft, or lowering the person down to retrieve the implement.

WATCHKEEPING

On small boats, any watchkeeping system can be used as long as it serves to provide enough people on duty at any time to work the boat and give everyone enough sleep. There is no point in having a system that gives only one hour of sleep as a body has only just relaxed in the first hour. At least three to four hours is a minimum to aim for, eight being a luxury. Obviously in a small crew the system will have to vary a bit, as there will be times when everyone is needed on deck, and it may not be possible to have regular watches. This does not matter as long as each member of the crew gets a good period of rest from time to time. The fundamental point in any watchkeeping system is to ensure that each person has the same quantity of rest. Once people get tired, the fact that they think they have had less rest than anyone else can build up into a major cause of resentment.

In the days of sailing merchant ships, where crews were small, the system operated was four hours on watch and four hours off, with all hands required for any major manoeuvre. Nowadays there are two standard British watchkeeping systems, which are basically similar, the Royal Navy and the Merchant Navy systems. The only difference lies in the fact that in the Royal Navy the 1600 to 2000 watch is divided into two, known as the dog watches, so that if there are only three watchkeepers, the watches they keep will vary from day to day. In the Merchant Navy, where it is rare for there to be more than three watchkeepers, a more regular system is preferred.

0000 to 0400	Middle Watch
0400 to 0800	Morning Watch
0800 to 1200	Forenoon Watch
1200 to 1600	Afternoon Watch
1600 to 1800	First Dog Watch
1800 to 2000	Second Dog Watch
2000 to 2400	Evening Watch

As a variation to this, in a Whitbread Round the World Race, we used a system that divided the day into five periods, starting from 0800 and shared between two watches. The daytime was divided into two six hour watches and the night into three four hour watches. The idea was to limit the time anyone was exposed to the cold at night and change the routine daily. Cooking and cleaning were carried out by one person from each watch every day which, with watches of six crew, meant that every sixth night each crew member had a full night's sleep.

With a smaller crew, six hours would be too long. A crew of three for instance, could do four hours on, eight hours off; but three on and six off would be more efficient. In this case, there would have to be an arrangement for calling someone else up on deck, and the fairest system is for the person just off watch to be the standby for the first hour and a half after they have finished their watch, and the person going on watch next is on standby for the one and a half hours before they go on. This means that with any luck at all, everyone gets three hours of uninterrupted sleep.

It used to be customary to sound the ship's bell at each half hour, starting with one strike half an hour after the beginning of each watch and adding an additional strike for each half hour. By the end of the watch of four hours, eight strikes or eight bells would have been reached. The only exception to this are the dog watches where the first watch would normally finish on four bells at 1800. However, eight bells is rung at the end of each dog watch to indicate the finish of a watch. It was also customary to sound sixteen bells at midnight on 31 December each year to indicate the year's end.

ROWING

For many people the preferred means of dinghy propulsion is an outboard engine. However, if this fails, the dinghy will have to be rowed, and a good dinghy rowing technique is something every yachtsman should develop. Sailors do not row boats as do scullers; they pull them, leaving the arms outstretched on the oars, and taking the weight on the legs, pivoting the body at the waist. Practised properly, this can be kept up for long periods without fatigue. If the oar is in a crutch, it should be 'feathered' after each stroke; that is, as the oar is lifted out of the water, the blade is turned horizontal for its sweep forward, and then turned vertical just before it is dug into the water for the next stroke. In many inflatable dinghies, with built-in crutches, feathering is not possible, but when the oar is held in an ordinary crutch it only requires a small turn of the wrist.

On multi-oared boats, which are not often seen nowadays, the rowers should take their time from the aftermost oarsman on the port side who is known as stroke, and all the oars should enter and leave the water in time with the stroke oar. When approaching a ship or landing stage, the order 'bowman' is given by the helmsman (or coxswain). The forward most oarsman takes one more stroke, and then 'tosses' his oar, by raising it into the air, blade uppermost. He then carefully 'boats' his oar by laying it down between the two lines of oarsmen, and picks up the boat hook or painter ready for going alongside. If the boat is going alongside, the oars on that side will need to be got out of the way. Normally an oared boat will approach an objective almost at right angles and when close, the helmsman will give the order 'oars' to the side going alongside, after which the oarsmen will take one more stroke and then hold their oars clear of the water. Their next order will be 'toss oars port/starboard', so that they bring their oars up in the air out of the way. The other side of rowers will receive the order 'hold water starboard/port', after which they will put their blades into the water to provide maximum resistance. The boat, which will carry some forward momentum, will pivot round the rowers holding water and, ideally, end up stopped parallel to the wharf or jetty. The order 'oars starboard/port' is then given to lift the oars holding water clear, then 'toss oars'; and finally 'boat oars', when all the rowers lay their oars down the centre-line of the boat, blades aft.

The only other oar orders are those required to bring the oars down from the 'toss oars' position to the rowing position – 'down oars', and 'rest on your oars' which is given when the crew have been rowing and need a rest. This latter order is given after 'oars', so the oars are already horizontal, and are now slid inboard so that they rest across the boat. On the command 'oars ready' the oarsmen lean forward so that their oars are ready to take a stroke, and 'give way together' is the order for all the oarsmen to put their blades into the water and pull. If the boat wants to be turned, 'give way port' or 'give way starboard' is used.

If approaching another vessel in a seaway, the boat's oars need to be brought inboard before getting too close as otherwise the rowers may be injured. The ship to be boarded should rig a boat rope from well forward which hangs down in the water and can be taken hold of from the boat. Once this boat rope has been caught, get all the oars out of the way, and use it to pull the boat alongside, making sure that there are good fenders on the near side. When boarding, the boat will probably be rising and falling in relation to the ship, and crew should grasp the boarding ladder at the top of the rise, and scramble further up as quickly as possible to avoid being injured by the boat rising again. The crew still in the boat should fend the boat clear whilst others are boarding; and as soon as a person has transferred to the ladder the boat's rudder should be put over to steer away from the ship's side. Assuming that the ship has slight headway, the pull on the boat rope will supply the steerage.

Before going alongside, crutches should always be removed as they can snag on an obstacle or cause damage. A single oarsman will manoeuvre his boat in exactly the same manner, boating his oars and removing crutches before coming alongside.

YACHT TENDERS

Although many yachts do little more than cruise from one marina to another, a tender is still an essential part of a yacht's basic equipment, and an essential part in certain emergencies. In small craft, stowing a dinghy has always been a problem as deck space is very limited, and the introduction of the inflatable dinghy has been a tremendous asset. In medium to large craft, dinghies can be stowed in chocks on deck or hung from davits over the stern.

The traditional clinker-built wooden dinghy is illustrated because although they are rarely seen nowadays, the names of the various parts of the dinghy have been passed on to its GRP or rubber successor.

There is no point in carrying a dinghy that is going to have a greater capacity than the boat requires as it will only present

Parts of a Clinker-built Dinghy

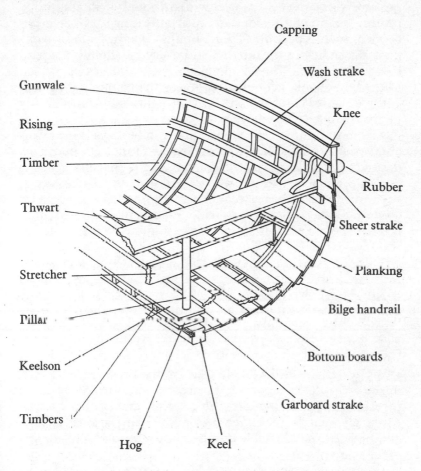

Capping

Wash strake

Gunwale

Rising

Knee

Timber

Thwart

Rubber

Stretcher

Sheer strake

Pillar

Planking

Keelson

Bilge handrail

Timbers

Bottom boards

Hog

Garboard strake

Keel

stowage and lifting problems. At the same time, some dinghies on the market are more suited to private swimming-pool use, and have no place on a yacht. A dinghy capable of carrying 2 or 3 people plus room for some stores is quite sufficient for the average cruising yacht. If more crew are being carried then more than one journey should be made. Never overload a dinghy; a passing wash can swamp it, causing panic in people unaccustomed to the water, and wet clothing to those who are.

When people climb into a yacht tender, the centre of gravity rises, so weight should be kept as low as possible. When boarding, always step in as near the middle of the dinghy as possible so that weight is evenly distributed. Climbing in by putting weight on the side can capsize the dinghy. Once in, sit down as soon as possible. There should never be more than one person standing in the dinghy, and everyone should be seated before casting off. When coming alongside, the nearest person to the bow should get out first, taking the painter with them. The rest should climb out one at a time, and should move slowly to avoid sudden shifts in weight.

The most common small boat dinghy nowadays is the inflatable, usually made of a rubber sealed fabric. Its buoyancy depends upon the air in the compartments that make up its gunwale, and it is susceptible to leaks if it strikes sharp objects, or through age and heavy wear. There are now numerous makes on the market, so the choice is wide. Pump up an inflatable until it is firm before use, but if it is pumped up in the morning, and the day is going to be warm, it may be necessary to release air in order not to strain the joints in the dinghy as the air expands. Most inflatables come with repair kits, and the instructions should be followed closely. Always carry an inflatable dinghy ashore, never drag it over the ground as this rapidly reduces its life, and whenever possible wash out any sand or gravel that has gathered in the bottom with fresh water. If the dinghy is to be stowed away for any length of time, it should be washed with soapy water, freshed off, allowed to dry properly, and then dusted with talcum powder to prevent the surfaces sticking together. Looked after properly, a well made inflatable can easily give ten or more years of use. Guard against anyone climbing into an inflatable dinghy with a knife or spike or any other sharp object.

When an inflatable dinghy is left tied from the stern of the boat the oars and pump should always be removed. In windy conditions, the dinghy can be flipped over by gusts, and all the contents lost.

GRP, wood or metal dinghies should be treated in the same manner as large boats of those materials, but they are of comparatively light construction and will not take heavy bangs. If the dinghy is not supplied with all round fendering, it is well worth fitting, as it will protect the dinghy's gunwale and also any boat's side to which the dinghy is moored. Soft rubber hose of about 16 mm (2 inch) diameter makes a good fender if ready-made fendering is not available or is too expensive. Usually most wear on a dinghy comes on its keel or bottom where it is drawn up over a beach or slipway. If the bottom has not been reinforced for this, have it done. On wood and GRP boats a rounded strip of brass screwed on from the stempost down along the keel to the stern is very effective.

Like any boat, a dinghy needs regular maintenance, but because of their work, dinghies tend to get knocked about more than most craft, and regular checks for damage should be made, bearing in mind their light construction.

The yacht's dinghy should never be towed astern of the boat when underway. The painter is usually too light for the strains imposed, and even if a heavy painter is used, the fastening point on the dinghy is likely to be strained or broken. A dinghy made fast to the stern is a hazard when manoeuvring, as it will bump under the stern and there is a risk of its painter entangling the propeller. Before getting underway always stow the dinghy on deck, therefore, even if for only a short trip.

When stowing a dinghy on deck, stow it upside down so that it does not become a trap for water which might affect the stability of the boat if it filled. If dinghies are to be left in davits, always remove the bung so that water will automatically drain out. If an inflatable dinghy, which has no bung, is stowed in davits, stow it at an angle so that water can slosh out of it, and this limits the amount of water that can be retained in the dinghy. A dinghy full of water is a very heavy weight, and could easily strain the dinghy falls or the davits. Always lash the dinghy down securely before going to sea.

Stowing a dinghy on a small boat is always a problem simply because it is comparatively large, and space on a boat is limited. Usually, the only possible space is on the cabin top. If a solid dinghy is stowed on deck, and *has* to be stowed the right way up, the bungs should always be removed. For short voyages, an inflatable may be stowed upside down on the cabin top, but on a longer voyage it should be deflated and stowed in its bag below.

The correct method of tying off a dinghy painter is by means of a round turn and two half hitches, pulled tight. There are other knots, but this is the surest. Always knot the painter to a secure holding point onshore or on the boat. The guardrail is not the place to secure the painter, as the dinghy's weight could damage it; a cleat is best, a strong stanchion base will do. If the dinghy is to be left for any length of time it should be tied near the stern, so that it cannot bump into the boat, or left on a boat boom.

A useful method of keeping a dinghy from banging the stern of the boat in a tideway is to hang a bucket in the water from the stern of the dinghy. The bucket acts as a drogue, and drags the dinghy down tide of the boat. When leaving the dinghy ashore, if there is no suitable holding point, draw the dinghy up clear of the high water mark as otherwise you may return to find that it has drifted away.

A dinghy should never be used without its oars aboard – the outboard may fail unexpectedly – and a baler, or sponge in an inflatable. If the inflatable is to be left for a while, take along its pump as well. At night, a dinghy should always carry a torch. An inflatable dinghy should also carry a repair bung that can be stuck into a tear in a hurry. If the dinghy is to be propelled by an outboard, some spare fuel should be carried.

Always ensure that the painter is stowed inboard when underway. If it trails in the water it can catch in the propeller of the outboard causing a jammed outboard, a torn propeller or a concertina'd dinghy.

It is not smart dinghy work to go racing through an anchorage causing a great wash, and approaches to boats and landing stages should be at slow speed.

Hoisting a dinghy aboard Most adults are able to haul an inflatable dinghy on board, but large inflatables and rigid dinghies will need to be hoisted using a tackle. There are two useful methods and both require a lifting strop. The ideal strop has three legs which secure to each corner aft and to the bow of the dinghy. These legs come to a central point a couple of feet above the centre of gravity of the dinghy where they are secured to a shackle, so that any hoist secured to the shackle will lift the dinghy on an even keel. With light dinghies a halyard from the masthead can be used as a hoist, with a member of the crew holding the dinghy clear of the boat's side and stanchions. Heavier dinghies are best hoisted using the main boom as a derrick.

Sculling It is useful to know how to propel a dinghy using only one oar, in case one should be lost or broken, or the rowlocks (crutches) are lost or come adrift. Any rigid dinghy should have a sculling notch cut into the middle of the top edge of the transom; but if not, a strop to hold the oar or a crutch fitted there will do. Sculling an inflatable is not possible over the transom, unless a crutch is fitted to an outboard bracket, as too much wear would result on the rubber; however, it is possible to scull an inflatable using one of the oar crutches at the side, since inflatables are so flat underneath that they can be driven sideways quite easily in calm conditions. Nevertheless, it is undoubtedly easier to scull a rigid dinghy which has greater inertia in the water.

To scull, balance the oar in the notch or crutch with the blade lying flat and the oar at a slightly steeper angle than for rowing. The blade should be mostly immersed. Work the oar from side to side, imparting a twist (about 45 degrees) with the wrists at the end of each stroke, so that the blade bites downwards and forwards with each sideways sweep. The blade should thus make continuous figure-of-eight progress through the water. The thrust of its forward bite will be transferred to the transom and the sculler himself, thus propelling the boat. The tendency of the oar blade to float upwards, and for the oar to jump out of the crutch, is counteracted by keeping constant bite on the water: the turns at the end of each stroke must therefore be quick, and the next stroke begun immediately. The sideways force imparted to the transom is cancelled out by successive strokes, and the remaining forward force propels the dinghy along.

It takes a few hours of practice to master this skill, but in time one can achieve considerable thrust with either hand, or both, without even having to look at what you are doing. If much sculling is envisaged, an extra leather should be put onto the dinghy's oars, as the fulcrum will probably fall a bit nearer the blade than for rowing.

3 EMERGENCIES

MAN OVERBOARD

Nothing is quite so alarming aboard as hearing the cry 'Man overboard!' or actually seeing somebody fall overside. The victim too suffers a devastating shock, and if he is singlehanded his error will almost certainly be a fatal one. Prevention is therefore, as in other aspects of seamanship, better than cure.

The layout and equipment of the deck can help considerably in preventing such accidents. Uncluttered decks mean less to trip on; strong pulpits at the bow give security when handling headsails or anchors, and a pushpit at the stern provides security aft. Guardrails should be high enough to offer real support and not just trip the crew at knee level. Adequate handholds and grabrails on deck are important especially in the working areas, and a good non-slip deck surface is essential. A decent toe-rail around the deck edge will save many potential crises, and jackstays – arranged as near the centreline of the boat as possible so that they prevent crew from falling off, rather than just allowing them to be towed along on their safety harness lines when they *have* fallen overboard – are further precautions. Strong rings or eyes in the cockpit for the attachment of safety harness lines should be positioned so that the crew can clip themselves on before they emerge from the companionway. When the boat is well heeled, the danger of falling down to leeward when climbing over the bridge-deck in heavy weather is to be guarded against.

In heavy weather the crew are perhaps more likely to be careful to stay aboard. There is an art to moving about on deck in such conditions, keeping body-weight low, and one hand for the ship, one for yourself. Safety harnesses and lifejackets should be mandatory at night, and no crew should go forward on deck without the knowledge of at least one other. But in fair weather the crew will be more off guard, and in some ways an accident is then more likely. Carelessness when moving on deck, or filling a bucket from the sea, or relieving oneself to leeward, or handling a fishing line, could prove a costly mistake.

However, if this serious accident occurs, it is vital to keep the crew's minds on the seamanship involved in manoeuvring the boat back to the casualty, and not give them time to think about their friend whose life is endangered. To avoid panic and confusion, the skipper must take charge immediately and keep calm, as the crew will be looking to him for guidance. He should keep talking and shouting to a minimum as it can cause a distraction, and if possible, keep the crew occupied. If the crew are busy on deck their minds are concerned with the tasks given them and the skipper is able to concentrate on supervising the work required to get the boat back as quickly as possible to the casualty. The skipper needs to be able to think, and a babble of voices shouting confusing and often contradictory orders is the ultimate in distractions.

For the crewman in the water there is the initial shock of contact with the water, the appalling worry as to whether he has been seen, and then whether the boat will return for him. For some this worry is too much, and they react by losing control or panicking, which shows itself in various forms, usually by frantic yelling and movement of the limbs. This has the effect of losing valuable energy, apart from the risk of getting a mouthful of water and choking.

The correct reaction for the casualty is to make as much noise as possible to attract attention, but controlled so that no water gets into the mouth, inflate the lifejacket, and look for the lifejacket light or whistle. By night, use both, and by day start to blow the whistle at short regular intervals as soon as possible. Look to see whether the crew have released a lifebuoy with a marker or light and if so, swim towards it and get the lifebuoy under your arms to provide support. If the lifebuoy is of the complete ring type, the correct method of getting it over your head is to place it in front of you, put both arms inside it, and then flip the furthest side over you so that it comes down behind your head. Rest your elbows on the outside of the ring. If the lifebuoy is of the horseshoe type, place the arms either side of your body from behind and pull the arms forward. You can then lean back into the lifebuoy. It does not matter too much how you get the horseshoe lifebuoy around you so long as you end up with the open end in front, and then you clip the two open ends together.

Remove items of clothing such as boots that can fill and weigh you down, and then float keeping a look out for the boat so that you can wave and whistle as it gets closer. If the water is cold, the need to preserve energy and body heat is of paramount importance. In warm water, a human can remain alive for a considerable period of time. In the tropics, for example, people have survived in the water for five days.

The crew may be able to throw the liferaft overboard immediately, which is particularly desirable in cold seas. The casualty should swim to the liferaft and climb in, then keep a lookout for the returning boat. If necessary he should break open the flares and ignite them to indicate the liferaft's position. As the boat returns for the pick-up, he should stay ready to receive the heaving line.

As the boat returns, the casualty should resist the temptation to swim towards it as the helmsman will be aiming to come close alongside, and your movement may force him to alter his course and therefore his aspect to the wind or seas which he will have chosen as ideal for his approach. Only when the boat is close by should you swim towards it.

In difficult conditions, the crew may not get as close as they would like in which case they will throw a line to you. Take the line around your body and then tie a knot in it, preferably a bowline. When the knot is tight, signal that you are ready to be hauled in.

On board the boat, the moment a crewman is seen to fall overside, sound 'O' in the morse code (three long blasts) on the siren or klaxon, and yell out as loudly as possible 'Man overboard'. At the same time, throw the person in the water a line, if the boat is moving slowly, or a lifebuoy if the boat is moving quickly. The helmsman should note the compass heading at the time the person goes into the water and the navigator the log reading or SatNav position, as if the boat loses sight of the person in the water, it will be necessary to sail back blind on the reciprocal course. Immediately post one of the crew as lookout, and this person is to do nothing but watch the man in the water, preferably pointing in his direction with an arm as this shows the skipper at a glance, and without unnecessary words, in which direction the person in the water lies.

In heavy seas the casualty will be quickly lost to sight behind wave crests. This is why it is so important that the boat's course is known. On one occasion in the Southern Ocean when we lost a man overboard, we had travelled at least half a mile before we had the spinnaker down, and the engine started. Although three crewmen were acting as lookouts, they could not keep the casualty in view. We eventually found him because the sea birds congregated over him and their tight wheeling over one spot led us back to the right place.

If the boat is under power at the time of the incident, the engine should be stopped immediately to avoid injuring the person in the water with the propeller. If the boat is twin screw, stop the engine on the side the person went in. If it is known on which side the man has fallen in, then the helm can be put over so that the stern swings away from him, thus reducing the chance that he will be struck by the boat as it passes him. Once the casualty has floated clear, the engine can be re-started.

When the boat is under sail, start the engine, let fly the sheet or halyards and go about and back towards the victim as fast as possible. Sometimes, and in a good blow in particular, it may be advisable to leave some sail up to help steady the boat – the mainsail, for preference, as it is more easily handled.

If the boat is under spinnaker it will be necessary to get this out of the way before the boat can be turned back. It takes time to get a spinnaker tripped and hauled in, and leaves the deck cluttered, so it is probably best to trip the spinnaker; let go the guy rope from the winch and allow it to run out completely and let the halyard go free and run out as well. This may seem a rather drastic and expensive manoeuvre, but it will be cheap when compared with the value of a life, and it has the advantage of clearing a major restriction on the boat's manoeuvrability at the time when seconds count.

Once all the obstructions have been cleared, the boat can be brought round and headed back towards the casualty. If he is no longer in sight, sail back on the reciprocal course, allowing for leeway, until the distance by log from where the incident occurred is reached, or you come up with the lifebuoy. If you cannot find the lifebuoy, drop the other one and watch your drift in relation to it. This should tell you if you have over or under allowed on your leeway, and you can then head away to compensate for it. It is a good idea to stop the engines, or if under sail heave-to, so as to minimise noise on the boat; this will make it more likely that the casualty's cries will be audible. If the casualty or lifebuoy are still not in sight, commence a square search. This involves going about a cable beyond the point where you thought the man went overboard, and then heading, say, north for a cable, east for two cables, south for two cables and west for three cables before turning north again for three cables, east for four cables etc. If the wind is strong, allow for the appropriate leeway. You do not have to use the cardinal points of the compass for this square search, but choose a first course that is easy to steer to and that has easily calculated right angles.

A cable is a good average distance to use, but in a short steep sea, it might be advisable to use a lesser distance. Once you have started a search pattern, use the entire crew as lookouts. Do not give up the search too quickly; the annals of human endurance are full of cases of people surviving in appalling conditions far longer than official medical tables would allow.

How best to make the approach will depend upon the weather conditions prevailing. Ideally, approach just upwind of the casualty, and stop the engine so that the boat will drift down, stopping with the casualty a few feet off the beam so that he can be hauled in from on deck. Sometimes however, the sea conditions will make this sort of approach dangerous as the boat might be thrown down on top of the casualty. In this case, throw the casualty a buoyant heaving line and tell him to tie it around his waist with a bowline. Try and get the boat head to sea so that the boat pitches more than she rolls, and haul the casualty inboard amidships. If the boat is lying beam on, it will tend to roll more than it pitches, in which case haul the casualty inboard at the bow or stern, whichever is quicker, although the stern will probably be easier. If the casualty is semi-conscious, it may be appropriate to send in a swimmer, tied to a stout line which can be paid out from the boat. The swimmer can get hold of the casualty and then signal the crew to haul him in.

If the boat has no engine, luff up to windward of the casualty, drop the sails on deck, and throw the heaving line towards him. Without sails, the boat will drift only slowly, and should move closer to the casualty.

When there are only two people in the crew, it will not be possible to keep such a good lookout. Throw the lifebuoy and follow the same recovery procedure. One way to help return to the right spot is to throw buoyant items such as cushions into the water at intervals, and then follow them back.

If a crewman goes overboard by night, the problems of locating him are far greater, even if he is conscious and has illuminated his lifejacket light and can blow his whistle. Lifejackets with reflective strips or patches have been demonstrated to show up well in the beam of a torch. Be careful in using a torch that night vision is not ruined by flashing it about haphazardly. In this case getting the boat round onto the reciprocal course is a matter of urgency, and good judgement is required to ensure that the boat returns on her previous track and not to leeward of it. Remember that the casualty will have no leeway but the boat will. In a single-screw power boat, the recognised method of achieving this is the Williamson Turn (described in Chapter 1) in which the helm is put hard over until the vessel's head is 70 degrees off the original course, and then hard over the other way until the reciprocal course is reached. The boat should come back within a boat's width of her previous track, but leeway must be taken into account.

The racing safety rules insist that there should be two lifebuoys on board a yacht and that one at least should have attached to it a danbuoy with flag, a drogue and a flashing light. The concept is excellent. The crew of the yacht should be able to see the buoy by day, or the flashing light by night. The lifebuoy should be close to the casualty who should equally be able to find it quickly. The drogue should prevent the buoy drifting too far from the casualty before he can reach it. The trouble is that all these pieces of equipment are inclined to get tangled and not perform quite as expected in an emergency. It is worth spending a little time and effort to try and arrange the whole package so that it does not get in the way of working the boat, and is yet in an easy position to release. The lifebuoy really has to be placed in a bracket on the guardrail, preferably outboard. Alternatively, it can be clipped onto the backstay or, on a ketch, onto a mizzen shroud. The drogue and light should be in a container or clipped on the lifebuoy bracket. In some boats tubes have been fitted through the transom into which the danbuoy is fitted, with a spring release to keep the buoy in the tube until it is necessary to release it. Some form of catapult is advisable on this system, as it is sometimes difficult to get the buoy clear of the tube.

A length of about 50 to 100 feet of buoyant line on the stern, kept coiled and ready to be thrown instantly, is probably as good as anything for an immediate response to a man overboard. If it is thrown to the man in the water, and the helm put down instantly to bring the boat head to wind, the casualty will hardly be towed any distance before the boat stops, and can be hauled in immediately. However, if the boat is moving at 4 or 5 knots or more, and is not brought up to wind quickly, the casualty will not be able to hang onto the line, due to the drag of his body. There is also a risk that if he does manage to hang onto the line whilst the boat is still moving, he will choke on water washed into his mouth. This is a system for instant response, therefore, which might work if circumstances permit, but it should not be considered as a substitute for a lifebuoy.

Once the casualty has been brought alongside, heave him on board as quickly as possible, taking care to avoid injuring him on the boat's side. Where there are three or four crew available on deck, heaving one person inboard is not too much of a problem. If the boat has a high freeboard, and the casualty does not have a rope secured around his chest, it may be necessary for someone to go into the water and tie the line around him. Sometimes, especially if the casualty is in a bad way, it will be preferable to launch the dinghy, particularly if it is of the inflatable variety, and place a crewman in the dinghy to recover the casualty. It will not necessarily be easier to recover him from the dinghy, but at least he is safe from drowning. If the casualty is in good shape he might be able to climb a boarding ladder. The fixed type is easier to climb, but difficult to stow in a handy position. When the boat is short-handed, probably the best method of recovery is to send down a halyard which can be tied around the casualty's chest. He can then be winched on board. Do not just pass the halyard around his chest and clip it back onto itself, as it will tighten and constrict his breathing. Many modern wet weather jackets have safety loops fitted into them, which are ideal for connecting the halyard. If a safety harness is worn, this has a buckle which is a secure fastening point.

Whilst the recovery is being achieved on deck, it is desirable to detail a spare crew member to go below and make preparations for the reception of the casualty. The first task is to put on a kettle and boil water for a hot drink of tea, coffee or soup. Do *not* use alcohol, because this causes further loss of body heat. As soon as the casualty is on board, strip him of his clothes and rough towel him. This dries the skin and the friction of a good towelling will help restore circulation. Do not try to dress him; place him immediately in a dry sleeping bag and then feed him hot, sweet tea for preference. If the casualty is suffering from hypothermia, which is basically loss of body core heat, ideally he should be placed in a hottish bath, but this is rarely possible on a boat, so have one of the crew strip off his clothes and climb into the sleeping bag to warm him with his own body heat; or, if a hot water bottle (hot, but not scalding) is available, place it in the bag close to the casualty's stomach and chest. The immediate objective is to avoid further loss of body heat. Another good method of achieving this is to place the casualty's sleeping bag inside a polythene or plastic bag. The bag effectively retains the heat that would normally escape through the sleeping bag, and thus allows the temperature within the bag to rise more quickly. A polythene bag large enough to encompass a normally extended sleeping bag, and a hot water bottle should be stowed on board for this sort of emergency. As soon as the casualty is able to take food, feed him something warm, light and nourishing, and if necessary spoon feed.

Effective reactions to a man overboard emergency can only be taught to a crew by practice. Before starting a season of racing, or setting out on a long voyage, the whole crew should be put through the drill. Run through the procedures and then go and practise, using a can or other buoyant object as a dummy. Try coming back to the dummy from a variety of situations, including being under spinnaker, and using both sail and power. When the crew understand the procedure, pick one of them privately and tell him to fall overside at some time when you are out on sailing trials, but tell him to do it without warning to you or the remainder of the crew.

This will concentrate minds on the problems, and bring home the need for sharp reactions; it will also make the crew more safety conscious when on deck. Once the 'casualty' is back on board, hold a wash-up and see if there is anything to learn.

Finally, if you are ever unfortunate enough to have a man overboard, write down exactly what happened and what action was taken as soon as the incident is over. At worst, you will need a report for the inquiry; at best, you will have a useful experience to pass on to others.

FIRE

Few threats at sea are as great as a fire on board. Most of the accommodation (and probably the boat itself) is made from highly combustible materials, and in addition there is the fuel for the engine as well as other fuels for the cooker, oil lamps, an outboard, and perhaps some paint – all these highly flammable items stored in a confined space. The utmost care is therefore essential in preventing a fire from starting. Even a small fire will spread quickly, and once it reaches the fuel tanks you are about three minutes late in starting the abandon ship procedure. The potential sources of fire hazard are readily identifiable: they are the galley, the engine room, the electrical circuits and fittings, oil lamps, heaters, and of course cigarettes.

Speed is essential in attacking a fire, as the longer it burns, the more it is likely to spread. The greater the heat created by a fire the harder it will become to extinguish. It is always better to over-react than otherwise. A mess in a boat can always be tidied up; although onerous, this is preferable to watching it burn to the waterline from the liferaft.

The solution to successfully putting out a fire lies in breaking the 'fire triangle' – oxygen, heat and fuel. Water directed at a fire will remove heat and create steam which displaces oxygen. Steam injection into holds has been standard equipment on merchant ships for years. Pumping water into a fire-filled compartment will eventually put out any fire; however, a small quantity of water directed accurately at the fire source can be just as effective, and no risk is run of losing stability or sinking the boat because she has been overfilled with water. Water pumped into the boat is going to have to be pumped out again.

There are five main types of fire extinguisher:

Water pressure   Usually comes in a two-gallon container, and directs a stream of water at a fire when a cylinder inside releases a gas to create a pressure, or the pressure is created by mixing two compounds that, when mixed, give off a gas. Suitable for larger yachts, and against fire in wood, painted surfaces, GRP and furnishings, but should not be used on oil or electrical fires.

Foam Usually comes in two-gallon containers, the foam is formed by the mixing of two compounds. The foam extinguishes the fire by sealing off the fire from oxygen. It should primarily be used for oil and electrical fires, but can be used on any fire. The foam should be aimed at an object above the fire so that it falls onto, and smothers the flames.

Chemical extinguishers There are a number of types available from the carbon tetrachloride hand pump type, which has largely been withdrawn because the gas given off is dangerous, to more modern pressure types which are controlled by a trigger. The sizes vary, but most come in a small convenient size for a yacht, and can be used on oil and electrical fires. The small chemical pressure type extinguishers are available from most chandlers, they should be checked regularly by weighing them to see that the contents are intact.

Dry powder This type of extinguisher uses a CO_2 charge to fire a special powder, (siliconised ammonium phosphate is typical) which interferes with the combustion chain reaction through a complex chemical reaction. It can be used on most fires.

CO_2 The carbon dioxide extinguisher fires CO_2 gas under pressure at a fire, and deprives the fire of oxygen. Once the CO_2 gas has dispersed however, if the cause of fire has not been traced and eliminated, the fire can be re-started, and extra CO_2 has to be applied. It works particularly well on fires on dry and wet materials where, once the flames are out, the fire will not re-start, and it has the great advantage of making no mess.

Electrical fires should be tackled by switching off the power on the affected circuit and then spraying the area with a CO_2, chemical or foam extinguisher. In 1982 I suffered a short-circuit between my two banks of batteries, with the result that the battery terminals became red hot and burned away all their insulation creating a vast amount of smoke. I managed to rip off one of the battery terminals before the fumes forced me out of the compartment, and it was fifteen minutes before the smoke had cleared sufficiently to allow me to start sorting out the mess and restoring power to the boat.

Apart from burns from the flames, the greatest danger from a fire comes from the smoke which can cause asphyxiation. Very few yachts carry smoke-breathing apparatus which allows the fire-fighter to draw air from a cylinder or from a hose led up on deck so remember that heat and smoke rise, and when tackling a fire in a compartment go in below the smoke, where there will still be oxygen to breathe. However, keep enough clean air in your lungs to allow yourself time to escape if the smoke thickens. Where crew are available, tie a safety line around your waist, and leave one of the crew on deck holding the line so that if the fire-fighter is overcome by fumes, you can trace his whereabouts with the line, or haul him out. Before going into a compartment to fight a fire, cover as much flesh as possible, and soak your clothing, prevent it being set alight by sparks or flames and protect the skin. This applies to all fires apart from high voltage electrical fires, but high voltage (240 volts) is usually only to be found in larger yachts.

If the smoke thickens to the point where it is impossible to remain in the compartment, try aiming extinguishers, or if dealing with a non-oil or electrical fire, buckets of water, at the source. If this fails, seal off the compartment to cut off fresh oxygen and wet down the areas near to the fire to stop it spreading to other compartments. Whilst waiting to see whether the fire will go out, start the abandon ship procedure.

If the fire is restricted to a cushion or other movable object, where possible, heave that burning object on deck or overside as it reduces the risk of the fire spreading. Inflammable items in the vicinity of the fire should always be removed to a safe place away from the fire to prevent the fire spreading and finding more fuel. Even though the flames of a fire may have been extinguished, there will still be residual heat around which could re-start the fire. Once the fire has been extinguished, swab the area to remove heat and dampen things down, and keep a watch on the fire source until the area is cooled and the danger of the fire re-starting has disappeared.

Certain areas of a boat are particular fire risks:

The galley This is the most common source of shipboard fires, as not only is there a naked flame, oil is often in use for frying etc. If a fire breaks out, get rid of the source of heat immediately by switching off the burners. If the stove uses gas, make sure that the gas bottle is switched off as quickly as possible. When the fire has reached cooking oil, it has found itself another source of fuel which is difficult to switch off, and some other member of the triangle will have to be removed. If the container in which the oil is burning has a lid, put it on. This will deprive the fire of oxygen and it will soon go out. If it is an open pan and not too full you can try moving the pan away on deck. If it is quite full, the risk is run of dropping burning oil on the way and starting a number of other fires. In this case, the best method of extinguishing the fire is to cover the pan with a fire blanket which will keep out the oxygen. Let the pan cool down before removing the blanket. Should the pan have only a little oil in it, then it may be possible to just let this oil burn off without too much risk, but turn off the burners and stand by with a fire blanket.

Never attempt to put out an oil fire of any sort with water. The water hits the oil and is turned instantly into steam, during which it expands 120 times. The result is an explosion of burning oil and steam.

When the galley is not in use it is advisable to switch off gas if that is the fuel used for cooking. Calor gas is heavier than air, and if there are any leaks in the supply system, the gas will find its way down to the bilges where a spark or light can set off an explosion of considerable force. A normal bilge pump will pump gas out of a bilge, and the bilge pump should be used to clear the foul bilge air or gas at frequent intervals and certainly after the boat has been left for a couple of days or longer.

Engine room An engine requires oxygen, without which it will not run. It also requires fuel and in operation it heats up. It is therefore a very likely source for fires. Most yachts with inboard engines use diesel or gas oil for fuel which is dangerous but only explosive when very hot. Petrol inboard engines are much less safe, as petrol can explode at comparatively low temperatures. If a fire develops in an engine room, the fuel to the engine should be cut off immediately, and the engine switched off and stopped. Then attack the fire with anything but water. If the engine compartment is small, it may be difficult to get at the source of the fire with an extinguisher, in which case deprive the fire of oxygen either by pushing in CO_2 gas as close to the fire source as possible so that the oxygen is displaced, or, in certain circumstances, such as when a lot of smoke is being given off, by sealing the engine compartment and allowing the smoke, which has lost its oxygen, to asphyxiate the fire. This latter method is only safe when the fire does not threaten to reach fuel tanks. Keep a close watch on the compartment when trying to starve a fire, and feel adjacent bulkheads and decks to assess the temperature. If the bulkheads become hotter, more active methods will have to be used.

An automatic fire extinguisher in the engine compartment is always a good investment. This is usually a difficult area to get at, and an extinguisher that goes off automatically when a certain dangerous temperature is reached, can stop a fire before it goes out of control.

Living quarters   Cushions, bedding, furniture, books and clothing are all inflammable, and probably the greatest danger comes from oil lights, electrical circuits and unextinguished cigarettes. Most oil lights carry limited amounts of fuel, but enough to start a fire in something else. If a light spills burning oil, it can be smothered with a blanket, or put out with a chemical, CO_2 or foam extinguisher. A quick reaction will reduce the damage. Electrical fires are best dealt with by switching off the affected circuit, and then putting the fire out with chemicals or CO_2. Only use foam if there is nothing else available as it has to be cleaned up.

Cigarettes can start a smouldering fire which can be treated with water, or any other extinguisher. If the crew includes smokers, make sure that there are untippable ashtrays on board and preferably of the type that has a spring top that seals off the contents. Apart from the fire risk, an overturned ashtray makes an unpleasant mess on board.

If a fire breaks out in a paint store or where lubricants are kept, foam or chemical fire extinguishers should be used, making sure that the foam is aimed so that it lands on the source, and keep spraying until the fire is out.

Every boat should carry at least two fire extinguishers and a fire blanket. In boats of more than 30 to 35 feet, where there are

likely to be more than two compartments, additional extinguishers should be installed, so that there is an extinguisher
within easy reach throughout the boat. Extinguishers should be
spread throughout the boat so that if a fire breaks out in any
compartment, there are extinguishers available from other
compartments to fight the fire. One extinguisher should be kept
outside the cabin, in the vicinity of the cockpit. Another should
be close to the engine compartment. The fire blanket should be
in an accessible place near the galley.

GROUNDING

The first thing to be said about going aground is that it should
not have happened. However, given that no hydrographer will
guarantee 100 per cent accuracy on his charts, and man's
explorative nature, groundings are a hazard that occur. One
should know what to do, therefore.

The first thing to try is to see whether she can be got off
immediately by using the engines going astern. If she will not
then a great deal will depend upon the prevailing tidal and
weather conditions and the nature of the bottom. When the
bottom is rock, clay or hard sand, the boat is not going to sink
into it and, unless she is got off quickly, she is going to heel over
when the tide ebbs. Where the bottom is soft, such as mud, then
the boat will sink in, and has probably already ploughed a
furrow through the mud before the increasing resistance
brought her to a halt. In these circumstances, the boat may
come to no harm at low water as she will sink into the mud until
her buoyancy prevents her sinking further, and the mud will
probably hold her upright. Always check the engine cooling
water filters as the boat floats off again though, as they may have
got blocked by the mud.

If the sea is calm at the time of grounding and there is no
wind, or a wind blowing the boat off the obstacle, and the tide is
rising, then keep the engine going astern and before long the
boat should come off as the water rises.

If the sea conditions are rough and the wind is blowing the
boat further aground, then immediate steps must be taken to

Grounding

Heeling the boat over reduces the draft.

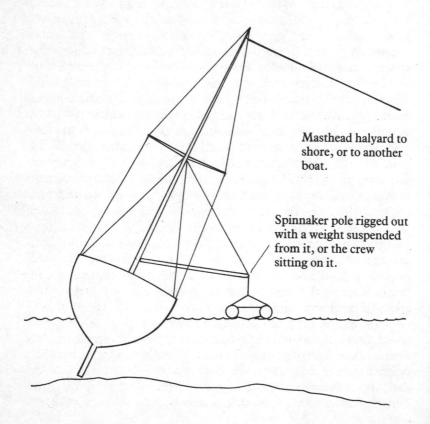

Masthead halyard to shore, or to another boat.

Spinnaker pole rigged out with a weight suspended from it, or the crew sitting on it.

prevent the boat being pushed further inshore, or swinging round beam on to the swell. The best method of securing the boat is by putting out her anchor upwind or up-tide, but so that the anchor is also in position to help pull off the boat. It will be necessary to use the dinghy for this. When putting out the anchor in this situation, put out the heaviest possible anchor and chain with as much scope as possible as the strains on the anchor and cable when being used for holding a boat aground are far greater than when a boat is using her anchor normally. Take up weight on the anchor cable on a winch or tackle. If the boat is pounding, she may move slightly each time a wave lifts her and by keeping tension on the anchor warp or chain, the boat can be inched out into deeper water.

A great deal will depend upon how hard the boat hit the obstacle and the nature of the bottom. If the boat gently comes to a stop, the chance of damage is slight; if she comes to an abrupt halt, the chance of the hull being damaged is greater, particularly if the bottom is rock. The point of impact is also important. When the keel hits the bottom hard, damage to the keel is likely, but unless the keel has been bent by the blow, or the keelbolts disturbed, the boat is unlikely to take water. When the hull hits the obstruction, as might happen on a power boat which has no keel but only a skeg, then the likelihood of holing is much greater.

Where the boat has been holed by the impact, there is no point in trying to move her until the leak has been stopped. If she fills with water she cannot sink because she is aground and salvage will be that much easier. If the leak can be plugged, then the first priority is to stop the ingress of water and pump the boat dry to make her more buoyant.

If she will not move, put all the crew onto one side of the boat, leaning outboard as far as possible to give the boat a list. With most boats this has the effect of reducing the draft, as it brings the bottom of the keel nearer to the surface. The greater the angle of heel the more the draft is reduced, and the point will come when the draft of the heeled boat is less than the depth of water and the boat will float clear. If the crew leaning out overside do not reduce the draft sufficiently, rig the spinnaker pole and swing it out overside with some of the crew at the outer end; this should increase the angle of heel.

Another method of heeling the boat is to take a masthead

halyard to a firm point abeam (which may be ashore or a heavy anchor laid out) and then winch in on the halyard. Alternatively, pass the halyard to another boat and get it to gently but firmly take the strain, pulling away abeam from the grounded boat. The more the other boat heaves, the greater the angle of heel. If the engine is kept going astern the boat should eventually come off astern.

Where a boat has a long keel, as is found on some cruisers and power boats, the draft is usually greater at the stern than at the bow. If the boat is aground at the stern but not the bow, the draft angle can be reduced by putting weight right at the bow. Remember to try and keep the deeper end of the boat towards the deeper water.

If the boat is a sailing boat without an auxiliary or a power boat which, because of the possible damage to the propellers, cannot use her engines, then attempts should be made to either get another boat to tow the boat clear, or kedge the boat off.

When the tide is ebbing at the time the boat goes aground, speed of action is essential. If none of the above methods has been successful, put a slight strain on the anchor cable so that it will tend to pull her off when the tide rises again, and check the bottom. The boat is going to heel over more as the water recedes; the extent of the heel will be dependent upon the state of the tide and how much more it has to fall. It will also be dependent upon the boat's type and hull shape. A power boat with a small keel will not heel over very far if the bottom is even, whilst on the same bottom a sailing boat with a deep keel will lie almost on its side. In both cases, the boat is going to rest on its side or bilge, and if there are sharp obstructions, such as rocks on the bottom, they could well hole the boat when she puts her weight on them. If the obstructions can be moved, then go overside and move them, if not, decide which side of the boat is safer, and heel her over that way, using one of the methods described earlier. When the choice is about the same, always heel the boat over towards the shallower side as this will give the boat less heel when she comes to rest. Where obstructions cannot be moved, place anything that will protect the boat overside between the boat and the obstruction. Fenders, bunk cushions, sails in bags, anything that will act as a cushion once the boat is resting on her side.

It may be possible to prevent the boat heeling over completely by the use of legs. Not many boats carry legs purpose-designed for drying out, but if they are available it is important to get them into position before the boat develops such an angle of heel that the lower side leg is impossible to put on. Jury legs can be rigged using any stout pole such as a spinnaker pole or boom. One pole is unsafe as the boat could pivot on it. Two should be used, preferably one each side so that the boat can be held upright, but if the boat has already taken a list, put both poles over the lower side. The poles must be very securely lashed to the gunwhale and then rigged with lines forward and aft so that they cannot slip. Temporary poles like this are not a safe long-term solution, and the poles may be damaged, but in an emergency they might just hold the boat long enough for the next tide to float her off.

The most difficult case occurs when the boat grounds at high water. Apart from having to wait twelve hours before the next high tide, there is no guarantee that there will be enough water then to give the boat the necessary buoyancy to float clear, whatever the optimistic figures in the tide tables may suggest. Use the time to strip the boat of all possible weight. Carry all the stores ashore, pump out the water tanks, and if containers can be found, pump or siphon the contents of the fuel tanks into them. Set out the anchor or anchors and, as high water arrives, heave in on the anchor warps and use the engine, if that is possible, to try and get into deeper water. If the boat still will not move, then she is stranded.

The prudent seaman always checks the chart thoroughly before entering an unfamiliar stretch of water, and if still unhappy, should only enter at slow speed on a flood tide. Any obstacle hit will then only be struck lightly, and the tide will soon lift the boat clear. When anchored in an unfamiliar anchorage, always check the depth of water beneath the boat, and in the anchor circle in which she could swing, to make sure that there is going to be sufficient water for the boat during low tide. If in doubt, move to deeper water or set up a grounding alarm. A simple alarm consists of a weight, the leadline will do, hung overside until it is a couple of feet or so below the keel. Run the line through a block to the cockpit or skylight, where the tension on the line is used to secure a pan or something robust, in such a way that the moment the tension is gone from the line, the pan will crash onto the deck.

CAPSIZE

A boat is capsized when a force pushes her over to the horizontal or beyond. The force can be external, such as a sudden squall of wind or a large wave, or it may be a shift of a load within the boat.

For the average monohull sailing yacht, a capsize need not necessarily present any great danger, provided that all openings in the hull are closed, as the weight of the keel will bring the boat back upright again once the force causing the initial heel has been removed. However, heavy objects which seem well stowed when the boat is upright or at a normal sailing angle of heel, can suddenly become insecure when the boat is laid on her side or rolled over, and may become lethal missiles which are hurled across the accommodation. Batteries, for example, should be immovably fixed in position. The rig of a sailing boat may be damaged in a violent knockdown, and large windows are liable to be stove in. In the event of a complete roll-over, dismasting would not be unlikely. But these are extreme events which the average cruising or racing yachtsman may not experience in a lifetime of sailing.

In a few rare cases a sailing yacht has remained upside down, but this has been due to the mast filling with water and counteracting the righting force of the keel, or the ballast keel itself falling off, as in the case of Simon Le Bon's *Drum*. A well designed yacht, with a sensible proportion of her ballast in the keel, is inherently unstable when upside down and will always spring back upright. However, if the boat has movable ballast, and this has not been secured properly so that it can break loose, its movement can slow down the righting of the boat, and, in extreme cases, keep the boat capsized. This is apart from any damage or injury that might be caused by the ballast as it moves about. If the ballast does move to the extent that the boat is held down, it will have to be shifted back, piece by piece, either to its original stowage position, or from the lower side of the boat to the upper side. The weights should be jammed in so that they will not fall out again when the boat comes upright. If this seems like hard work, remember the case of a barque, rolled in the Southern Ocean so that her ballast of gravel shifted. The crew spent two days shovelling the gravel back up to the other side of the hold, literally shovelling for their lives.

A monohull rolled by a large breaking wave, is unlikely to remain upside down for long, as she will be unstable in this position. A small nudge, such as would be supplied by another wave, would start her moving from the totally inverted position, and her natural stability will do the rest to bring her back upright.

On power boats, the weight of the engine and fuel will normally pull the boat back upright after a capsize. Again, the watertight integrity of the deck and superstructure is of vital importance. A large superstructure, if sealed, will help the boat to right itself, as it displaces a great deal of water when it is submerged. This provides considerable resistance to the boat turning over beyond the horizontal. This is the principle used to provide self-righting ability with the Arun class of British lifeboats, owned by the Royal National Lifeboat Institution. The high, box-like superstructure is designed to be sufficiently watertight so that in the event of a capsize, the boat is unstable upside down and wants to right itself. Other lifeboats, without a large superstructure, have large inflatable bags on their upperworks. These bags automatically inflate when the boat capsizes, and this buoyancy pushes the boat round to a point where the boat's righting lever operates positively.

Multihulls, once they pass beyond the horizontal, are as stable upside down as the right way up; in fact, the weight of the mast and rigging, if still standing, makes them more stable upside down. In nearly every case, once a multihull has capsized, it must have outside assistance to be brought upright again, and this usually means a large crane or derrick.

There was a very successful righting of a capsized catamaran, during the 1984 OSTAR, in the middle of the Atlantic by Philippe Jeantot. He received assistance from a French research ship for the operation, which took just over two days.

He started by flooding one hull, by opening the deck hatches which were under the water, and then allowing the trapped air to escape through the hull fittings. To compensate for the air still trapped in the hull, about two tons of cement was hung onto the waterlogged hull, which now floated well below the other hull. Next some air balloons were attached to the mainmast halyards, and hauled to the mast head. This had the effect of bringing the boat almost horizontal. Tow lines were then lead

Righting a Catamaran

Boat capsized. It is necessary to send down a swimmer, or find another means to attach some flotation to the mast. Then ballast one hull to start the boat coming upright.

Boat horizontal. Some exterior force will be required to bring her the rest of the way up. Jeantot used a hawser from another boat.

Boat finally upright, and the ballasted hull can be pumped out. With any luck the boat can sail home.

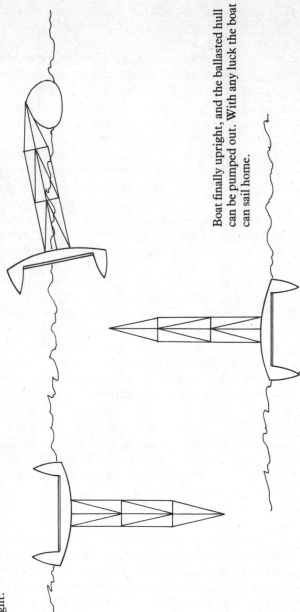

over the uppermost hull, down over the deck and secured to the submerged hull, and the strain taken by the research ship to pull the boat upright. The strain was maintained whilst the cement weights were cut loose and the waterlogged hull pumped dry.

The whole operation was dependent upon outside assistance and a spell of reasonable weather, but the boat was recovered in remarkably undamaged condition.

There have been a number of experiments righting capsized multihulls in the fore and aft plane using the same principle. The forward parts of the hull were flooded to push the bows below water, and then an air bag used to bring the mast up out of the water. By flooding the aft end of the boat, a righting moment was created which brought the boat upright, requiring only to be pumped out to be serviceable again.

In nearly all cases, multihulls, because of their lack of a heavy keel, will float quite safely in the upside down position, provided all hatches and openings have been closed. Modern race requirements insist that multihulls be positively buoyant, and fitted, in each hull having accommodation, with a watertight hatch of a minimum of 45 cm (about 18 inches) diameter which can be opened from inside or outside the hull, and so placed that it will not be underwater when the multihull is capsized. There have been a number of cases where the crew of a capsized multihull have survived quite safely until rescued, and they were undoubtedly safer in their upturned boat than in a liferaft.

As an anti-capsize device, some catamarans are fitted with a float at their masthead which is designed to prevent the boat from going beyond the horizontal. The disadvantage of this is that the float has to be quite large to be effective. Even if the float is streamlined, it still represents wind resistance and weight at the masthead, which is the last place a boat wants excess weight, and although the float may prevent the boat going right over, a boat on its side is little better off than one completely upside down and harder to live in. The only advantage is that it is half way to being righted, but it is a high permanent price to pay for making salvage a little easier.

JURY STEERING

All boats should be fitted with an alternative means of steering in case the rudder, tiller or wheel is damaged. The simplest form of emergency steering, which was standard issue in ships' lifeboats, was an oar, which could be put into a crutch, rowlock or strop at the stern, and used in the manner of the Viking ships. When planning a long cruise it is advisable to equip the boat with a lifeboat oar or similar for this purpose. If an oar is not carried, then it is worth spending some time in advance working out how a jury steering system is to be set up, and if necessary, putting extra fittings on the boat in readiness.

When the rudder or tiller breaks, the first thing to do is stop the boat, by handing all sail or stopping the engines, and then investigate the cause. If the rudder is thrashing around, immediate steps must be taken to control it, or it is likely to damage its gudgeons and pintles. Again there is a lesson to be learned from ship's lifeboats, which had a hole drilled through the outer lower end of the rudder blade through which a line was led from each side of the gunwale, and knotted either side of the hole. This served as an emergency steering system. Yachts will not want to sail around with lines hanging over the stern, but it is worth considering having the hole drilled in the rudder blade at the next re-fit, so that it is there if necessary.

If there is no hole in the rudder, one method of restraining it is to put a rope over the stern, secured on each side of the stern, and haul it tight against the rudder blade. If figure-of-eight knots are put into the rope, the blade will not be able to slip beyond the nearest knots. An alternative is to put lines on each side of a large shackle, from which the pin has been removed, and haul the shackle in tight over the aft end of the rudder blade. This method can be used as a rudimentary steering system, provided the shackle can be held in place, easing on one line as the other is taken up to alter the rudder angle. In a dire situation, even the anchor can be used to restrain the rudder by putting one line on one arm, and another line on the cable ring, and lowering the anchor down the rudder so that the blade is caught between the shank and arm.

If the tiller has broken, an emergency tiller can be set up by lashing any suitable piece of wood or metal to the rudder head.

Jury Rudders

A line lead either side of the boat, from the rudder up, via a
block on deck to winches in the cockpit.

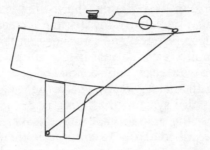

The same basic system can be used with a shackle if there is
no hole in the rudder blade.

Use of spinnaker poles

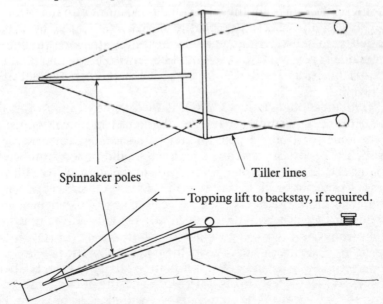

Spinnaker poles

Tiller lines

Topping lift to backstay, if required.

Wood bunk board or similar.

Where the boat has wheel steering, the usual cause of failure is one of the tiller lines. A spare wire, already spliced to fit the system, should be carried but if not, a replacement will have to be made up on board. With hydraulic steering systems, the usual cause of failure is a leak in the hydraulic pipe lines. If insufficient spare oil is available, the manual back-up system should be installed. All hydraulic steering systems should have stop valves in the pipe lines, and a method of isolating the wheel from the hydraulic rams, so that if the failure is due to some other cause, the wheel can be disconnected.

The most difficult repair is where the rudder stock has broken, as any jury system of steering is going to have to be rigged directly to the rudder blade, and this means using one of the methods described earlier to control the angle of the blade.

Where the entire rudder is lost, it is most unlikely that the modern fin keel and skeg yacht will be able to steer herself by balancing the sails, as was occasionally possible with the older, long keel yachts, or with two-masted boats. However it may be possible to control direction by setting the jib, and hanking a small jib or storm sail to the backstay. The jib will provide power and hold the bow off the wind. By trimming the sheet on the small sail, the boat will tend to come into the wind, by easing the sheet, the boat will pay off. If the boat is fitted with self-steering gear which has an auxiliary rudder, this might just work, but it would be unwise to put too much strain on it, and sail should be reduced to keep the speed down.

The most obvious jury rudder is made up by using a spinnaker pole, or a similar spar, over the stern like a steering oar. The inner end of the pole should be lashed to the backstay which then acts as a pivot. Two lines should be led from the outer end of the pole, one to each side of the stern, where they pass through a block and then into the cockpit. Experimentation will show whether these lines need to be led to winches, or whether they can be pulled and eased manually. If the pole is long enough, it may be possible to lash it to the backstay at a point on its length which allows the inner end of the pole to be operated like a crude tiller, with the fulcrum being at the backstay. However, this is hard work and the lines should be rigged for back-up. The pole on its own will steer the boat as it is moved from side to side (this is how punts are steered) but it will be much more effective if a plank, such as the ubiquitous bunk board, is bolted or lashed to it.

Where the stern of the boat is narrow, and the angle of the lines from the spinnaker pole back to the stern is acute, the tension required to pull the pole from side to side will be considerable. It can be lessened by widening the angle, and the easiest way to do this is to lash another spinnaker pole square across the stern of the boat, with blocks at each end, and lead the tiller lines through these blocks instead of the ones on the boat's gunwale.

JURY RIGS

Being dismasted is a serious misfortune for a sailing boat, because the rig provides her motive power. It will tend to occur in extremely heavy weather, but could equally be due to the failure of some part of the rigging. In the quest for aerodynamic efficiency some modern racing boats are rigged rather too lightly, and whilst modern materials are immensely strong they are not indestructible. It is important to avoid personal injury when the mast breaks or falls wholesale over the side. One consequence of the loss of the mast in a monohull will be a much quicker motion of the boat, due to the loss of the inertia aloft; this makes remedial work all the more difficult. If you are not far offshore, then it is best to make for port under power, once you have sorted out the mess, but if this occasion arises when you are in mid-ocean and beyond the reach of outside help, then you have got to improvise some kind of jury, or temporary, rig. Even if you have large fuel tanks, restoring some sail area will steady the motion of the boat and provide a modicum of sail-power.

If the boat is a ketch, yawl or schooner and the mainmast breaks, it may be possible to move the other mast into its position. Before my singlehanded circumnavigation I replaced *Suhaili*'s wooden mizzen with a lighter aluminium spar, so that if I broke the mainmast, I would have an easier task of moving the mizzen up into its place. Provided one mast is left standing, the task of stepping a jury mast in the other position is made

Jury Masts

Setting up a jury mast by means of sheer legs.

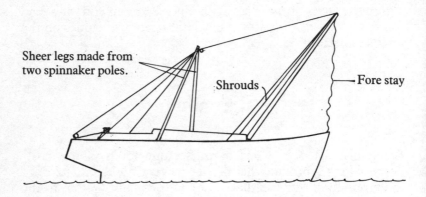

Sheer legs made from
two spinnaker poles.

Shrouds

Fore stay

Simple jury rigs

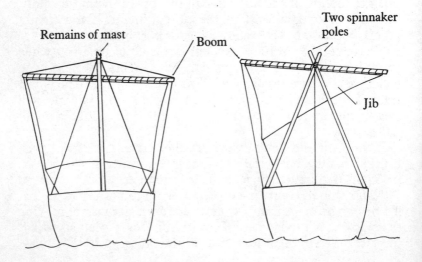

Remains of mast

Boom

Two spinnaker
poles

Jib

much easier because there is already a high point to attach a line to take the jury mast up to a parallel upright position from where tackles can be used on the stays to finish off the job.

Of course, in a ketch or a yawl, it may not be necessary to replace a broken mizzen mast, as the boat may sail perfectly well under the sails on the mainmast alone.

In the event that the only mast has broken, and been lost, then a jury mast will have to be set up from what remains on board, such as the main boom, spinnaker poles or bowsprit. If there is a stump of the mast remaining, a spar, previously dressed with its shrouds, stays and halyards, can be lashed upright to this stump.

A reasonable mast can be made by using two spars as sheer legs, and setting up fore and back stays, but this rig is only suited to a square sail, and another spar will be needed as a yard of sorts.

Jury masts When a mast breaks the first job to tackle is clearing the wreckage, and recovering as much usable rigging and bits of the mast as possible as these may come in handy for making a jury rig.

If part or all of the mast has gone overside, it will be attached to the boat by shrouds and stays, so check that it is not endangering the hull of the boat. The next move is dependent upon the sea state. In anything worse than a small chop, it will be difficult or impossible to try to haul the mast on board, and the wreckage cannot be left lying alongside as it is likely to knock a hole in the hull. If conditions permit, try to recover the sails intact and release all the rigging, but leave a stout line attached to a part of the mast or rigging, and then let go. A wood mast should float clear of the boat, an aluminium one will sink beneath the boat. Either way, the mast should be well clear of the boat, but still attached so that it can be recovered to be used as part of the jury rig when the sea conditions improve.

Where the sea conditions are bad, and it is therefore danger-ous to try and keep the mast attached, all the wreckage will have to be let go completely, and other items that remain on board used to make up the jury rig.

When conditions allow, or if the mast breaks in a reasonable sea, haul the mast in alongside. Start by putting fenders overside between the mast and the hull and lash the mast to the boat to reduce the relative movement between them. Next, remove the rigging by disconnecting it from the mast and then from the deck by undoing the rigging screws and coil it down. This reduces the weight hanging overside, and makes the load to be heaved on board less; it also tidies up the deck and makes working easier.

Hauling the mast on board, unless it is small and light, is not an easy task, and so should be tackled methodically. Move the mast fore and aft until its centre of gravity is level with the midship section of the boat. Pass strops from the deck, down round the mast and back onto the deck again, and attach tackles to the upper end of the strops to form a simple parbuckle.

If no suitable tackles are available, take a line from the upper part of the strop to a snatch block on deck in line with the strop's position and back to a winch. Alternatively, instead of using a strop, take a line from the winch, through a snatch block, and then down over the mast and up from beneath the mast to be secured to some strong point on deck.

On a large boat, more than two strops could be used, but on a boat of, say, 30 feet in length, two should be sufficient; the strops should be placed between 6 and 10 feet either side of midships, depending on how the hull curves. If the hull is fairly straight, the strops may be further apart.

Having rigged the tackles, start to take up the weight. If the mast refuses to come up the side easily, the job can be made easier by fitting a temporary ramp, angled down from the deck into the water, up which the mast can slide. Spinnaker poles, or the main boom will do for the ramp. They should be dropped down overside between the hull and the mast, and then the top end hauled inboard. This will have the effect of moving the mast upwards and away from the hull. The ramps should be fitted with fore and aft guys so that they cannot slip. Once the ramps are in place, hauling the mast onboard with the parbuckles should be a lot easier. Once the mast is aboard, lash it down to the deck, and start to work out what you have with which to set up your jury rig.

Mast intact   If the mast is deck-stepped and has only gone overside because of some rigging failure, then it will probably still be intact. First repair or replace the broken rigging. Even if the only material available is rope, set up temporary rigging replacements with this rope, and make it as tight as possible. It is unlikely to be as strong as the original rigging, but it will provide some support, and if reduced sail is subsequently set, it should take the strain.

Mast broken If the mast has been broken, the first decision is which part of the mast should be used for the jury rig. Normally it would be sensible to use the longest remaining section, as more sail could be set, but sometimes it is advisable to use a shorter section because it will be easier to set up, as when, for instance, the top part of the mast is available, as it has halyard sheaves and tangs intact for the rigging.

When a lower section of the mast is to be used, if the break is just above a spreader, then the spreader level will make a convenient point for the attachment of the fore and backstays. They can either be knotted directly to the mast just above the spreader, or tied off to a strop placed around the mast above the spreaders. Either way, the spreaders will prevent the stays from slipping downwards.

Where the temporary hounds are to be put clear of an obvious point like the spreaders, a jury mast knot will serve to provide good holding points for shrouds and stays. If you are worried that the jury mast knot might slip downwards, you can always put a turk's head around the mast just below the jury mast knot.

Once the temporary hounds are set up, put on shrouds and stays. Blocks will also have to be secured to the hounds to take the temporary headsail and mainsail halyards.

Where the mast has broken close to the deck, thus leaving a stump, it is usually advisable to leave this stump, and lash the jury mast to it. When stepping the mast, make a secure lashing to hold the foot of the jury mast to the bottom of the stump at deck level, and, once the mast is upright, lash it to the stump. The best system of lashing is to take at least a dozen tight turns around the two pieces of the spar, and finish off by frapping the lashing between the two spars and tying it off. If there is space, put more than one such lashing round the spars.

Stepping the mast There are two alternative methods when re-stepping the mast. The first is to push the mast forward, its head projecting out over the bow, and its heel lashed to hold it at the mast step. Set up two spinnaker poles, or a spinnaker pole and the main boom, as sheer legs over the deck, aft of the mast step, and hang a block from the apex of the sheer legs. To avoid damaging the deck, place pieces of wood beneath the heels of the spinnaker poles. Next, put lashings around the bottom of the poles and take them to secure points fore and aft so that the heels cannot slide. Lead a line from the masthead, or a point on the mast that would be the same height as the top of the sheer legs block when the mast is upright, through the block on the sheer legs, and down to a winch on deck. Attach the shrouds and the forestay to their rigging screws and then winch up the mast. The moment it is upright, secure the backstays and then dismantle the sheer legs.

The alternative method, which will almost certainly have to be used if the mast is intact because it will be too long to extend safely over the bows, is to lay the mast on deck with its head over the stern. Rig sheer legs again, just forward of the mast step, and follow the same procedure, but this time it is the forestay that will have to be attached once the mast is upright.

In both systems, all the standing rigging, halyards, running backstays etc., should be secured to the mast before it is stepped.

Topmast broken   Where the upper part of the mast breaks off, leaving a substantial length of the mast still standing, the remaining length can be used to set sail. First remove the wreckage, and, if it has not already fallen, lower the broken piece of the mast as gently as possible to the deck. If the break is clean it may be worth keeping this broken section, as a mast maker might be able to repair the mast, which will be cheaper than buying a new one.

If there are no halyards left below the break, it is going to be necessary to make a means of getting aloft to rig temporary stays and halyards. Where there are two lower shrouds, the simplest system is to make ratlines. Where the mast has only a single lower shroud, make a ladder by tying off lines between the mast and this shroud. This task may not be easy, as the boat will become more stiff without the extra weight aloft and this will reduce her rolling period, making her motion more jerky.

Once it is possible to climb to the top of the broken mast, either put a jury mast knot around the top to attach stays, shrouds and halyard blocks, or, where the break is close above a spreader, attach these to the mast on a strop around the mast just above the spreader.

Sprit and gunter jury rigs A very handy jury rig can be set up once a mast is stepped, using either the sprit or gunter rigs. In the case of the sprit rig, this is practical when the lower part of the mainsail is intact. Any suitable spar can be lashed roughly in the position of the main boom gooseneck, so that it can rotate a little, and then its outer end lashed to a suitable point on the leech of the mainsail. The mainsail should be sewn along its new head, and, if necessary, a rope should be sewn along this seam to provide extra strength.

The gunter rig is slightly more difficult to set up, but will work when the upper part of the mainsail survives, and there is more length of mainsail than the mast remaining or the jury mast. The gunter rig is simple to handle and allows a higher sail to be set where the jury mast is short and it is not possible to put parrels on the upper part of the sail because they could not be hoisted above spreaders.

Jury sails If you are lucky, sufficient of the mast will remain to allow the mainsail, suitably reefed, to be set. However, if the mainsail is so badly torn that it cannot be repaired, some other sail will have to be set as a mainsail.

On a ketch, this could be the mizzen. On any boat, a jib or staysail can be used, and set loose footed, with the clew taken out to the end of the main boom. Where possible, the sail should have its luff secured to the mast, be this its usual luff or its leech if it happens to fit better back to front. If the mast track remains, it is a simple job to sew the sail slides onto the jury sail. If the track is unusable, it will be necessary to make up parrels to go around the mast; however, this will only work if there are no obstructions, such as spreaders, in the way.

Where it is not possible to make up any form of fore and aft sail, a square sail, or a lateen sail may be the only answer. In both cases a spar will be necessary. It is advisable to rig up a halyard for this yard, and secure the halyard directly to the pivot point of the yard, or onto slings, so that both the sail and the yard can be lowered easily to the deck when necessary.

If none of the sails left on board will fit as a mainsail, it may be necessary to adapt them for the new rig. No-one likes to cut up a perfectly good sail, but there may be no alternative.

ABANDON SHIP

Abandoning a boat at sea is very much a last resort, and to be avoided if at all possible. The boat is the best shelter and more seaworthy than a liferaft or dinghy. When you leave it, you cease to have active control over your destiny, and instead, become passive and totally dependent upon other people's activity.

The only possible excuses for abandoning the boat are if it is on fire, and the fire is out of control; if it is holed, and nothing can stop the ingress of water; if it is on rocks or a lee shore, and neither the anchor nor sails nor the engine can save her. In all other circumstances, stick with the boat. If the boat is swamped, it can be baled out; if it is dismasted, it can be jury-rigged once conditions improve; if it loses its keel, the mast can be cast overside and the boat laid to a sea anchor. A boat has shelter, food and equipment, and is designed for its element; a liferaft or dinghy may have shelter, might have food, but is not designed to be sea comfortable.

Nevertheless, in circumstances where all measures to keep the boat afloat have failed, organised preparations to abandon her should be put in hand.

If the radio is still functioning, put out a May Day call and keep transmitting it until the last possible minute. A May Day should run as follows:

> Mayday Mayday Mayday
> This is yacht – Name
> Sinking in – Position
> Taking to the liferaft

Make sure that the message is delivered slowly and clearly and that the position given cannot be confused.

First make sure that all the crew put on their lifejackets then collect the boat's flare pack and medical kit and all the stores, water and food that you can; make sure that the crew, if not warmly clothed, at least take some warm clothes with them. Some liferafts have double bottoms but not all, and the crew are going to feel the cold which, in time, is a killer.

The liferaft should have in its pack the following items:

Sponge for baling	Hand pump
Flares	Rescue quoit
Repair kit	Buoyant knife

The most important store to get on board is fresh water. The human body can survive for a remarkably long time without food, but without water death comes much sooner. Water should be kept in small emergency containers, and these should be taken into the raft along with any other water containers. Large jerrycans should be not quite full, so that they will float easily and can be retrieved if they accidentally fall into the sea in the scramble to take to the raft. Almost any food will preserve life, but concentrate on taking those that are easily digested and have a high nourishment value such as dried fruit.

When all is ready, attach the operating cord to some strong point on board the boat, throw the raft overside to leeward and pull the cord. The cord is connected to the air cylinders within the canister or valise, and releases air into the raft which will inflate quite quickly. The operating cord is attached to a towing bridle so that once the liferaft has inflated, the cord is acting as a painter.

If sea or fire conditions permit, haul the raft alongside, and put one of the crew into it. Then pass across the stores that have been collected. When all that is worth salvaging, and which might be useful, such as fishing line and emergency radio has been passed across, the remainder of the crew can board.

If it is not possible to get the crew straight into the raft from the boat, then they will have to jump into the water and swim. Make sure that the lifejackets are inflated, and that the crew jump in feet first with one arm crossed over the top of the lifejacket and the other holding the nose. If the crew have to jump from a considerable height, lifejackets should not be inflated until in the water. If at all possible, keep a safety line on each crewman as they swim across to the liferaft, but if this is not possible, make them hold onto the painter. Once one of the crew has got into the liferaft, he should assist the others to get on board. Good swimmers should try and take extra stores across to the liferaft. Alternatively, if the boat has a dinghy, this should be launched, loaded with the extra stores, then floated across to the liferaft and tied firmly to it. The extra buoyancy may come in handy, and the dinghy will give extra space for the crew. It will also help rescuers to see the survivors as it doubles the visual target. (This is a good reason for having a bright orange or yellow dinghy). If more than one liferaft is carried, the liferafts should be tied together as soon as possible for mutual support.

In strong winds, liferafts can be rolled over, unless well weighed down with people. Tests have shown that, until the liferaft's drogue has taken a grip, the raft is susceptible to the wind or breaking waves, and the period between launching the raft and the drogue gripping is particularly dangerous.

There have been cases where the liferaft has been launched and has been blown downwind, spinning round like a kite, and drawn back to the boat upside down. To avoid this danger, it is best to board enough people before letting go of the boat, so that their weight stabilises the raft or leave so...cone in the water to hold onto the upwind end of the raft until everyone else has got in. Where the inflatable support for the canopy is a single tube, it is particularly important that this lies at right angles to the wind, as the shape of the canopy helps hold the raft down. If the tube lies down the line of the wind, the raft tends to veer about, putting additional strain on the drogue hawser.

Once all the crew are in the liferaft, the painter attached to the boat can be cut. Immediately check the raft for leaks or damage. The safety topping up valves may blow because of the warmth created by the survivors, but they will stop once the right pressure in the raft is reached. Next check the crew for clothing and injury, giving medical attention as required. Share out clothing if necessary. Stow the stores safely and take stock of what is on board. Work out the possibilities of rescue and calculate a ration that will last as long as possible. Even if there is plenty of food on board, try not to issue any rations for the first 24 hours as the stomachs will shrink and the survivors' food requirements and desires will be lessened as a result. When issued, all food should be chewed, sucked and eaten slowly. Water should be taken in carefully controlled sips.

Issue seasick pills to all the crew and keep up the issue for the first 48 hours, thereafter giving them out as required. A liferaft is not comfortable in a seaway, and it is desirable not to empty the survivors' stomachs. If the weather is cold, huddle the survivors together for mutual warmth. Pick up any flotsam that is drifting around from the boat. Bits of wood, clothing, rope or containers may be invaluable.

If there is a chance that a distress signal has been seen or heard, or the boat was on an obvious route which will be the first area to be searched by rescuers, stream the sea anchor so that the raft stays in the vicinity of the position given. Do not worry about the surface drift of the sea, this will be calculated by the searchers. Only if the boat has sunk close to a shore, or where the currents or winds will blow the raft towards a shore or shipping lane, should the raft be allowed to drift.

Finally, post a lookout and set up a watch system for lookouts. Do not blindly set off flares and distress signals unless you are in the middle of a shipping lane. Keep them for when something is sighted or heard. Remember that when people have been adrift for some time, they often imagine that they can see a ship or hear aircraft. All such reports must be checked by another crew member before a flare is ignited as otherwise a flare can be needlessly fired. If an emergency radio is carried set it up and transmit distress signals.

Every effort should be made to supplement the food and water supplies. If rain squalls appear, use the canopy of the liferaft to catch the rain water, or if in a dinghy, mop it out before the rain, and then collect as much as possible. Fish, birds and turtles can all be caught and eaten, but beware of eating raw fish or bird meat without having water on board, as they are protein-rich and can ruin the liver.

Above all, attempt to keep up the morale of the crew in these very difficult circumstances.

Where crew have to take to the water because there is no time to launch the liferaft, or the dinghy or other buoyant apparatus are not immediately available, the crew should jump into the water as previously described, and then swim away about 100 yards from the boat, keeping together. The reason for getting clear of the boat is that once it sinks, buoyant pieces of equipment will free themselves and float to the surface, sometimes at quite a speed, and could cause injury to the swimmers.

The swimmers should tie themselves together and then lie back with the back of the head in the sea. The length of time that people can survive in the sea varies with conditions, and in particular the temperature of the water. There are records of swimmers surviving for 4 or 5 days, but remember, the real limits of human endurance are not really known, and the orthodox views about survival limits are often proved grossly pessimistic.

RESCUE BY HELICOPTER

These days the removal of an injured crew member, or the rescue of the entire crew if the boat is in danger, is frequently carried out by a helicopter rather than another boat. Although the helicopter crews are highly trained in rescue techniques, the crew on board can make the task much safer and simpler by means of a little preparation:

1. Leave the VHF set to Channel 16 or the MF set to 2182 kHz.

2. On a large boat clear a suitable area of the deck so that the helicopter can hover above but clear of any masts or obstructions. Make sure that there is nothing with which the helicopter's hoist wire can become entangled. On small boats, particularly sailing craft, the helicopter may have difficulty making a close approach because of the mast. In this case prepare the dinghy with a long, strong painter and put the casualty and another 'minder' in the dinghy and allow it to float clear when the helicopter arrives.

3. When abandoning a boat, the helicopter crew may prefer to pick up the crew from the water. In this case, put everyone into lifejackets and leap from the boat one at a time, waiting for each person to be picked up before the next person enters the water. It is advisable to have a line on each crewman when they go into the water so that they can be hauled back to the boat if necessary.

4. At night illuminate the dinghy or person in the water by means of a powerful light. Keep the light from shining at the helicopter as it will blind the crew.

5. When the helicopter is sighted, try to establish contact on the radio, and bring the boat round onto a comfortable course. It is easier for the helicopter to adjust to the boat's course and speed if it can come in upwind from the boat's starboard quarter, so hold a course with the wind on the port bow if possible.

Rescue by Helicopter

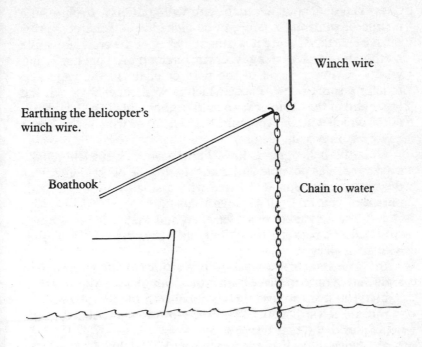

Winch wire

Earthing the helicopter's
winch wire.

Boathook

Chain to water

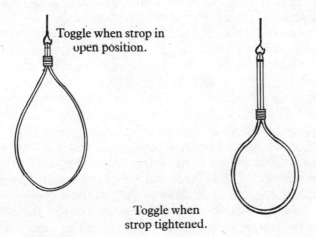

Helicopter lifting strop

Toggle when strop in
open position.

Toggle when
strop tightened.

6. Reduce speed, but keep enough headway to allow steerage way.

7. The helicopter's winch wire will contain a strong static charge; if someone is going to be picked up off the deck, this must be earthed before it is caught by any of the crew. A simple method is to attach a length of wire or chain to a boat hook, and whilst leaving the end of the wire or chain in the water, or touching some metal object which is well earthed, touch the other end of the chain or wire on the other end of the boat hook to the winch wire. Never make the helicopter winch wire fast to anything on board the boat.

8. If the helicopter is lowering a basket or stretcher, take hold as soon as possible and guide it onto the deck. Sometimes the basket or stretcher is fitted with a small trail line for this purpose. This line will not give a shock.

9. Place a casualty in a lifejacket, and then strap him into a stretcher. If a basket is to be used, place the person in the basket with arms clear.

10. The standard rescue strop is a thick, wide strop with a toggle fitted onto it. Place both arms through the strop and then tighten the strop around the chest beneath the arms by pulling the toggle towards you. When the strop is tight, signal to the helicopter that it may heave away.

11. Once the helicopter winch has the weight, the person in the basket, stretcher or strop should relax, and let the air crew do the work. They have practised the drill many times and know exactly how they want to take you up and into the helicopter.

BREECHES BUOY

The Breeches buoy was developed as a method of recovering the crew from a stranded vessel to the shore. It is unlikely to be very effective from a small boat, but could be used in a dire emergency. It is, however, an interesting piece of equipment, and may have other applications of use to the seaman.

In the original system, a line was sent out to the stranded vessel by means of a rocket, and once this line had been

Breeches Buoy

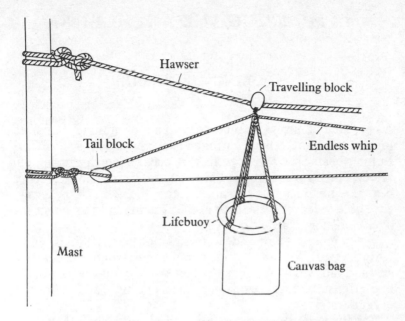

recovered on board, and secured, the rocket line was used to haul out to the boat a tailed block with an endless fall. The block's tail was made fast to some firm object, such as the mast, well above the deck. After signalling to the shore that the block was secure, a hawser was hauled out to the boat and secured about two feet higher than the tailed block.

The shore party then set the hawser up taut, and hauled out to the vessel a sling lifebuoy, attached to the endless fall, and suspended from the hawser by a block. The crew were then taken off one by one in the sling buoy. The system was used only from high ground ashore, and, if conditions did not permit the hawser to be set up, it could be effective, but less safe, just using the whip on its own.

4 MOORING AND ANCHORING

MOORING ALONGSIDE

A boat should always be moored with a minimum of four stout lines; a head line, a head spring, a back spring and a stern line. In long boats, say above 70 feet, it may be worth putting out more. The lines can be too light, but within reason, never too heavy. The lines should not be too short, as it is always advisable to leave a little give in the system, and the longer the lines, the more elasticity.

When mooring alongside a floating pontoon the lines can be set quite taut. When alongside a wall or pier where the boat will rise and fall with the tide, sufficient slack should be left in the lines to ensure that they do not become overtight at extreme low or high water.

The lines should be made fast securely on board. If they are on a cleat, the line should have at least three turns before putting on a locking turn. On a bollard five turns and a locking turn is about right. When tying up to a ring bolt, the correct knot to use is a round turn and two half hitches. A bowline or fisherman's bend can be used, but it is important to make sure that there is at least a round turn on the ring to reduce the chafe on the mooring line. If the boat is to be left moored up for a while, the tail of the rope should be whipped back onto the standing part.

The springs should be led outside the fenders so that they will not tend to lift the fenders. If there is no fairlead, the lines should be led in as straight a line as possible between their two fastening points, and should avoid passing round or over corners, as they will chafe. Where there is a risk of chafe, a chafing piece should be fitted to the mooring line. This can be a piece of canvas, leather or other suitable material, wrapped around the line and whipped onto it so that it will not move. Its purpose is to protect the mooring line and take the wear itself. Nowadays we have various sizes of polythene hose which can be

Mooring Lines

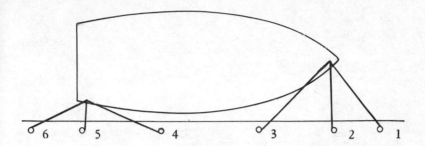

1 The headline
2 The forward breast line
3 Head spring
4 Back spring
5 The aft breast line
6 The stern line

Slip Lines

Slip lines are mooring lines led from the boat, round a
mooring bollard or eyebolt, and back on board again. They
are set up to be let go from on board when there is no one
ashore to let the boat's lines go, or when the boat is secured to
a pile.

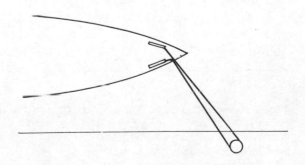

Mooring to a Short Pontoon

Tie off line to keep boat
off the pontoon.

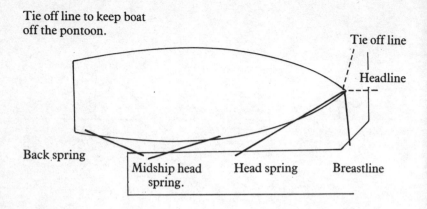

Tie off line

Headline

Back spring

Midship head
spring.

Head spring

Breastline

Mooring Lines in a Basin with High Tidal Range

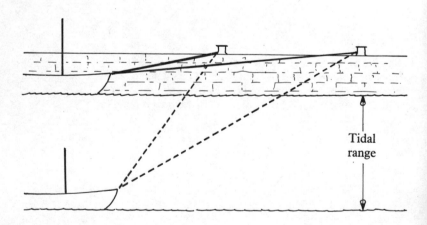

Tidal
range

The short mooring line would have to stretch 50% to allow
for the range of tide, the longer would have to stretch 12½%.
When alongside a quay wall in these conditions, mooring
lines should be made as long as possible.

Mooring Alongside Other Boats

Wrong

The elasticity of the
mooring lines
means that those at the
outer side of the trot
will be swept back
and forward each
tide, putting a
crushing force
on the inside
boats.

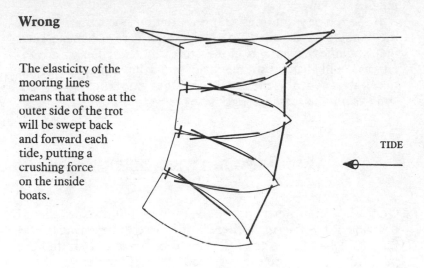

TIDE

Right

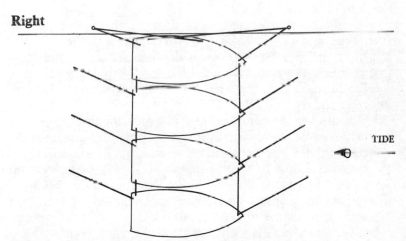

TIDE

Lines are led from each boat to the shore, so that each is
holding itself. This will steady the trot of boats and reduce
the crush on the inner boats. The same principle applies
when boats are moored to piles. Although the outermost boat
might get away without putting lines onto the shore or pile,
one never knows when another boat is going to come
alongside for a berth. It is normal for each boat in these
circumstances to be responsible for the fenders on its inner
side.

slipped over a mooring line and lashed into place to make a very efficient chafing piece.

If there is any doubt as to the strength of the mooring lines, they should be doubled up. Nylon and Terylene make good mooring lines; nylon has more stretch in it which is an advantage as it will give to a sudden load, and will not snap or tear out the cleat. Polypropylene can be used, but it does not last as well, and has not the same strength size for size.

MOORING BETWEEN PILES

Only a head and stern line will be required. Stout lines should be made fast to the ring if there is one, or to the mooring bar. If the pile is bare, then the line should be made fast around the pile. In all cases, a round turn and two half hitches should be used for securing.

The advantage of a ring on a vertical mooring bar on the pile is that the ring will ride up and down the bar with the tide, and the lines can be left quite taut. If the line has to be fastened to one point on the pile, try to get the knot at roughly half tide level, and make sure that there is enough slack in the lines to allow for the rise and fall.

Quite often when coming onto a pile mooring there is a hurry just to get a line made fast. In this case, put a slip line from the boat through the ring or round the pile and back on board. Once the boat is midway between the piles, and held by lighter slip lines fore and aft, the dinghy can be launched to carry out the heavier mooring lines. These slip lines will be needed again when the time comes to depart, but if they are to be left set up, make sure that there is plenty of slack in them and they do not take the weight instead of the proper mooring lines.

If the boat is regularly kept on a pile mooring with a mooring ring or bar, it will be worth splicing special mooring pennants. These should have a hard eye round a galvanised thimble at the end to take a shackle which will secure around onto the ring or bar. The other end can either be left to be made up around a cleat, or can have an eye spliced in that fits over a bollard or king post. In the latter case it is worth slipping a length of polythene

Rigging a Plank Outside Fenders for Lying Alongside Piles

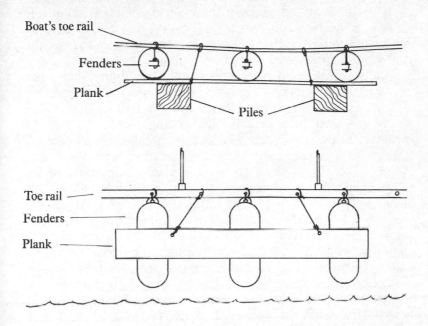

tube over the rope before making the permanent eye-splices at each end; the tube will fit in the fair lead and save the rope from chafe. Special mooring pennants like this will last a lot longer than ropes tied to the piles, and can be made up to the length required.

MOORING TO A BUOY

Many buoys have their own mooring pennants already attached. If the buoy is a large one the pennant will be attached to a ring in the top of the buoy; if a small one, the pennant should be attached directly to the buoy riser chain. Often there is a small pick-up buoy attached to the pennant. Motor or sail to the buoy, pick up the pennant pick-up buoy or the pennant, haul it inboard and make fast to a strong point such as a king post or heavy anchor cleat. If necessary, fit a chafing piece over the pennant where it comes inboard over the bow roller.

If the boat has a bowsprit, the mooring pennant should be taken to the bow roller *under* any bowsprit guys. It may be necessary to rig a spring to keep the pennant from chafing the bobstay, if the bobstay cannot be temporarily removed.

Should there be no mooring pennant on the buoy, then if the buoy is a large one with a mooring ring, make the mooring line fast to the ring with a round turn and two half hitches. If the buoy is a small one, even if it has a ring on top, be wary of securing to the buoy itself. Haul the buoy inboard and take the rising chain direct to a cleat, bollard or king post. Make sure there is plenty of slack left in the riser chain, however; a mooring chain should never be taut vertically, it should always have some slack in it to act as a spring. If the riser chain is too short to allow it to be brought inboard, then secure the mooring line to the riser chain direct, using a rolling hitch, and take two half hitches with the tail around the standing part. The rolling hitch will tighten on the chain, and if tied properly, will not slip.

If the boat is to remain on the mooring for some time, or heavy winds are expected, then the anchor chain should be used. Unshackle the anchor, and use the anchor shackle to secure to the mooring ring, or the riser chain.

MOORING MULTIHULLS

Catamaran   There are three places from which a catamaran's moorings can be led, the two bows and the centre of the forward beam. To moor effectively, the boat has to be as balanced as possible. If she yaws on her mooring she puts more strain on her mooring lines and the ground tackle. Mooring from one of the hulls is unbalanced and should be avoided where possible. Mooring on a yoke from both hulls is much to be preferred. If a mooring is taken from the centre of the forward beam alone, the catamaran can still yaw and to prevent this springs should be led out to the buoy from each hull. These will prevent the hulls from striking the buoy, which is particularly undesirable if the buoy is a heavy one. When anchoring it is worth leading springs to the anchor chain or warp as well, as it tends to stabilise the boat and cuts down the yawing.

Trimaran A trimaran can be moored like a monohull, with lines led out from the main hull alone. However, because of the width of the boat, it is advisable to put lines out from the two outriggers as well. Alternatively, the boat could be moored by lines from the two outriggers only.

The point to bear in mind, particularly if mooring alongside other boats, is that the outriggers are comparatively light in comparison with the construction of any other boat, and should be well fendered.

FENDERS

Fenders, or 'fend-offs', as they are sometimes known, are used to protect the hull of a boat from shock, impact and abrasion when going or lying alongside a jetty or another boat. They also serve to keep the boat a safe distance off a jetty or another boat. However, their main purpose is to absorb shock, and so it follows that they should have give, and be placed over a strong part of the boat's topsides when coming alongside. Ideally, they should be placed so that they lie in line with a bulkhead or stringer but this is not always possible with the modern GRP boat, in which case a larger fender should be used to spread the load over as big an area as possible.

Fenders should have their own lanyards, spliced to the eye provided on the fender. The other end of the lanyard should be whipped, as back-splicing it doubles its size and makes it difficult to put through small eyebolts. Secure fenders to a firm object on or near the rail, such as the base of a stanchion or the toe rail. Avoid securing them to the guardrails if these are wire, as the weight of the fender when trapped and pulled downwards will stretch the guardrail, or cause the stanchions to bend.

The most popular type of fender for small boats is the plastic inflated pudding type, which comes in a variety of sizes and colours. Although there is a small risk from puncturing, these fenders provide a smooth surface which is kind to the boat's topsides. It is a mistake to buy fenders too small, the rule should be to buy the largest that can be conveniently stowed and handled on the boat. The larger the fender the greater area over which it will spread the load, the further it will keep the boat off, and the more give it can provide.

Inflatable fenders should not be inflated too hard. Apart from wanting them to be spongy to absorb shock rather than transmit it, soft fenders seem less likely to jump out of position when the boat rolls or moves. Chandleries can usually inflate fenders if they become too soft, alternatively a special adaptor can be purchased which connects to a car foot pump or air line.

Fenders inevitably pick up dirt and oil, and unless this is cleaned off, it will transfer itself to the boat's topsides and abrade the finish. Fenders should always be washed before being stowed away, and if the boat is left lying alongside for long periods, they should be removed and cleaned at regular intervals. When oil or tar gets onto a fender, clean it off with a solvent or petrol, and then wash the surface with a detergent.

When lying alongside piles, or a pier which is piled, the fenders will move out of position as the boat surges or moves up and down with the tide. To protect the topsides, place a couple of fenders overside, and then hang a heavy plank outside the fenders. The plank will slide up and down the pile, and the boat is kept protected.

Inflatable fenders have largely replaced the coir fender, which was made up of a hessian sack filled with cork shavings or old rope, such as Turk's head or a continuous wall knot. These fenders were soft, but very heavy to handle once they became wet. Another fender that has been replaced by plastic was the canvas bag full of old rope or cork shavings, often painted and seen mostly on large yacht tenders.

If standard fenders are not available, or lost, there are a large number of alternatives. Any alternative should be strong and resilient, and have a non abrasive surface, the smoother the better. The simplest is a car tyre, but do not tie the lanyard round the tyre where it can be chafed and broken. Cut two holes in the tread and put the lanyard through these. Car tyres will mark the topsides, leaving black marks which can be cleaned off with detergent. Since tyres come in a wide variety of sizes, it is possible to select one which will suit the boat.

If a heavier fender is required, a number of rubber tyres can be slipped over an old spar or pile and lashed in place by means of holes in the walls of the tyres. The spar should be hung horizontally overside by a lanyard attached to each end. This type of fender is too heavy for usual on-board use, but is very effective when put between two laid up boats, or alongside a jetty.

Another type of fender, known as the apple ring fender, is made up from rope cheesed down into a coil, and then lashed together. This fender is strong and durable, and can always have a canvas cover sewn over it to provide a smoother and less dirt-attractive surface.

Fixed fendering Where a boat is in continuous use as a tender or work launch, it is often easier to fit continuous fendering around the gunwale so that it does not matter which part of the boat comes into contact with another boat or jetty. Heavy coir rope used to be a favourite for this, or canvas hose pipe filled with old rope or cork shavings, but both of these have now largely disappeared to be replaced by special heavy rubber or plastic fendering.

The best method of attaching rope to a boat's gunwale was by putting twine or small stuff through the rope and then through holes in the gunwale. Lashings around the rope fendering were liable to chafe through. Canvas hose required canvas straps, placed at sensible intervals, that passed around the hose and then secured to the boat's gunwale. The heavy rubber or plastic fendering can be screwed or bolted into position, but it is better to use a lashing of some sort if possible as this will give, rather than break when it is hit hard.

Boats used for pushing should be well fendered at their bows to avoid damage to a boat being pushed. It also helps to hold the boat in place if the fendering is flat at the front. Inflatable fenders will do for the outer layer, but, because of the risk of puncture, they should be backed up by something more substantial such as coir fendering.

DRYING OUT ALONGSIDE A QUAY

There are times when it is desirable to go alongside a jetty or quay and remain there even though the quay dries out at low water.

If the boat is a power boat, check that the propellers do not project below the skeg before attempting anything, as if the bottom is hard, the whole weight of the boat will be taken on the propellers and the shafts and cause damage. If the bottom is reputed to be soft, check it for yourself; the helpful local expert will become unhelpful and deny responsibility for information given if it leads to damage.

Going alongside to dry out with a sailing boat is quite simple. Put out good stout fenders on the side of the boat next to the quay and moor up with head and stern lines and springs. Then run a masthead halyard onto a firm point ashore. It is probably best to use a spinnaker halyard as it usually runs from a turning block at the masthead, whereas a genoa halyard is usually designed to lead fore and aft, and a sideways pull can damage the masthead sheave box.

Keep the boat tight against the fenders on the quay and as the keel touches the bottom, heave up on the halyard and give the boat a slight list in toward the quay so that the weight of the boat leans against the quay. The boat should be quite safe until the tide begins to come in when it will be necessary to ease off the spinnaker halyard.

A boat can also be laid quite safely alongside a single pile to dry out. In this case put a good strong lashing from the gunwhale or toerail around the pile, and make it tight as the keel grounds. Then place a good tackle or lashing from the gunwale to the top of the pile so that the boat cannot sink downwards.

The only risk when drying out on a single pile is that the boat might slew. This can be prevented by putting lines out to strong points ashore or putting out the anchor and taking up weight on the cable or warp.

Where the boat is left regularly alongside a quay wall that dries, a system of weights can be set up on the halyard which has been secured ashore to ensure that the boat leans slightly into the quay as the keel grounds each low water. The weight, and experimentation will show how much weight is required by a

Grounding Alongside a Quay

A method of giving the boat a list into the quay

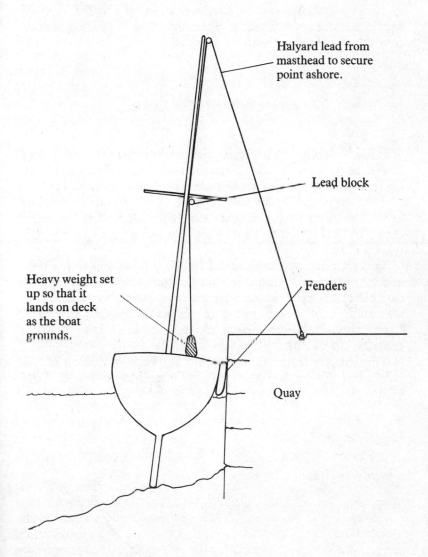

Halyard lead from masthead to secure point ashore.

Lead block

Heavy weight set up so that it lands on deck as the boat grounds.

Fenders

Quay

particular boat, is lashed onto the downhaul of a masthead halyard just above deck level when the boat is aground. The halyard must be led down outside the mast. As the tide rises, the weight will be hauled up towards the masthead, and as the tide falls the weight will descend, but the weight should put enough weight onto the halyard to induce a slight list in towards the quay. This system is quite effective, but an off quay wind could cancel out the inward pull of the halyard, and in these conditions, the boat will have to be watched.

GROUNDING ON LEGS

Where a boat is left on a beach or in a harbour that dries out, legs can be fitted to each side so the moment the keel grounds, the legs ground as well and prevent the boat from keeling over.

A lot depends upon the type of boat. A power boat is generally wider than a sailing boat, and not having the same depth of keel underneath it, puts less weight on the legs if it tends to heel.

There are various methods of securing these legs to the boat and all require a strong point on the hull at deck level that is capable of taking the boat's weight. A strong toerail might be man enough for the job, but the chain plates certainly should be strong enough. Never use stanchion bases as an anchor point, they are just not strong enough.

The legs, at least one on each side about one third of the boat's length from forward, should be securely fastened to the boat so that there is no movement in them when in position.

Grounding on Legs

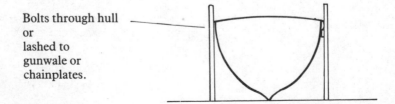

Bolts through hull
or
lashed to
gunwale or
chainplates.

Nevertheless, lines from the foot of the legs should be taken to the deck forward and aft to provide extra support.

On some boats, a special bracket is fitted to the hull to take the legs. Remember that the legs are designed to stop the side of the boat slipping downwards, and so the boat's weight is going to fall onto the legs.

Unless you are really confident about securing the legs, seek advice from the boat's manufacturer or a boatyard before trying to fit them.

GROUNDING IN A CRADLE

It is a small step from fitting legs to a boat to having a special cradle made for the boat so that she will lie in the cradle at low water.

The cradle should be robust, and the top cut to the shape of the boat where the cradle fits, so that you can make sure of getting the boat snugly into the cradle each time. If the boat is not exactly positioned in the cradle, it can be damaged or its weight might be offset and it could cause the cradle to topple over.

The cradle should be built so that it is just heavier than water, and it should have lines attached to it so that it can be drawn ahead or astern to get it into position, and it can be hauled up snug to the boat and lashed when the boat is correctly positioned. These lines are usually attached to small pick-up buoys so that they can be retrieved by the boat as she floats in towards the cradle.

The cradle must always be lashed tightly against the boat, as any slack in the lashings can cause the boat to move relative to the cradle and damage can result.

In some ports, this system of mooring boats is in regular use and the cradle has mooring lines attached to it from up and down the beach. The only disadvantage is that the boat can only leave and return to its cradle when there is sufficient water to float the two together. However, it does provide a safe method of mooring where there are no alternatives, provided that the beach is fairly level and even.

JURY SLIPPING SYSTEM

Where there are no slipway facilities and no firm vertical surfaces against which a boat can lean, and it is difficult or impossible to rig legs, the Indians use a simple method of keeping a boat upright which can be used for either mooring in an area that dries out, or to allow bottom repairs or painting to be effected. This system will work for a boat with a long keel, or a motor boat, but should not be attempted with a fin keel boat.

Four stout pieces of timber are required, about six feet longer than the boat's maximum beam. Two of these timbers are floated beneath the boat athwartship, and the other two are placed on top of the deck so that each is over one of the lower beams. Putting the lower beams into position beneath the keel takes a bit of doing if they are of buoyant timber, but with lines to each end, the beam can be juggled beneath the boat. Once the beams are in position, lash the upper and lower ends together firmly with a number of turns. Then take a stout bar, preferably of wood, and place it through these turns and twist it round. This has the effect of tightening the lashings even further. Once the lashings are really tight, the bar can be allowed to rest against the hull to prevent it untwisting.

A Jury Grounding System

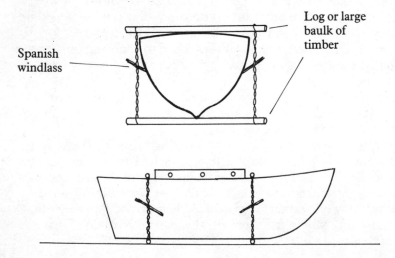

Log or large
baulk of
timber

Spanish
windlass

Effectively the boat is now resting on two beams, but is held upright on them by the lashings to the two upper beams. The quality of the beams is important. I once tried this method using palm trunks, but the weight of a ten-ton boat crushed the trunks beneath the keel, and the boat fell over onto her side.

ANCHORING

Anchoring and anchor work is one of the most basic of all the seaman's skills, and must be thoroughly mastered if a sailor is to proceed to sea safely and with confidence.

The anchors and cables on the boat (anchor chain or warp is known as the anchor cable) should always be of the best quality available, and of a sufficient size to hold the boat safely in even the most adverse conditions. When in doubt as to the weight of the ground tackle, it can never be wrong to equip the boat with a larger anchor and bigger cable than recommended.

An anchor relies for its holding power on the type of bottom, the anchor weight and shape, and the anchor being allowed to grip the bottom. Anchors are designed to take a hold when pulled horizontally along the bottom, so it is essential to ensure that sufficient chain or warp is put out so that the pull on the anchor shank is horizontal.

Most boats have chain anchor cables, and the weight of the

Boat Lying to an Anchor

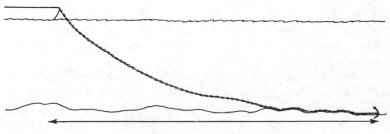

Three times the depth of water

chain will ensure a horizontal pull. Where a warp is used instead of chain, at least 30 feet of chain should be attached to the anchor between it and the warp to weigh the anchor cable down, and because chain is much more resistant to wear, it will not be subject to chafe from a bottom obstruction.

When anchoring, a boat should stem the strongest prevailing force, whether wind or tide, and should be stopped when the anchor is let go. Initially let go just sufficient anchor chain to allow the anchor to rest on the bottom, but the moment the boat begins to move backwards, pay out chain. The boat can be moved backwards by either wind or tide, or by putting the engines astern for a short burst.

Usually it is sensible to pay out sufficient anchor chain or warp to equal three times the depth of water at high tide. However, provided there is sufficient space, it can never be wrong to pay out a little more. If the bottom has poor holding characteristics, it will be necessary to pay out more cable.

Choosing the anchorage   Find out from the chart what sort of bottom your chosen anchorage has before you let go. Gravel and mud are usually good holding, but an anchor can drag easily in soft mud. Sand is good provided the anchor can get a grip. A rocky bottom varies, and usually you have to wait for the anchor to snag a rock before you are properly secure. The danger with this is that when the tide turns, the anchor may drag until it snags another rock in the opposite direction.

Secondly, there must be sufficient water for the boat to float safely at all states of the tide. Bear in mind also that, if the wind or tide changes, the boat will swing round, and you must make sure that there are no obstructions in the 'swinging circle'. An easy way to check this is, after anchoring and fixing the position of the anchor on the chart, draw a circle round this position the radius of which should be equal to the length of the anchor cable out, plus the length of the boat. If there are no obstructions in this circle, then – provided the boat does not drag – the boat is anchored safely.

When anchoring in a crowded anchorage, there will not always be sufficient space for a clear swinging circle. Anchor in the clearest spot, noting how all the other boats are lying. If the wind or tide changes, all the boats should swing together and a collision should not occur. However, a watch should always be

Anchor Transits

Ideally, two sets of transits, at right angles to each other. If
the boat yaws on her anchor cable, the transits will open,
giving the impression that she has dragged although the
anchor may be holding firmly.

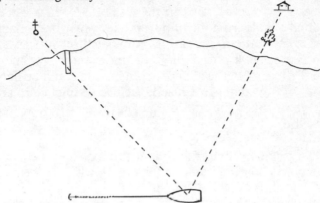

Swinging Circle

The anchor is positioned so that
whichever way the boat swings
she will clear all
obstructions.

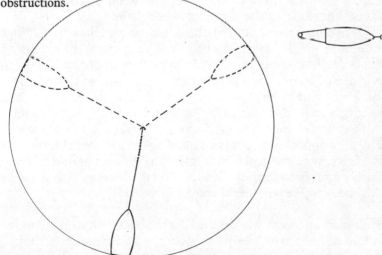

kept when the tide turns just to make sure, and have someone available to fend off if necessary, or use engines to swing in the correct direction.

Make sure that you are not going to drop the anchor close to mooring buoys, underwater pipelines or power cables. Mooring buoys have large chains on the sea bottom which can extend up to half a cable from the buoy, and there may be as many as three or four of them spreading equidistantly outwards. If your anchor snags a power cable or underwater pipeline, you will have to sacrifice the anchor, because you could be liable for the cost of any damage caused. Before letting your anchor go, however, buoy the end so that a diver may be able to recover it for you.

Dragging the anchor It is most important to ensure that the anchor is holding before snugging down. The best method of doing this is to take a 'transit' on the shore of two fixed objects, one close to the shore, and one some distance behind. If the relative position of these two objects remains the same, the anchor is holding. If it changes, the anchor is dragging and it will be necessary either to pay out more chain until it holds or to up anchor and re-anchor in another spot. If the boat is swinging, the transit will appear to change because of the boat's movement, and you may not necessarily be dragging. To check this, watch the transit when the boat is on a particular and average heading on the compass in each swing.

If the wind rises, always check that the anchor is holding. The extra weight on the anchor chain may cause the anchor to drag. Try letting out more cable to give the anchor a chance to grip again, but let it out gently, under pressure, as if you just let out a lot of cable, the boat will run back quite quickly and then suddenly snag. This snagging can break out the anchor again.

Two useful methods of discovering whether an anchor is dragging or not are to put your hand on the anchor cable outside the hawse pipe and feel for vibrations as the anchor moves along the bottom, or to drop the lead line on the bottom with slack on the line, and see whether it moves forward.

Weighing anchor Make sure that the boat is all ready to move before starting to heave up the anchor, as, once the anchor is up, you will be fully occupied manoeuvring.

If the boat is going to sail from the anchorage, the sails should be hoisted, but the sheets left free so that the sails cannot draw or be blown aback until the anchor is raised. If the boat is a power boat, or a sailing boat with engine that is going to motor clear of the anchorage, the engine should be warmed up before weighing anchor.

The prudent seaman will not sail out of a crowded anchorage unless his boat is without an engine. There is little room to manoeuvre, and the sudden appearance of another boat (manoeuvring) will possibly necessitate violent action on the part of one's own boat which is not so easily or safely carried out under sail and can cause confusion or a collision.

In a power boat, once the boat is ready to weigh, the anchor should be hauled in. If hauling in by hand, do not try and haul the anchor up with one great heave, you will probably damage yourself. Take the weight on the anchor cable and give a steady pull, the boat will slowly begin to move forward and you can pull in the slack as she does so. If there is more than one person on the fo'c'sle, the second person can help to heave and be prepared to take turns with the cable if a rest is required so that all the progress made so far is not lost. The helmsman should keep the boat heading straight along the line of the anchor cable. If the fo'c'sle party are finding the strain a little much, then the helmsman can assist by coming slowly ahead on the engines, but the boat should not overrun the cable.

Once the cable is up and down, the anchor might have to be broken out of the bottom, which can be achieved by either giving a big heave or if it is well stuck in, by making fast the cable and motoring slowly in the opposite direction to which the cable was leading. Do not motor too hard or too far, as there is always the risk of overdoing things so that the anchor breaks clear and digs in afresh in the other way. Once the anchor is aweigh, i.e. clear of the bottom, it should be hauled up as quickly as possible. If the boat has to move to avoid other boats, it should only move at slow speeds until the anchor is clear of the water as any movement makes the anchor heavier for the fo'c'sle party.

When you wish to sail from your anchorage, haul up short on the cable before setting sail. If the weight on the cable is too great it is possible to sail up onto the anchor, but this requires quick reactions on the part of the anchor party. Hoist the sails, sheet home on one tack or the other and gather way. Once the boat is moving ahead, she will be moving diagonally to the anchor cable, put the helm over and tack. The boat will now be moving in towards the anchor, and the chain should be hauled in as quickly as possible. Just before the cable draws abeam, cleat up the cable, because the anchor party will not be able to hold the weight, and tack again. As the boat comes into the wind, it should be possible to take up some slack on the cable if it is taken in quickly. Once the boat is about, wait until she has gathered way and then tack again, taking in slack on the cable as she goes and again cleating up as the cable draws abeam.

It is hard work, and requires quick reactions on the part of the crew, but is sometimes the only sensible answer if the boat has no engine and the pull on the cable is too great for the crew to take up direct.

If the anchor appears to have stuck, or become fouled, cleat up the cable, stop engines, or make sure the sails are not pulling and take stock of the situation.

False fouling   Firstly, make sure that the boat is not underway by checking for any drift. You will not be the first crew to think that the anchor is fouled when all that has happened is that the extra weight of the anchor as it comes away from the bottom makes it feel as if it is stuck. This is particularly likely when the crew have had a hard heave and are tired.

The most likely cause of trouble is that the anchor has dug itself in too well, or it has snagged on an obstruction such as a boulder or rocks. Make the anchor cable secure, as near up and down as possible, and if the engines are available try motoring the boat in various directions to see if the anchor will break clear. Do not be too ferocious with the throttles, a steady pull is what is required, a sharp pull could break the cable or the anchor.

If the water is clear, it may be possible to see the anchor and discover what the snag is, and take action accordingly. Alternatively, it may be possible to dive down and check the situation.

If after pulling the anchor in every direction it will still not move, one can cut the cable and tie a buoy to it, and leave it for a diver to recover. As a last resort however, wait for low water and heave up on the cable until it is taut up and down and firmly secure the cable to a strong object on board. As the tide rises, the boat will act as a 'camel', and pull the anchor clear. There is a danger in this that the bow will be pulled well down, in which case there comes a point when you will have to carefully ease the cable, cut it, and leave a buoy on it so that it can be recovered later. It is worth trying to accelerate this by taking all the crew and easily moved weights forward, whilst the anchor is being tautened and secured, and then moving all the weight and crew aft. The lift this will apply to the anchor cable might free the anchor.

Sometimes the anchor may have snagged on a heavy object that will not come free. If it is not possible to haul up the anchor and clear it, get the anchor cable up and down and secured and then try moving into deeper water to see if the obstruction will fall off. If it will not, wait for high water and move into shallow water, preferably on a firm sandy bottom, dragging the anchor with you and pausing periodically to take up the slack in the cable as the water becomes more shallow. Drag the anchor in as close to the shore as possible and break the cable and move back into deep water and anchor on your kedge anchor. As soon as the fouled anchor has been exposed by the falling tide, you can row ashore to free and recover it.

Clearing a Fouled Anchor

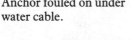

Anchor fouled on under water cable.

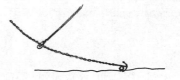

Rope, knotted into a loop, tied round cable.

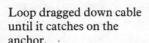

Loop dragged down cable until it catches on the anchor. ·

Rope pulled from dinghy or another boat lifts anchor clear of obstruction.

Old cables and chains left on the bottom are a frequent cause of fouling. Try and haul the anchor right up and then disentangle it. If it is too heavy to lift, the cable will have to be cut and buoyed. Remember, if you find you have snagged a cable it might be a telephone or power supply, in which case you *must* abandon your anchor to avoid damaging the cable.

One successful method I have used to clear an anchor fouled on a cable was to run a heavy rope with a large loop down the cable to the anchor, having hauled the cable up as tight as possible. Then we passed the rope to another boat ahead of us and he hauled it in by going ahead slowly on his engines. The flukes of the anchor were pulled clear of the obstruction and we recovered the anchor.

TYPES OF ANCHOR

The number of anchors to be carried by a boat will depend upon its size. A small dinghy will need only a grapnel; for yachts of 20 to 70 feet, a bow anchor which will be its main anchor, and a kedge anchor used from the stern when the boat is to be held in a particular line, or as a back-up for the bow anchor. Larger yachts should carry two bow anchors in addition to the kedge anchor. The above are the generally accepted minimum, and there can be no harm in having an extra anchor on board for emergencies.

There are various types of anchor available, because no one anchor can give a secure hold in all types of sea bottom. Generally, it is a good idea to carry different types for bow and kedge anchors to provide for a variety of anchorages.

The kedge anchor should be 66 to 75 per cent of the weight of the bow anchor.

The fisherman anchor   The traditional anchor is the fisherman anchor. It should be cast or forged in one piece, and not made up by welding.

Nowadays it is rare to find a fisherman anchor that does not have a removable stock. The stock will be removed for ease of stowing. Before the anchor is used, however, the stock must be

The Fisherman's Anchor

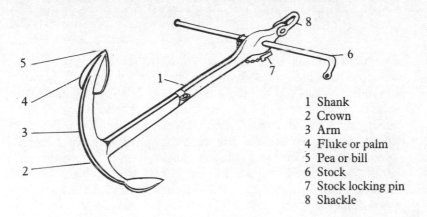

1 Shank
2 Crown
3 Arm
4 Fluke or palm
5 Pea or bill
6 Stock
7 Stock locking pin
8 Shackle

set up and pinned or lashed into place. The stock's purpose is to turn the anchor so that the flukes can dig into the bottom. When the anchor hits the bottom and begins to be drawn along by the chain, the stock tends to trip and lie flat. As the stock is at right angles to the flukes; when it goes flat, the flukes are slightly curved into the ground. As the pull increases the flukes dig deeper into the bottom.

The main disadvantage of the fisherman anchor is that one of the flukes is always left standing up and as the boat moves round, the anchor cable can get caught on this fluke and trip the anchor. Also when this type of anchor is let go, care must be taken not to drop too much chain initially with the anchor, as this chain can become tangled with the stocks or flukes, and if this happens the anchor will not dig in. So, when using a fisherman anchor lower it to the bottom and then pay out chain as the boat drifts away, not putting any weight on to the anchor until there is plenty of cable out, as a fisherman will pull out of the ground with a vertical pull.

The fisherman is a good standard anchor, but more modern anchors have been developed for sand, mud and gravel bottoms. The fisherman is still the best in rocky bottoms or in kelp.

Stockless anchor The introduction of the hawse pipe led to the development of stockless anchors. The flukes are hinged onto the shank so that the head can turn on its axis up to 45 degrees either side of the shank. The usual type, seen on large merchant and warships, is not very reliable in its smaller sizes. It does not dig in very well, and if it starts to drag, does not grip again easily.

Danforth anchor   An American design, basically similar to a stockless, but the flukes are longer. It will grip particularly well in sand and mud and has the advantage of stowing flat. Its main weakness, in my experience, is that if it digs in very well it can sheer off where the shank connects to the bar that joins the flukes. In many versions the shank is galvanised mild steel, which can bend if it has a sideways load put on it. These shanks should be watched for fractures once this has happened. When hauling them up, put a gradual upward strain on the anchor, not a desperate pull.

CQR   Designed originally in Britain and first used on the Mulberry harbour, and named from the word 'secure', it is sometimes known as the plough anchor as its fluke resembles a ploughshare. These anchors are robust and have good holding power on most bottoms. As the weight comes on the shank the fluke digs into the ground. The more weight applied, the better the anchor digs in. They are not usually difficult to break out, but when used, there should be sufficient chain out to ensure a horizontal pull on the shank.

CQR Anchor   Bruce Anchor

Danforth Anchor

Bruce anchor A recent design which digs into the bottom very quickly, and like the CQR, the harder it is pulled the deeper it digs in. In many respects its action is the same as the CQR, but being cast in one piece there is nothing on it to break.

The Stockless, Danforth, CQR and Bruce anchors have no stock so once they are down, the anchor chain cannot catch on the anchor itself. However if the boat swings, or the tide turns, the anchor will break out as the weight comes on from the opposite direction. Usually the anchor will dig itself in again pretty quickly, but for security, an anchor watch should be kept when the boat is likely to swing.

Table of Approximate Anchor Sizes

Boat length (ft)	Weight of anchor (lbs)				Size of chain (inches diam.)
	Fisherman	*CQR*	*Bruce*	*Danforth*	
15	20	15	4½	15	³⁄₁₆
20	30	20		20	
25	40	25	11	25	¼
30	50	30	16½	30	⁵⁄₁₆
35	60	35	22	35	⅜
40	70	40	33	40	⁷⁄₁₆
45	90	45	47	45	½
50	120	50		60	½
60	140	70	63	70	⁹⁄₁₆
70	200	100		100	⅝

ANCHOR CABLES

The approximate size of chain cable used for the anchor is shown in the Table. Although there is a tendency to use anchor warps instead of chain, particularly in small boats and in racing craft where weight is at a premium, there is no substitute for chain cable. Even if a warp is used, at least 5 fathoms of cable should be shackled onto the anchor before the warp is attached, as not only does the cable's weight act as a spring and prevent the boat jerking the anchor out of the bottom, the chain is much more resistant to the wear and chafe which a line on the bottom would suffer from obstructions. A cruising yacht should have all its anchor cable of chain, and on boats of up to 30 feet, 30 fathoms of chain would be safe. On larger boats the length of anchor chain carried should be greater.

Chain used to come in 15-fathom lengths, known (confusingly) as a shackle. Nowadays it can be bought in greater lengths. Always buy short link chain for an anchor cable. If more than one length of cable is required the lengths should be joined with a special joining shackle, as an ordinary shackle can catch on obstructions as it is paying out.

When paying out anchor chain, it is not always possible to tell how much cable has run out, as the joining shackles may not be immediately obvious. It is a great help to mark the anchor cable every 5 or 10 fathoms. Painting one link of the cable white at 10, two links at 20 etc, is the usual method, and it also pays to put a strand of seizing wire around the stud of the link so that if the paint wears away, the link can still be found. The anchor chain should always be washed off when the anchor is being weighed, otherwise the chain locker will slowly fill with mud. Sometimes it will be necessary to scrub it and hose it off or sluice it with buckets of water to get really sticky mud off.

From time to time, and at the annual re-fit is the most obvious, the anchor cable should be ranged out and inspected. The anchor should be unshackled from the cable and end for ended, that is the end that was attached to the anchor becomes the bitter end and is shackled or lashed to the boat in the chain locker and the bitter end is shackled to the anchor. This evens out the wear on the chain. If the cable is made up of a number of shackles, the joining shackle should be removed at the next re-fit and the shackles of chain end for ended.

There is nothing more embarrassing, and potentially dangerous, than standing watching the bitter end slip overside because it has not been secured properly in the chain locker. In some modern boats a securing point is not always remembered by the builders, or if it is, it takes the form of a small eyeplate screwed into anything handy. The securing point must be capable of taking quite savage jerks and if it does not look strong enough, do not rely on it. Either put in something strong such as a large eyebolt or, as a fall back, lash a piece of hard wood to the bitter end which is too big to pass through the spurling pipe.

ANCHOR STOWAGE

When the boat is underway, an anchor should be stowed in a special locker, or securely lashed on deck so that it cannot break free and fall overside. In large yachts, which have hawsepipes, the anchor's stock can be hauled up into the hawsepipe so that the head and flukes lie snug against the ship's side, but on smaller yachts, where the anchor cable runs out over a bow roller, the anchor must be stowed.

Usually, the anchor is stowed on special chocks on the deck, which are shaped to take it, and restrain any tendency to move. If no special chocks exist, then the anchor should be lashed to some firm object such as the windlass. On some boats, the bow roller is fitted with a pin which can be inserted through the anchor's shank and thus hold it in place.

On long voyages, it is often best to unshackle the anchor from its cable and stow it below. This has the advantage of clearing one obstruction from the deck, lowering the weight in the boat, and removing the risk of the anchor lashings breaking whilst at sea.

Kedge anchors are not usually kept on deck, but kept stowed away in some convenient locker.

THE ANGEL AND ITS USE

An angel is a heavy weight, usually of between 50 and 70 pounds, with a large eye on its top. To this eye is attached a line, strong enough to take the weight of the angel, and a shackle which is passed around the anchor cable.

When anchored in a confined space, where there is not a great deal of swinging room, the angel helps to reduce the swinging circle of the boat. Put the large shackle around the anchor cable, and then lower the angel onto the sea bottom on the end of its line. Make sure that there is enough slack in the line so that the weight of the angel does not come onto the line again whatever the tide. The line should be left fastened to a cleat on deck to be used again when the angel is to be recovered.

Once on the bottom, the angel's weight helps to restrain the

The Angel

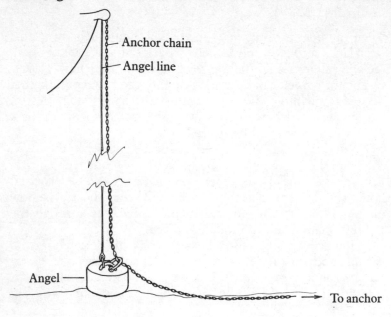

Anchor chain

Angel line

Angel ──────

To anchor

anchor cable, and, because the weight holds the anchor cable down, and makes it lie more horizontally, the anchor gets a better chance to dig in. In light weather conditions, the boat will probably swing around the angel itself, which reduces the swinging circle. In a blow, the weight of the angel on the cable helps to give the anchor cable 'spring' and lessens the chances of the boat snubbing to the anchor.

Although sometimes awkward to handle, an angel is a very useful piece of equipment for the cruising yachtsman, and can easily be made up from an old weight, or by casting with concrete.

BOW FITTINGS FOR ANCHORS AND CABLES

The main requirements for the anchor cable lead are that it be strong enough to take the very considerable loads that can be exerted by a vessel yawing and snatching whilst at anchor, and it should provide an easy lead for the cable when it is being paid out or hauled in.

Larger boats solve this problem by having hawsepipes, round, usually cast, metal tubes, which connect from the deck and come out through the hull. Hawsepipes have to be robust, as they take a great deal of wear, not just from the cable when going out or in, but also when at anchor, as the cable leads from the hawsepipe. The deck and hull must be reinforced around a hawsepipe.

On average sized yachts, the anchor cable usually leads out through a lead on the bow, and to reduce wear and friction a roller is often fitted at the bottom of the lead. Although an ordinary fairlead will be sufficient on a dinghy, the lead on a yacht of 20 feet or more should be more robust, and should be of the Panama type, enclosed so that the cable cannot jump out of it. This lead, often a part of the Gammon plate, must be strong enough to take sideways loads when the boat yaws or snatches at the cable.

The anchor cable should not be secured to the bow lead, but to a more substantial strong point on deck, such as the windlass or well secured bitts.

If the boat is lying at anchor with a warp as cable, it may be necessary to bind the cable with cloth or leather in way of the lead to prevent the cable from chafing. Alternatively, a piece of polythene tube placed around the cable provides good protection.

PERMANENT MOORINGS

When a boat is to be left at anchor for prolonged periods, or where the boat is going to be in a particular location as a base where no facilities exist, it is worth considering laying a permanent mooring to tie the boat to, rather than leaving her at anchor. The advantages are that it is easier to cast off a mooring pennant than haul up the anchor, and a permanent mooring, if properly laid, is safer than an anchor.

Before laying a permanent mooring, ascertain that it is permissible in your chosen site. A river or port authority may control mooring rights, in which case you will need to obtain their permission. The waters may be privately owned, or be claimed by the Crown Estate Commissioners (in the UK only).

Check that your chosen position is sheltered, allows the boat swinging room, does not interfere with a fairway or fishing grounds, and that the anchors and chains will not foul underwater cables or pipelines.

The strongest traditional permanent mooring consists of three anchors, set out at 120° to each other from a central ring. The chain known as the ground chain should be substantially heavier than the boat's normal anchor chain. When the bottom is of rock, then a 'halved' fisherman's anchor should be used. This is to prevent having a fluke extending upwards from the bottom to catch other lines or chains, and in shallow water to avoid boats hitting the exposed fluke and damaging themselves. Danforth, CQR and Bruce anchors can be used in sand, shingle or muddy bottoms, but all anchors used for permanent moorings should be heavier than the boat's normal anchor.

The facing table gives the weight of anchor and size of chain that should be used where winds of up to 65 knots are anticipated.

A permanent mooring should never be put down on a single anchor, as each time the tide or wind changes, the anchor will tend to break out. The Mushroom anchor was designed for a single anchor mooring, and these have tremendous suction when they have dug in, but a mushroom anchor will need to be at least four times the weight of anchor shown in the table, and should be given time to dig itself in before weight is put on it. A mushroom anchor will only work effectively on a bottom which allows it to dig in, it is no use in rock or other hard bottoms.

On a single anchor mooring, heavy chain should be used for the bottom part of the mooring chain, and lighter chain for the remainder. Chain of the weights shown in the table should be used. The length of the lighter chain should be equal to the maximum depth of water. The heavy chain should be of the same length as shown in the table.

To avoid the chain twisting, a swivel link should be placed between the light and heavy chains.

Another method of making a mooring anchor is to use a very heavy weight as a sinker instead of an anchor. The weight must be considerable as it has no holding power, purely relying on its

Boat length (ft)	Anchor weight (lbs)	Ground chain		Riser chain size (ins diam.)	Mooring pennant size (ins circum.)		
		Length (ft)	Size (ins diam.)		Manilla	Terylene	S. steel
Power boats							
25	45	30	⅞	3/8	2½	2	1¼
35	100	35	1	7/16	3	2½	1½
45	140	40	1	½	4	3	2
55	180	50	1	9/16	5	4	2½
65	240	60	1¼	5/8	6	4½	3
75	300	70	1⅜	3/4	7	5	3½
Sailing boats							
25	35	30	3/4	5/16	2½	2	1¼
35	80	35	1	3/8	3	2½	1½
45	140	40	1	7/16	4	3	2
55	200	50	1	½	5	4	2½
65	275	60	1¼	5/8	6	4½	3
75	350	70	1⅜	3/4	7	5	3½

Permanent Moorings

Mooring buoys

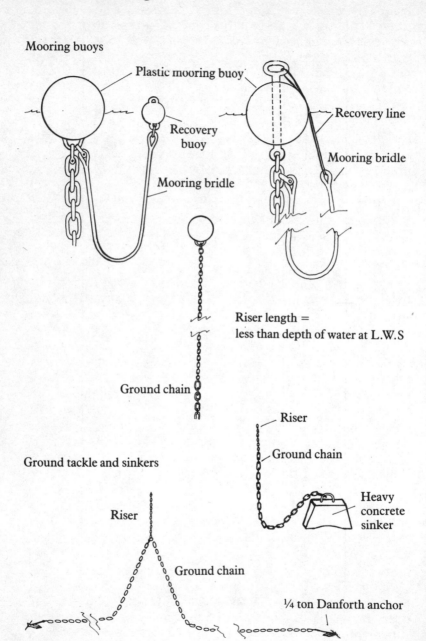

Plastic mooring buoy

Recovery buoy

Recovery line

Mooring bridle

Mooring bridle

Riser length =
less than depth of water at L.W.S

Ground chain

Riser

Ground chain

Heavy
concrete
sinker

Ground tackle and sinkers

Riser

Ground chain

¼ ton Danforth anchor

mass to hold the boat in place. A simple sinker can be made from a 45 gallon oil drum filled with cement, with a piece of heavy chain set into the concrete to provide a securing point. However a better shape is a dome with a concave bottom, again with a piece of chain set into the top. Once this type of sinker has set into a soft bottom, its concave bottom creates suction and holding power.

Where more than one mooring is required, a linked system of moorings can be set up using common ground chains. In a simple form, a two buoy system can be made using the triple anchor system. However instead of the third anchor in each, the ground chains on the third arm join each other. The moorings are just as strong but use only four anchors.

Where more than two moorings are required, the end anchors are moved further apart, and the connecting chain lengthened. For three mooring buoys, just lengthening the connecting chain will be sufficient, and the third riser is shackled on to the middle of the connecting chain. However, where more mooring points are required, then extra anchors must be placed along the connecting chain to provide lateral support.

Iron and steel corrode underwater, and mooring chains should be given an annual check. Even if the chain is galvanised, in one season this zinc coating will corrode away. In many cases moorings are taken up out of season for cleaning and checking, and painted with a bitumastic paint. Ground chain, because of its greater size will usually last longer than riser chains which can be expected to have a life of two to four years depending upon conditions. If moorings cannot be uplifted each season they should be inspected by a diver. If the chains show the slightest sign of wear, they will have to be renewed.

Mooring buoys   The mooring buoy is shackled on to the top end of the riser chain, and should have sufficient buoyancy so that it is only half submerged when supporting the weight of riser at maximum tide. Some buoys are designed to mark the position of the riser, and there will be another smaller buoy close by which should be picked up. This buoy will be attached to the mooring pennant, which is connected directly to the riser, not to the mooring buoy, whose main purpose is to support the riser.

Where a buoy is designed to be fastened to directly, it will have a mooring ring on top which connects directly to the riser, usually by a strong steel rod. Unless a mooring pennant is attached to the ring, the boat should secure itself to the buoy using its own pennant. For a short stop, a rope will be sufficient, but if the boat is to be left moored to the buoy for any length of time, the yacht should use its anchor cable as a pennant, unshackling the anchor and shackling the cable on to the mooring ring.

A boat should never moor to a buoy by just passing a line through the mooring ring and back on board. The line will chafe on the buoy.

The mooring pennant should always be checked for chafe on a bobstay, or where the pennant comes on board. If the pennant is likely to be chafed as it passes through a lead, it should be wrapped round with a chafing piece where chafe is likely to occur. This can be leather or canvas, and the modern equivalent is polythene pipe which the rope or wire of the pennant is run through before being made fast.

5   ROPES, KNOTS AND TACKLES

TYPES OF ROPE

Rope is one of the sailor's basic materials, and a knowledge of its properties and how to work and handle the various types available, is one of the fundamentals of good seamanship.

Rope is manufactured from three materials, vegetable fibres, man-made fibres, and steel.

Vegetable fibres   There are five main natural fibres used for making rope: manilla, sisal, hemp, cotton and coir.

Manilla   Comes from the leaf of the wild banana tree which grows extensively in the Philippine Islands. It makes a strong flexible rope, which stands up well to wear and to the weather.

Sisal   Comes from the leaf of the agave plant, a form of cactus found in East Africa. It is as strong as second grade manilla, but not as flexible, nor does it stand up to the weather and wear and tear as well.

Hemp   Obtained from the skin of a nettle-like plant which is widespread. Italian hemp is the best, and is the strongest of all the vegetable fibres. Hemp rope wears as well as manilla but is far more flexible.

Cotton   Used to be used for yacht cordage and fancy work, but was expensive although very flexible. Not as strong as manilla or hemp.

Coir   Made from the fibres in the husks of coconuts grown, principally, in Sri Lanka. It is the weakest of all the vegetable fibres, about one fifth of the strength of manilla, but only half the weight. It is buoyant, very flexible and springy. Tarring coir rope reduces its strength.

Man-made fibres The three synthetic fibres used are nylon, polyester (Terylene or Dacron) and polypropylene.

Nylon This was the first of the man-made fibres to be used for rope making. It is stronger than any of the vegetable fibres, but will stretch considerably when under load which makes it unsuitable for running rigging. It is best used where its shock-absorbing properties are an advantage such as in mooring or anchor warps.

Polyester Made up from multifilament fibres. Although not quite as strong as nylon, it does not stretch as much, and is more resistant to wear. It is the most common of all the ropes used on boats. It can be obtained in pre-stretched form, where it has been heat treated during manufacture to reduce its stretch even further.

Polypropylene The lightest and weakest of the man-made fibres, but it has the advantage that it is buoyant. When used for mooring lines, a larger size than the equivalent in polyester or nylon should be used. Polypropylene suffers from light degradation, and should be replaced annually if used for moorings, and more frequently in the tropics.

Types of rope
Hawser-laid rope The most common type of rope is made up of three or four strands and is laid up right-handed, i.e. twisted from left to right. If the rope has four strands, it is usually given a small strand as a heart. A simple method of deciding whether a rope is left- or right-handed is to look down the rope. If the strands, running away from you, go from the left side of the rope to the right, the rope is right-handed, and vice versa. A right-handed rope is always coiled down clockwise.

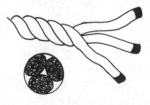

Hawser-laid Rope

Cable-laid rope   This is constructed by laying up three hawser-laid ropes from right to left.

Ratline stuff   Composed of 18 to 21 threads (yarns) and is the smallest rope made. Below that, there are various types of line, codline, marline and spunyarn (either 2 or 3 stranded).

Braidline   A method of rope making that came into use at sea with the introduction of man-made fibres. The rope is made up of a large number of strands plaited together. It has considerable strength and considerable resistance to wear. The most common, and strongest form of braidline rope is double braidline, which has a plaited core and a plaited sheath around it.

Braidline

STRENGTHS OF ROPE AND WIRE

A rough formula for calculating the breaking strain of a wire rope is:

$$\text{Breaking Strain} = 3 \times \text{Circumference}^2$$

A rough formula for finding the breaking strain of hemp, sisal and manilla ropes is:

$$\text{Breaking strain} = \frac{3 \times \text{Circumference}^3}{7}$$

In order to prolong the life of the rope or wire, strains taken by the rope should not exceed one sixth of the breaking strain in normal working usage. If the strains are exceeded the life of the rope will be shortened.

Wire rope   The flexibility and strength of wire rope is dependent upon its size and its construction. Wire rope is made with six strands around a core. The number of wires in the strand dictates the flexibility; the more wires there are the greater the flexibility. Thus for standing rigging, a 6 × 7 (seven wires to each of the six strands) would be used, whereas for running rigging a 6 × 19 or 6 × 24 wire would be more suitable. All steel wire rope should be galvanised for use at sea. The core of small wire rope, and flexible wire rope is usually of hemp, but large ships' shroud wire will have a copper core.

In yachts, stainless steel wire is now common for both standing rigging and, in a more flexible form, for running rigging. Standing rigging wire in stainless steel is usually of the multi-strand form and the ends are swaged rather than spliced. Although stainless steel is slightly stronger than ordinary steel wire rope, it work-hardens more quickly, and gives little warning before it fails.

ROPE AND WIRE PROTECTION

Ropes should always be protected against wear, chafe and corrosion. They should always be stowed well clear of a source of heat or of anything corrosive; a life may depend upon it.

Man-made fibres can be damaged by chemicals, dirt or salt crystals, and should be washed regularly in fresh water avoiding detergents. The most usual source of damage to rope comes from a bad nip; that is, a bad lead or a sheave that is too small, narrow, or has seized up. A rough guide for wire ropes is that the diameter of the sheave should be at least 720 times the diameter of the smallest wire in the rope, but as a general rule, use as large a block as possible for a rope lead.

Where a rope, other than a man-made fibre, is used in an exposed position, unless it has been rot-proofed it is often tarred as although this reduces the strength slightly, it retards decay due to salt water. Ropes used for standing work may be protected by worming, parcelling and serving.

Wire rope, except stainless wire, should always be treated. The treatment depends upon the purpose to which the wire is put. If it is a part of the standing rigging it will not be required to flex, and a hard-skinned protection such as paint or boiled linseed oil may be used. The wire should always be soaked or slapped down first with tallow or oil. A good protection for galvanised standing rigging is to immerse the wire in melted tallow before setting the rigging up. After a month a crewman should be sent aloft to slap down all the standing rigging with a 50/50 mix of tallow and white lead paste or putty. This process should be repeated as necessary thereafter. In warm weather this mix melts slightly, lubricating the wire, and in cold weather it hardens up to protect the surface of the wire. On merchant vessels the shrouds and stays are often treated with a mix of tallow, white lead and white paint and sometimes candle grease is added. Running rigging wire should be well greased with either special lubricants such as waterproof grease or tallow. A mix often used in merchant ships is tallow, fish oil and black lead powder, but this is not recommended for small boats as it stains clothing.

KNOTS

Most knots were originally developed by seamen so it follows that most of the important knots owe their origins and names to the requirements of a ship. There are five basic types of knots:

1. Bends. The name of a knot used to unite two ends of rope.
2. Hitches. The name given to a knot that ties a rope to an object such as an eyebolt, bollard, bar, etc.
3. Fancy Knots. Work with rope, developed over the years by seamen in their spare time.
4. Splices. The long and short splices are multi-stranded bends; an eye splice is a multi-strand loop.
5. Knobs. The name of any rope work which is designed to prevent the rope unreeving.

The modern sailor no longer has a need to know all the tens of thousands of knots that were developed in sailing ships one hundred and fifty years ago, but he does need to know a dozen or so which are relevant today, and these knots should be well learned and practised until they can be tied swiftly and surely even at night in difficult conditions.

There are a few technical terms used in knotting. Two ropes

are 'bent' together, a hitch is 'taken' or 'made fast', a knot is 'put in' or 'made'. A splice is 'put in', whilst a Turk's head would be worked. A rope is divided into three parts, the 'standing part', the 'bight' and the 'end'. The 'end' is the end of the rope to be worked. The 'bight' is the piece of rope in the middle between the end and the standing part, and the standing part is the rope beyond the bight, possibly made fast to something. A 'turn' is taken when a rope is wound completely round an object, or curved round itself once, and if it is taken round twice it is known as a 'round turn'. If a further turn is taken although there would be three turns, it is known as 'two round turns'.

Overhand knot   This is the simplest knot, and forms the basis of many others. Hold the standing part in one hand, and take the end back over the standing part to form a loop, and then pass it through the loop. The overhand knot is used in a rope's end temporarily to stop the strands fraying, and can also be used as a stopper. When pulled tight, it can be difficult to undo.

Overhand Knot

Figure-of-eight Knot

Figure-of-eight-knot   Sometimes called the Flemish knot. A more ornamental knot than the overhand knot, used for the same purposes, but easier to undo. Take the end of the rope back over and round the standing part, and then down through the loop.

Reef knot or square knot   Probably the most common and well known of all knots, but should never be used as bend to join two ropes together, as it can easily spill. It is easy to make, secure when made, and easy to undo. Hence its use and name, for tying together reef points on a sail. It is an excellent binder knot; however, it will *not* hold when made up of rope of different sizes. The simple rule for making a correct reef knot is: right over left and tuck it under, left over right and tuck it through. If the ends of the reef knot are not passed through correctly a granny or lubber's knot is formed. Although a

Reef Knot

Granny or Lubber's Knot

granny knot looks like a good knot, in practice it will slip the moment weight is put on it.

Sheet bend This is the best knot for tying the ends of two ropes together as it pulls tight, and can be used with dissimilar sizes of rope. Make a loop in one of the ends of rope. Take the other end up through the loop round behind the standing part of the loop and back over the top underneath itself.

Sheet Bend

Becket hitch Basically a sheet bend, but one of the ropes, the loop, is replaced by the becket, or any eye.

Double sheet bend This is a more secure version of the sheet bend. The end is passed twice round the back of the loop before being put under its own part.

Double Sheet Bend

Bowline Probably the most useful knot of all because, if made properly, it will not slip. The name derives from the 'bow line', a rope that held forward the weather leech of a square sail. Take the end in the right hand and lay it across the bight, which is held in the left hand. Loop the bight over the end, and then take the end down, round behind the standing part and back up and then down through the loop. WIth practice, this knot can be tied very quickly. It is a safe knot, and is used when sending a man aloft or overside, and can be used in a hawser to make a loop to go over a bollard, or to tie up a painter. Two interlocked bowlines forming a bowline bend make a good method of joining hawsers. A running bowline is formed when the knot is tied after it has been passed around the standing part. This forms a loop that can be tightened when the standing part is pulled.

Bowline   Carrick Bend

Carrick bend This knot is beautifully symmetrical, and, when worked round a number of times, is very decorative. It is used for joining two hawsers together. Put the end of one rope over its own bight to form a loop. Take the end of the other rope over the loop, then round under the standing part, over the other end, under the loop again but over its own part.

Clove hitch Basically two half hitches, but so that both ends come out of the centre. It is used where it is not possible to pass a hitch over the end of a pole or something similar. It is made by taking the end round the pole, over itself and round the pole again and underneath itself. It resists lateral movement, which was why it is used for ratlines on shrouds.

Clove Hitch   Rolling Hitch or Magnus Hitch

Rolling hitch Used when it is necessary to make a rope fast to another rope or bar so that it will not slide sideways along the rope, as in a stopper. Take the end of the rope around the spar twice in front of the standing part, then back, round the spar the other side of the standing part and under itself.

Round turn and two half hitches A simple method of securing a rope to a ring or spar, often used for securing a boat's painter.

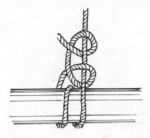 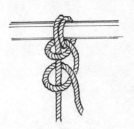

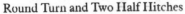

Round Turn and Two Half Hitches   Fisherman's Bend

Fisherman's bend A misnamed knot, because it is a hitch. Similar to a round turn and two half hitches, except that when taking the first half hitch the end is passed beneath the round turn first. It locks better than a round turn and two half hitches, and is used for the same jobs.

Marlinespike hitch Useful for getting a grip on a standing part of a rope, but originally used for giving a hold on marline with a marlinespike when serving a wire or rope. Make a bight and bring it back over itself. Then pass the marlinespike under the standing part.

Marlinspike Hitch

Jury mast knot, or double pitcher knot Used to provide an emergency hounds on a spar, the bights of the knot being the

Forming the jury knot

The jury knot in use, showing the guys made up to the loops with sheet bends.

attachment point for temporary shrouds and stays, which should be attached using a becket hitch. The knot will tighten around the spar as tension is put on the loops, but will hold better if horns are nailed beneath it, or the spar is parcelled beneath it. The simplest way to make the knot is to make three loops as shown, and then weave the inner bights of the two outer loops in regular sequence to the opposite side of the knot. The ends of the knot can be seized to the side loops, or used for additional stays.

Turk's head Often thought of as a decorative knot, and used on the vertical spokes of the wheel, stanchions etc, as such. However it has many practical uses, such as on a spar or rope as a bole to stop another rope slipping, as a drip guard on oars, and as a very firm seizing on a spar when the spar is springing. There are many-stranded turk's heads, but only the three-strand version is shown here. Lay the end of the rope against the spar,

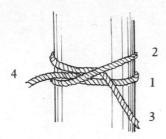

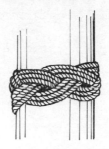

Beginning Turk's Head   Turk's Head

and take a turn, coming up underneath and to the right of the standing part. Go across the standing part and take another turn, coming up on the left of the standing part. Go over the top of the beginning of the second turn and underneath the standing part of the first turn, so that it comes out to the right. Then turn the rope round until looking at the two parallel strands of the two turns, and tuck the right hand of these two strands under the left. Now take the end, pass it over the new right hand of these strands and under the left, so that it comes out to the left. Next take the end, beyond the crossover of the two strands, and take it down between the strands coming out to the right. A simple Turk's head is now formed, and the end should be lying alongside the original standing part. Tighten up the strands, and then, if a more substantial Turk's head is required, take the end round following the same path as the standing part.

Monkey knot The knot used at the end of a heaving line to give it weight. It is normally made around the fingers of the left hand. Take three turns around the fingers, the middle and index finger being slightly separated. Then take three more turns, at right angles to the first three turns, through the two separated fingers. The last three turns are wound round outside the second turns and inside the first turns. The knot is worked taut, around some hard round object, such as a large marble or golf ball. To finish, splice the end of the rope to the standing part.

Crown knot This knot is used to stop the ends of a rope fraying, and is also the beginning of a back splice. Unlay the rope for 2–3 circumferences, take the centre strand over the top

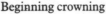

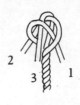

Beginning crowning   Crowning complete

of the rope and hold it down on the other side so that a loop is
formed. Take the right strand around the loop and bring it back
between the standing part of the first strand and the end of the
third strand. Take the third strand over the end of the second
strand and through the loop made by the first strand. Pull the
ends tight.

Wall knot   A more effective stop on the end of a rope than the
crown knot. Unlay the strands, and make a loop with one of
them, holding its end to the standing part of the rope. Take the
next strand to the right over the end of the first strand and back
against the standing part. Take the third strand over the end of
the second and up through the loop formed by the first strand.
Then pull all the strands evenly.

   If the ends are taken round once more, and brought up in the
middle, a stopper knot is formed. To make a man rope knot,
make a crown knot, and then put a wall knot beneath it.

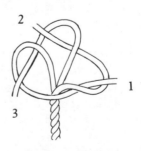

Wall Knot

TACKLES

Tackles are a simple means of obtaining increased power by use of blocks and rope. The power gained is directly proportional to the number of sheaves in the tackle, and a simple method of calculating the power gained, or the mechanical advantage, is to count the number of parts of rope at the moving block, or the top block. This gives the factor for the power gained, but 10% should be deducted for each sheave in the tackle to allow for friction.

A tackle can be anything from one block, to a two block multi-sheave arrangement. All the main types of tackles in use have separate names, many of which date back to quite early usage.

Parts of a tackle The drawing shows a gun tackle, made up from two single sheaved blocks, one fitted with a becket. The mechanical advantage of this tackle is two or three, depending upon which end is used as the moving part. If used as shown in the drawing, the mechanical advantage is three; if used the opposite way round, it is two.

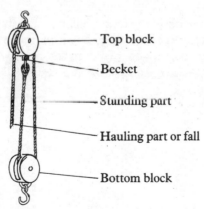

Parts of a Tackle

- Top block
- Becket
- Standing part
- Hauling part or fall
- Bottom block

Single whip A rope rove through a single sheaved block. There is no mechanical advantage; it merely acts as a lead block.

Double whip A tackle with two becketless blocks which gives a mechanical advantage of two.

Gun tackle Two single blocks, but one with a becket to which the standing part of the rope is made fast. The mechanical advantage is two or three, depending upon which way the tackle is used.

Handy Billy A single block with becket and a double block. The mechanical advantage is three or four, depending upon which way round the tackle is set up. This tackle is also called a Jigger.

Watch tackle Basically the same as a Handy Billy, but it has two hook blocks instead of one hook block and one tail block.

Double luff tackle Two double blocks, one with a becket. The mechanical advantage is either four or five, depending upon how the tackle is rigged.

Three and two tackle Sometimes known as a Gyn Tackle. The mechanical advantage is five or six.

Three fold purchase The mechanical advantage is six or seven. The method of reeving shown in figure B is the better as the pull on the hauling part is from the centre of the block, and the block is less likely to capsize as a result.

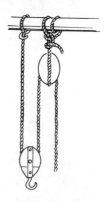

Single Whip   Double Whip

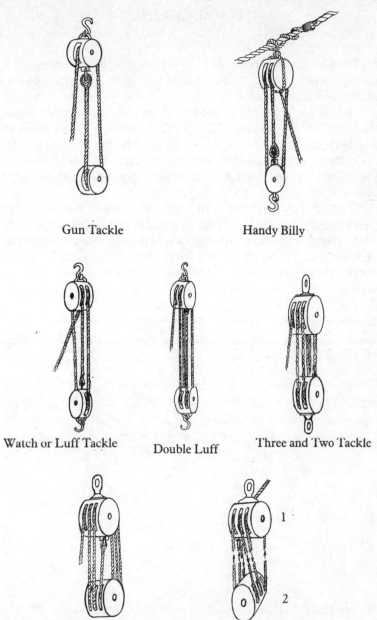

Gun Tackle

Handy Billy

Watch or Luff Tackle

Double Luff

Three and Two Tackle

1

2

Threefold Purchases – Alternative Methods of Reeving

PARBUCKLING

Parbuckling is an old, and surprisingly effective method of gaining a mechanical advantage of nearly two, when moving a heavy object.

The classic example is the movement of some heavy object, such as a barrel, up an incline. Two ropes are secured at the top and laid out down the inclined surface. The barrel is then rolled onto these ropes, which are then taken round and over the barrel and back to the top of the incline. As the ropes are pulled, the barrel is wound up the slopes.

It has its uses for moving any round load, but a modern example of a form of parbuckling is the uphaul on a leeboard. The uphaul is made fast on one side of the leeboard case, and led down into the case, through a sheave in the board and back to a block on the other side of the case from whence it is led to a winch.

Parbuckling

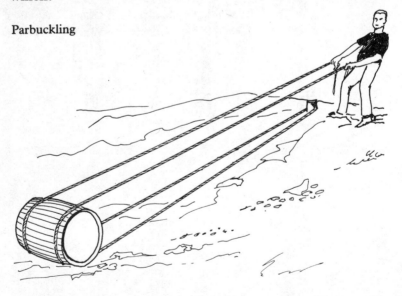

Whippings   All ropes' ends should be secured so that the rope will not fray. Although synthetic materials can be sealed by heating the ends, which melts and fuses the filaments, the best method of securing a rope's end is by means of a whipping.

Common whipping   Make a loop, with twine, along the rope and make a dozen or so turns around the rope over the loop. Place the end of the twine through the loop and pull on the loop so that the end is pulled out of sight beneath the whipping. Cut off the ends.

Common Whipping

Sailor's whipping   Also known as an ordinary whipping. Lay the end of a length of twine along the rope and then take 5 or 6 tight turns against the lay back over the end. Now take the other end of the twine and lay it along the rope over the other turns. Continue the tight turns over both ends of twine until just short of the rope's end, and then pull tight on the twine, so that the loop of twine at the end disappears. Provided the turns are made tightly, and the twine is pulled tight at the finish, a very firm whipping is formed. Cut off the surplus twine where it comes out of the whipping.

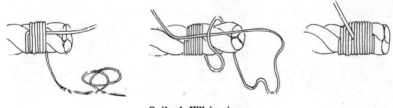

Sailor's Whipping

Palm and needle whipping   Also known as a sailmaker's whipping. This is the best type of whipping, as it is firmer and

Palm and Needle Whipping

more permanent. Take the required amount of twine and thread it through a needle, and knot the other end. Place the needle between two strands of the rope, and then through the middle of the next strand and draw the knot into the rope. Take a dozen or so tight turns towards the end, and then put the needle between two strands, pulling the twine tight. Follow the groove in the rope to the other end of the whipping and pass the needle and twine between the strands. Follow round until the three grooves in the rope are filled, frapping the turns in the whipping, pass the needle beneath a strand again, and then knot it with a half hitch to its adjacent frapping. Pulling the twine taut buries the knot in the rope. Repeat the knot and cut off the end.

West Country whipping   Middle the twine around the rope and half knot it over the rope. Repeat half knots at every half turn, so that each half knot is on the opposite side of the rope. When the whipping is long enough, finish it off with a reef knot. This whipping is a very effective temporary whipping on rope and wire.

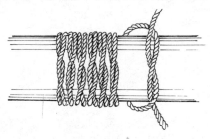

West Country Whipping

SEIZINGS

A seizing is a lashing used to hold two parts of rope together, either permanently or temporarily. It can also be used to hold two parts of rope together to form an eye, particularly where a hard eye is used, and the thimble is likely to suffer more wear than the rope or wire, and may need to be renewed. There are two basic types of seizing, Round seizing and Racked seizing.

Round seizing Place the two parts of rope or wire to be seized together, and take a clove hitch around one part, with marline for a rope seizing, and seizing wire for a wire seizing. Then take between ten and fifteen turns around both parts of rope as tightly as possible. Finish off by taking two or three frapping turns over the seizing between the two ropes, and then knot the seizing to the part left free from the clove hitch, but so that the knot lies hidden between the two parts of rope. This type of seizing works well when both parts of the rope are taking an equal strain.

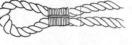

Round Seizing   Racked Seizing

Racking seizing Start as for a Round seizing, but then take figure-of-eight turns round the two parts of rope ten to fifteen times. Finish off by taking frapping turns as before. If the rope parts are being seized around a thimble, start the turns close up to the thimble.

WORMING

Worming a rope prior to parcelling and serving is not often done nowadays. It is a method of filling the grooves between the strands of a rope or wire with marline or other small stuff, to make it more round. It would be used on fancy work, where a smart finish is desirable.

PARCELLING

Parcelling serves two purposes; it helps to level off any unevenness in a rope or wire before serving, and it also helps to keep the weather out. Parcelling is made up of strips of hessian from

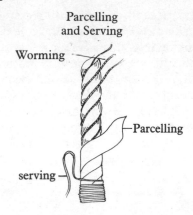

bags, which is then wound tightly round the rope or wire like a bandage. To provide protection to a wire, the wire should be well tallowed before parcelling, and the parcelling well tallowed before serving. Hold the parcelling in place with a series of half hitches with sailtwine.

Parcelling is wound round a rope or wire *with* the lay, in accordance with the old rhyme: 'Worm and parcel with the lay, turn and serve the other way.'

SERVING

In order to protect a rope or wire, or to protect skin or clothing from the snag ends of a wire splice, the rope or wire is 'served' with marline. A serving is simply a number of turns around the wire, rope or splice, but to make a good job, a serving mallet is used to keep the turns tight and packed well together.

Place the end of the marline on the wire, so that its end is pointed towards the direction to be served, and then take about four or five turns back over this end, by hand, and as tight as possible, as in a simple whipping. Then place the serving mallet on the wire, and take the marline over the mallet, round behind its handle, and back down the front and round the wire to the handle. Take a turn of marline around the handle again, as the tightness of the serving will be adjusted by the amount of tension put on the marline as it passes around the handle.

To make serving simple, an assistant should hold the ball of marline and follow round the wire as the serving mallet is turned, as this will avoid a tangle of loose turns of marline.

Continue turning the mallet, and putting turns around the wire, until about six turns from the end, making sure that each turn is tucked tightly against its predecessor. Then stop, and take six loose turns with the ball of marline ahead of the mallet. These turns should be large enough to allow the ball of marline to be passed through them. Pass the ball through, from the end towards the mallet, and then serve six more turns over this end of marline. There should now be a large loop of marline at the end of the serve. Pull on the end where it comes out in the middle of the serve so that the loop is drawn into the serve, and then cut off the marline where it comes out in the middle of the serve.

A serving provides a professional finish to a splice. To preserve the serving it should be given a good coating of Stockholm tar.

SPLICING

Splicing is the means of joining two ropes or wires permanently or for bending the end of a rope onto itself to form a permanent loop.

Short splice This is used to join together two ropes' ends, when the rope is not required to pass through a block. Unlay the two ropes ends for a distance of about 3 to 4 times their circumference, and then clutch them together so that each

Short Splice

strand passes between two strands of the other end. Then take each strand in turn from one end, take it over the strand of the other rope lying to its left, and under the next strand of the other rope, in other words against the lay of the rope. When all three strands have been passed in this manner, gently but firmly pull all the strands until they are even and tight. These are called the locking tucks. Now take each of the six strands in turn and pass it over its left neighbour and under the next strand. To make a good splice, three tucks should be taken with each end.

Long splice   Used to join together two ropes where the rope is expected to pass through a block. Unlay the ropes for 12 to 16 times the circumference, and clutch them together as in a short splice. Now unlay one strand and fill up the gap thus caused by twisting in the strand opposite to it in the other rope. Next, unlay a strand in the other end, and fill its gap with its opposite strand. The ropes should now appear as in the diagram. To finish, tuck the ends as in a short splice, but with the lay of the rope, so that the two end strands are wound round each other and not their neighbours. To make a really tidy job, reduce the strands gradually in each end so that the extra thickness tapers.

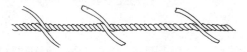

Long Splice

Rope eye splice   Used to form a permanent eye in a rope. Unlay the rope for 3 to 4 times its circumference, and then lay it alongside the standing part at a point which gives the desired size of loop. Lay the three strands upon the standing part, and put the middle strand under the closest strand in the standing part, against the lay of the rope. Then take the strand on the

Rope Eye Splice

left, pass it over the strand beneath which the first strand was tucked, and underneath the next strand. Take the third strand and tuck it beneath its opposite number in the standing part. All the strands are tucked against the lay. Pull the three strands firmly, and then take two more complete tucks. On the next tucks the strands can be tapered.

Backsplice A method of preventing a rope from fraying, where the rope does not have to pass through a block. Form a Crown knot, and then take tucks in sequence as for a normal splice.

Splicing braidline Braidline splicing is much easier if the proper fids are available, as not only are they designed to put in the tucks; but are also used for measuring out the lengths for the splice. The fid has a mark on it for this purpose, and a short fid length is the distance between the mark and the open end of the fid.

Eye splice Tape the end of the braidline and cut off the end if it has been heat sealed. Make a mark R on the sheath, one fid length from the end. Form the desired size of loop from this mark and place another mark X on the opposite side of the loop, on the standing part. Having put a knot, or made the rope fast at a distance about 5 fid lengths down the rope from the core extraction point (mark X), remove the core of the rope from mark X to the end, and tape the end. From the first mark R, count off ten double strands towards the end and make a mark all round the sheath, T; slide the sheath back towards the knotted point and mark the exposed core as follows: mark 1 at the extraction point X, mark 2 one short fid length (this is indicated on the braidline fid) toward the knot, mark 3, 2 long and one short fid lengths down the core. Place the sheath in the fid, insert it into the core at the second mark and out at the third. Pull the sheath through until the mark T on the sheath is at mark 2 on the core. Take the core, and run it through the empty sheath from point T to the point where the core comes out of the sheath at point X. Now pull the core until it bunches the sheath back against mark T and then the sheath so it bunches the core back. Finally pull on the sheath, away from the knot, so that the part of the splice where the core is on the outside is drawn into the standing part's sheath.

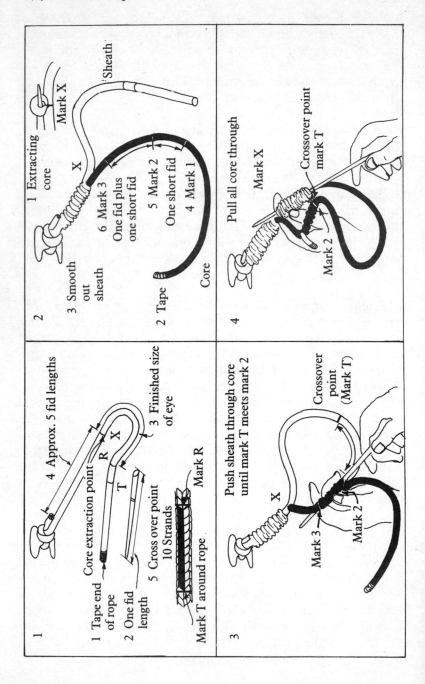

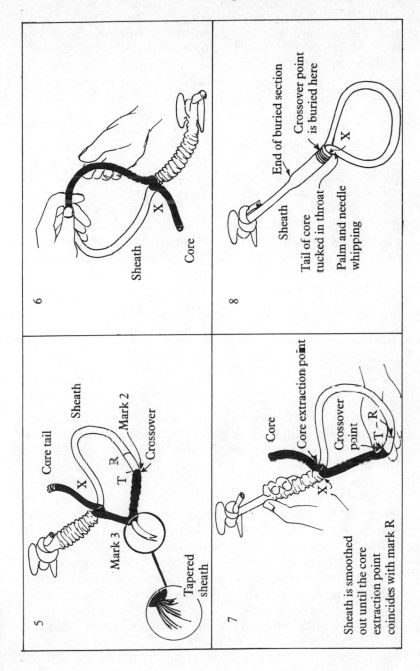

5

Core tail

X

Sheath

Mark 2

T R

Crossover

Mark 3

Tapered sheath

6

Sheath

X

Core

7

Core

Core extraction point

Crossover point

X

T – R

Sheath is smoothed out until the core extraction point coincides with mark R

8

End of buried section

Crossover point is buried here

X

Sheath

Tail of core tucked in throat

Palm and needle whipping

Smooth out the rope, and then put a palm and needle whipping around the neck. After one or two practice splices, the ends can be tapered to make a very even splice. To put a thimble in the splice, measure the loop around the thimble from mark X to mark Y, and then make the splice as described. If splicing used braidline, soak it in water to lubricate and loosen the fibres.

Wire splicing　Always work carefully with wire to avoid kinks in the wire or its strands. Before working the wire, put a seizing at the point to which you intend unlaying the wire. Put whippings on the ends of each strand before starting to splice. When splicing a wire use a long, well tapered, steel marline spike, and once it has been placed under a strand, it should not be removed until the tuck has been made, and the strand pulled firmly through. The Swedish type of spike can be used on smaller wires.

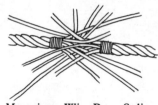

Marrying a Wire Rope Splice

Short splice　Short splices are not often put in wires, except when making slings, as they will not pass through a block. However, if it is required to join two ends of wire with a short splice, prepare the ends as described above. Clutch the two ends together so that each strand is lying between two strands of the opposite wire. Then, in order, tuck the strands of one of the wires under the strands of the other, and repeat this in the same manner as for splicing rope until there are at least three tucks either side of the join. Hammer the splice so that the wires snug down together, and then cut off the surplus ends using a hammer and cold chisel. Cover the splice with tallow before hammering it, as the tallow will help to preserve the wire.

Long splice　Seldom used on small boats because it is usually easier to provide a new wire as the lengths involved are small, and a long splice in wire requires a considerable length of wire if

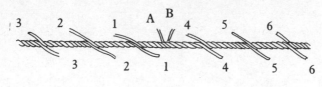

Long Splice

it is to work safely. For instance, on a colliery lift wire, the splice would extend over 60 feet. In a 1-inch circumference wire, the splice should extend over about 10 feet. Start by putting a whipping on each wire, the required distance back from the end equivalent to half the total splice length. Then unravel one strand on each wire back to these whippings. Take the strand from one wire and wind into the gap left by the unravelled strand in the other wire. Miss the next strand in sequence in the wire and repeat with the following strands, but to just over half the distance between the clutch and the end. Miss the next strands in the wire, and repeat with the following strands for about 1/10th of the distance from the clutch. Then repeat with the remaining strands in the other direction. The wire should now look as shown in the diagram.

Finally, tuck the wire ends into each other with the lay, and cut off the surplus ends with a cold chisel and hammer, after having hammered the tucks in the splice to bed down the ends.

Eye splice Whip the wire about 12 times the circumference from the end, and unravel the strands. Take the end level with the whipping, and bend it back alongside the standing part to give the desired size of loop. Clamp the wire into a vice at this point so that the loop is below the vice, and the standing part and unravelled strands are above the vice. It will help if the standing part has been looped over something above the vice so it is standing vertically. Then divide the strands so that three go one side of the standing part and three the other. Looking from the strands' side, take the right-hand strand closest to the standing part, and tuck it, with the lay, under the nearest two strands in the standing part. Take the next strand and tuck it with the lay beneath the nearer of the two strands which the first strand went beneath. Take the last of the three strands on the right side and place it against the lay beneath the next strand in the standing part, in a clockwise direction looking down on the

Left-handed Splice, First Tuck

standing part. Next, take the strand on the left side closest to the standing part, and pass it beneath two strands in the standing part, so that it comes out one strand away from the first strand. Put the second strand beneath the closer of the two strands used by the fourth strand, and finally, put the last strand, with the lay beneath the same strand in the standing part as the third strand, but with the lay. The first tucks are now complete. To put in the tucks, put in the marline spike under one strand of the standing part, and take the strand to its right, and place it through the gap from left to right. Pull it taut – run the marline spike up the standing part, and repeat the tuck. Repeat until at least four tucks have been taken this way, and then repeat with each of the strands in turn, but so that the number of tucks varies between adjacent strands, one having four, the next five, the next four and so on. Once all the tucks have been taken, remove the splice from the vice, smear it with tallow, and hammer it to bed in the strands. Then cut the ends with a cold chisel.

Rope to wire splice – braidline   Very common nowadays for halyards, where the standing part is of wire, and the tail of rope. Start by tapering the wire by cutting off each strand by a different amount over a length of about 3 feet. Tape over the end of the wire. Tie a knot in the braidline about 9 feet from the end to be worked, a marline spike hitch will do for this. Pull back the sheath of the braidline to expose the core, and cut off about 1–1½ feet of the core. Unbraid the core, and divide the strands into three, and put tape over the three ends. Insert the wire inside the core, until the last of the cut strands is at least 1½ feet down the core. Using a marlinespike or Swedish fid, open

Rope to Wire Splice

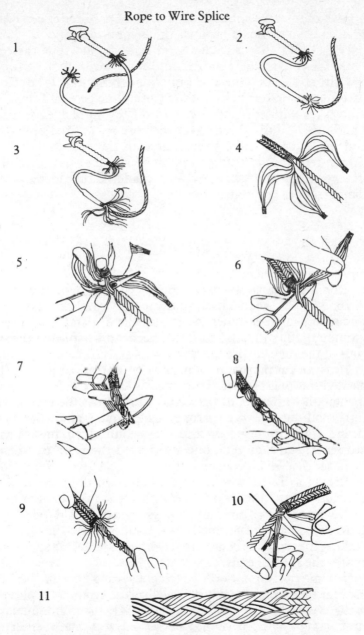

This splice is very strong, and when properly made, hardly increases the diameter of the rope at all.

up two of the wire strands together, and pass under one of the braidline core strands, against the lay, and laying the strands flat. Pick out the next two wire strands, and put the next braidline core strand beneath, and repeat with the last two of the wire strands and the final braidline core strand. Take at least two more series of tucks with the braidline core and then one more tuck with core tapered. Cut off the surplus ends of the braidline. Pull the sheath over the core splice, and unbraid it and make it into three strands as with the core. Splice these three strands in exactly the same manner as the core. This splice is very strong and when properly made, hardly increases the diameter of the rope at all.

GROMMETS

A grommet is a strop made up by twisting one long strand of rope or wire round itself and tucking away the ends as in a long splice. It is much easier to make a small strop as a grommet rather than try to form the strop by splicing the two ends of the rope or wire together.

Measure out the length of rope or wire required to make the desired size of grommet. Then measure off six and a half times the length with wire, or three and a half times the length with rope, and cut the wire or rope. Unlay one strand. Bend this strand round into a loop the size required for the finished grommet, and then tuck one end round the main part of the loop so that it lays against the standing part of the loop naturally, as it did when laid up before in the rope or wire. Continue round the loop twice with rope, or five more times with wire. If done carefully, the grommet should look like a continuous circle of normally laid rope or wire. Finish off by tucking the two ends beneath each other as for a long splice, and cut off the surplus ends.

In some cases it is worth putting a seizing over the tucks to prevent them from unlaying. A well-made grommet is pleasing to the eye, and very satisfying to make. Where the grommet is to slide along a spar, it should be served with marline. Before applying the serving the grommet, if made of wire, should be well soaked in tallow for its protection.

6 SAILS

MAINSAILS

Sails provide the horse power that drives a sailing boat, and are just as responsive to adjustment as an engine is to tuning. Modern materials have made the sailor's lot much easier, as today's sails, made from synthetic fibre, have much more strength and will last longer than canvas. This means, of course, that they can be set longer, as their strength will sustain the sudden strain of a squall which would have blown a canvas sail to pieces, even if the boat is driven over on to her side by the force.

There are very many differing types of sail that can be set from a small boat, but apart from the bermudian type, and light modern spinnakers, most were in use a couple of hundred years ago. Like most things associated with sailing small boats, experimentation with sails is both fun and rewarding, and teaches one how to get the best performance from the rig.

The mainsail is the boat's driving sail, although not necessarily the largest. It is the one sail that is set in nearly all weather conditions and sail combinations, and therefore must set well in calm conditions, yet be strong enough for the heaviest weather. The weight of the cloth to be used will depend upon the size of the boat, but 8 to 10-oz cloth is a good mean, for a medium size cruising boat. It is a false economy to save money by buying a cheap cloth for the mainsail, as the work required to make it is the same, but the life of the sail will be shorter.

All points that take wear or strain on a mainsail should be reinforced such as the head, tack, clew, reefing points, batten pockets, and where the mainsail will come into contact with the spreaders or running backstays. On my mainsails, I have recently taken to sticking a strip of cloth over the seams, to protect the stitching from chafe. If this is not done with a machine-sewn sail, it is a sensible practice for long distance sailing to put a few hand-sewn stitches in each seam at about one metre intervals, as this will stop the machine stitching running out for a whole seam if the stitching starts to break.

The normal number of reefs provided in a mainsail is three, but I have found it a distinct advantage to have a fourth reef. This is the storm reef, and gives just a small amount of mainsail for manoeuvring in bad weather. It is far simpler to put in a fourth reef than to set the trysail. You should be able to reef 60 per cent of the sail area.

Modern bermudian mainsails often have a small triangular panel of light cloth sewn into the foot of the sail which gives the sail belly for light weather when the sail should not be flat. Once the wind rises, this is removed by putting in the flattening reef, which may lie between 6 and 18 inches from the clew. In very calm conditions too the flattening reef should be taken in to help stop the crack of the sail as it slaps from side to side.

Battens are usually put into a mainsail to prevent the sail falling away at the leech, particularly if the sail has much roach (curve of the leech). The racing rules limit the number of battens allowed to four, and there are restrictions on their length, but these rules need not affect a cruising boat or any designed to sail in non IOR races.

Fully battened mainsails   Battens extending right from the luff to the leech help to give the sail a better shape, but the main purpose of having such full length battens is usually to allow the sail to be given much more roach and thus increase its area for a given mast height. A properly designed mainsail with good roach and well made battens can be set just as well to windward as one with little roach, and also gives more power when reaching or running.

The secret of a good set to such a sail lies in the shape and strength of the battens. They should be thinner at the luff end so that they can curve more easily. Most of the problems with fully battened sails come from the battens being insufficiently flexible to take the strains put on them when the sail is gybed, or not sufficiently strong to take the thrashing given to them when the sail is being reefed or tacked, and in particular when there are running backstays in the way. Full length battens put large forward force at the luff of the sail, and this has to be checked or it will force the batten through the sailcloth of the batten pocket. The usual method of controlling this force is to put a strong slide in the point where the batten and luff meet, and then connect the batten directly to the slide. Battens then behave like a gaff boom, and need to be treated in rather the same way. Their connection to the slide must enable them to pivot up and down and swivel from side to side, the same as a boom gooseneck. Some sailmakers supply small plastic end-pieces that bolt either side to the end of the sail so that the batten is secured in a plastic pocket. The problem with these is that they only trap a small part of the batten which will, sooner or later, break off level with the plastic pocket and then tear through the sail cloth and stick out forward of the luff. The batten is then a hazard because it can become caught on spreaders. A better system is to have a stainless steel strap made, that bolts either side of the batten and connects directly to the sail slide on the mast track.

The main disadvantage with a large roach fully battened mainsail is that it will usually foul a fixed backstay unless the boat has a great deal of length astern of the main boom. This means that when tacking or gybing, the halyard has to be eased until the sail clears the backstay, and then re-hoisted. Not only is this a laborious task, it also allows the sail to thrash about and risks breaking the battens. It is therefore usual to do away with standing backstays and fix running backstays in their place. A fully battened mainsail with running backstays supporting the mast is not ideal for the cruising boat, and they are mostly to be found on the large racing multihulls where the IOR does not apply and the crew are experienced in their use.

Gaff mainsail A gaff mainsail has the advantage of a large area for down wind work, but this is countered by the extra yard and rigging which increases top weight and maintenance. It is still to be seen on older vessels, but is rarely fitted with modern craft as the simpler and cheaper bermudian mainsail allows a lighter mast, and less ballast.

Bermudian mainsail The bermudian rig crept in at the beginning of this century and was soon in favour because of its simplicity and its higher aspect ratio than the gaff rig enabled boats to point closer to the wind. The sail is attached to the mast at its luff either by means of slides on the sail that fit onto a track on the mast, or by a luff rope sewn onto the sail which fits into a

Gaff Mainsail

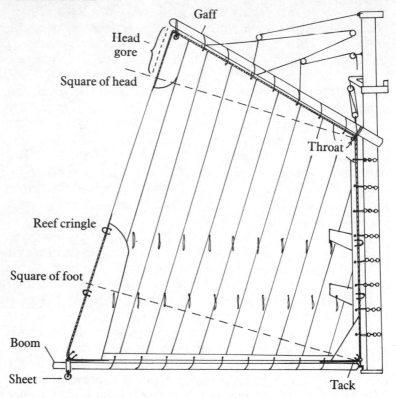

grooved channel up the aft side of the mast. The luff groove system is popular with ocean racers, but requires more care when hoisting or reefing, so the slide system is to be preferred for cruising and short-handed sailing. It is worth having the lowest reef of sail slides attached to the sail only by means of a rope lashing which passes through eyelets in the luff and the slides. This lashing should be taut when the sail is fully set, but as the sail is lowered to reef, the rope eases, and allows the sail to fall away from the mast. This saves removing the sail slides from the track when pulling in the first reef.

There are two views on the shape of cruising mainsails. A battenless mainsail is preferred by some as battens do break and can tear the sailcloth. Without battens the sail cannot have roach, and the leech must be cut in a straight line from head to clew. With modern battens however, made from stronger

Bermudian Mainsail

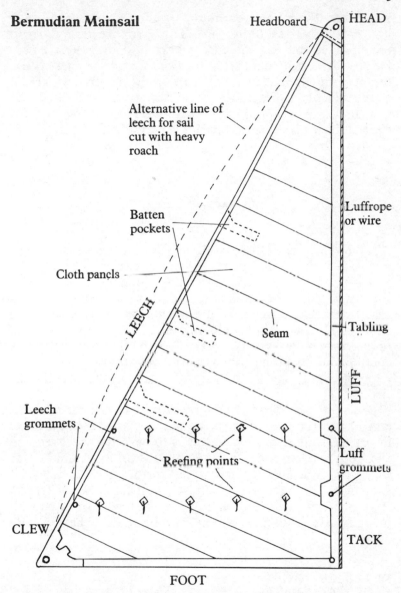

materials than the traditional wood (hickory is the favourite), this argument has less validity. On *Suhaili* both of my mainsails had battens and it was tearing seams that gave me problems, not tears caused by broken battens.

The heads of modern bermudian mainsails are usually made up to an aluminium headboard. This gives greater rigidity to the head of the sail and also allows a slightly longer sail. Headboards are hard on both sides and their fastenings should be wired onto the slides and the wire lashing covered with hide. If the sail fits into a luff groove, the headboard should be similarly sewed to special slides that fit into the groove. Unless the headboard is supported in this way, the sail is likely to tear down its luff.

MIZZENS

The mizzen on a ketch or yawl is usually a smaller version of the mainsail. On a ketch, the mizzen can be almost as large as the mainsail, but it is usually comparatively small on a yawl. It will usually be gaff or bermudian rigged as the mainsail and set in exactly the same manner. On yachts where the boat will manoeuvre under a jib and mizzen, this provides a useful reduced rig for heavy weather. On *Suhaili* I frequently used this combination in strong winds, as the mizzen was made of the same strength of cloth as the mainsail to give it sufficient strength.

A common problem with mizzen sails is that their booms extend over the stern of the boat, and they are difficult to sheet in properly. One solution to this is to have the sheet secured short of the boom end. The alternative is to rig a bumkin over the stern of the boat. In its simplest form, a bumkin is a sprit sticking out of the stern of the boat, but it can be a bracket or a stern platform. It should, in any case, be made strong enough for the loads it will take, if necessary by rigging chain or wire supports.

REEFING MAINSAILS AND MIZZENS

There is a modern trend amongst racers to keep their boats over pressed the whole time, the thought being, presumably, that if the boat is being hard pressed she must be going flat out and achieving her best performance. This is not always the case, and most boats will respond with a better speed and less leeway if their angle of heel is reduced. Reefing down the sails to reduce the power, as the wind rises and would otherwise increase power, is both sensible and practical. If the crew are new and inexperienced, there is nothing more frightening than the boat heeling over and bashing into the seas, and it is both a kindness, and in the interest of maintaining their enthusiasm for the sport, to ease up. Knowing when to reef a particular boat comes with experience, but with new sails, or a new boat, it is best to reef earlier rather than later.

The system of reefing a mainsail is usually the same for a mizzen. There are three basic types of reefing, standard, slab and rolling.

Standard reefing This is the same basic form of reefing as used in the days of commercial sailing ships. The halyard is eased and the luff reef cringle is secured by a shackle or lashing to the boom gooseneck. The leech cringle for that reef now becomes the clew, and is hauled down by means of a reefing pennant or tackle, onto the boom, and made fast. The reefing points, the small ropes set on either side of the sail along the line of the reef, are then tied together beneath the boom using reef knots.

It is important to get the reef pennant tight so that the foot of the sail is not baggy once the reef is in as, apart from the fact that the sail will not set properly, this tends to put extreme strain on the reefing points. Once the reef is in, put a sail tie around the boom and through the leech cringle. This acts as a preventer in case the reef pennant parts. The standard type of reefing is the kindest to the sail.

Slab reefing This is a racing development of the standard reef. Modern man-made fibre sailcloth, being stronger than flax or cotton, can take greater loads, and this has allowed reefs to be put in which depend upon the reefing pennant to hold the foot, not a series of reef points. An open hook is fitted onto the boom at the gooseneck, and the tack reefing cringle is slipped over this hook and the halyard tightened. The reefing pennant is led from an eye on one side of the boom, through the reef clew cringle, and then back to a block, either at the boom end, or on the other side of the boom. From there the pennant usually goes into the boom, along to the gooseneck and over a sheave and down to the deck where it leads to a winch. A stopper, on the boom at the gooseneck, is used to lock the pennant once the clew of the reef is in position so that the boom is free to move up and down without upsetting the pennant's tension. The reef is now in, and it only remains to put the preventer in the clew, and gather up the bunt of the sail and tie it to the boom. The reefing points in slab reefing should not be too tight as their sole purpose is to hold the bunt of the sail. A slab-reefed sail usually sets well.

Roller reefing   This is the least efficient form of reefing, but arguably the simplest to implement. The sail is reduced by revolving the boom, and winding the sail up around it. The halyard must be eased as appropriate.

The normal method of roller reefing is by means of a turning screw on the gooseneck. As the reefing handle is turned, the boom revolves. There are numerous types on the market. If the boom is to revolve, the sheet and topping lift must be placed on a slip ring on the outer end of the boom, so that they do not turn at the same time.

The problem with most roller reefing is that as the sail rolls up around the boom, there is more sail close to the gooseneck so more sail gets taken up near the luff and the boom end tends to drop as a result. The answer is to taper the boom so that it is thinner at the gooseneck than at the outer end. However, it is still very difficult to roll up the sail evenly, and the sail usually tenses or bags in the middle which spoils its shape.

HEADSAILS

The headsails are those set forward of the foremost mast, and can be jibs, genoas, staysails and running sails such as spinnakers. Apart from running sails, headsails are usually set attached to a forestay, either by piston stay hanks, or in a luff groove. Shackles can be used if hanks are unavailable in an emergency.

On racing boats, the jibs, genoas, yankees or staysails, are often set in specially adapted stays which have an aluminium extrusion around them containing a luff groove. The sail has a bulbous tape sewn to its luff which fits into this groove. This is a very efficient and simple method of securing the luff of a sail to the stay, but has disadvantages for the short-handed and cruising sailor, as the sail, when being changed, has nothing holding its luff to the boat and, as a result, can blow off to leeward.

Roller furling   The introduction of roller furling headsails has been a boon to the cruising and short-handed sailor. Instead of having to change the headsail as the wind increases, it is just necessary to revolve the stay so that it rolls up the required amount of sail, and vice versa. One can thus effectively reef the headsail, and without leaving the cockpit too.

The principle is simple. Bearings are fitted at the top and bottom of the stay which allow the whole of the stay in between to revolve. At or near the lower bearing a reel is fitted to the stay,

Headsail Roller Furler

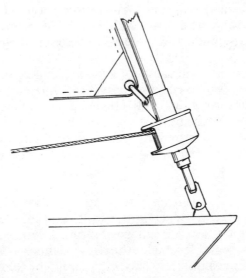

The furling rope is shown going into a cover which protects the drum attached to the forestay.

and a rope or wire wound onto the reel with the other end being taken to the cockpit. By pulling on this rope or wire, called the furling pennant, the reel, and therefore the stay to which it is attached, is revolved. A halyard traveller is fitted onto the stay, the centre part of which is held onto the stay, and the outside can revolve around it. The halyard is secured to the outside and the head of the sail to the inside part of the traveller. This prevents the halyard from being twisted round the stay as it is revolved.

Rolling forestays will only work effectively with a luff groove system, as hanks would slip around the stay as it revolved, and although the sail would start to roll up at the head and tack, the centre would roll later, making the sail baggy in the middle.

As, with a roller furling system, one headsail will cover a wide range of wind strengths, the sail should be made sufficiently strong to cover all conditions from very light to gale force winds.

When reeving on the furling pennant, the line should have only about three turns on the reel when the sail is fully rolled up, and the turns should wind on as the sail is let out. Bear in mind that in light conditions, more sail is taken up in each roll than in heavy weather when there is greater tension on the sail. Because the bearings in a rolling furling system are under very considerable tension, as they are taking the full tension off the forestay, the sheet should always be eased before rolling up the sail.

Jib   The generic name for a sail set hanked or attached onto a forestay. Where a jib is set outside the forestay, say from the end of a bowsprit, and not attached to a stay, it is known as a flying jib. Jibs can come in a number of sizes and weights to suit varying wind strengths. In modern terminology, a jib is a working headsail whose cut is a compromise between a genoa and a yankee.

Genoa   This is usually the largest working headsail and will usually extend well abaft the mast. The amount of this overlap is referred to as a percentage of the foretriangle area. The foot of a genoa comes level with the deck. Genoas were developed for the racing community and if they are to be used by the cruising boat, their foot should be cut well above the deck to allow the helmsman to keep a lookout.

Genoa and Yankee

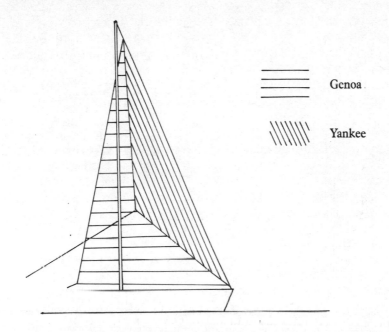

Genoa

Yankee

Because they fill the foretriangle, genoas give the maximum possible headsail, and are usually designed to be set in winds up to about 16 knots. Then the boat would change down to a jib.

Yachts with an unlimited budget, or racing yachts, would carry a No 1 and No 2 genoa, as well as a light genoa and possibly a very lightweight drifting genoa.

Yankee jib This is a high-cut jib, the clew normally being about halfway up the sail. It is a windward sail, and set in conjunction with a staysail gives a good pointing performance. A yankee is normally unsuitable for reaching or running, as its comparatively small area gives less power. Being high-cut, the sheet is led well aft on the boat, and the practical limits of the shape for a yankee are governed by the ability to sheet it at the stern. If the sail is cut too high, the sheet would need to be set beyond the stern, and since this is not possible, the foot of the sail would be too slack, and the leech too taut when hauled right in.

Self-tacking Staysail

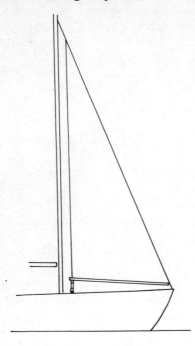

Staysail cut so that it
clears inside the mast.
A simple tackle, secured
to a deck bolt in the centre
line of the boat, will
allow the sail to set
without adjustment on
either tack.

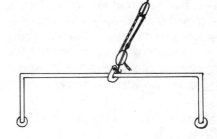

Old-fashioned horse rail.
The sheet slides on a
shackle to the rail.

Modern method with track fastened to
the deck with slider attached to the
sheet.

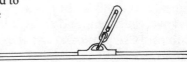

Staysail Any sail that is set on a stay is a staysail, but the description does not apply to the foremost staysail in the boat, which is the jib. Quite often, loose-luffed sails which are not secured or hanked on to a stay, but rely for their luff tension on the halyard being set up taut, are referred to as staysails. Examples are spinnaker and light weather staysails.

The usual staysail is set on an inner forestay, and helps fill the gap between the jib and the mainsail. It should be trimmed in conjunction with the other sails, but in practice it is easier to get the main and genoa pulling, and then trim the staysail to match them. The classic use of staysails is on a square-rigged ship where, particularly when beating, staysails are set on all the stays between the masts.

Self-tacking staysail In cruising boats, it is often simpler to have the staysail self-tacking, as it reduces the work involved in going about. The simplest method of doing this is to put the staysail on its own boom, with the gooseneck attached to the stay's bottlescrew or some other convenient object on the deck. The sheet can be cleated forward by the sails, or led aft from a central sheeting point When the boat is put about, the sheet will be set up for the other tack without any adjustment. A better alternative is to have a track or rail across the deck to which the staysail sheet is secured. This enables the clew to be held down when the sail is eased out, which makes trimming simpler. If the sheet leads from a block on the centre-line to a block on the slide on the track the sail is still self-tacking as the slide will cross over when the boat goes about, and set the same on the other tack.

STORM SAILS

Any boat contemplating a voyage of more than a few days should carry storm sails, in order to provide some manoeuvrability and windward capability if the existing sails cannot be reduced sufficiently by reefing, or are not of very strong material. The type, size and weight of sail will depend upon the size and weight of the boat, but the sails should be of good quality heavy material, and preferably hand sewn. The sails will be given greater strength if they are roped, by having rope sewn around their entire edges. The exact shape of the storm sails is of less importance than their strength and ability to withstand being consistently thrown aback in very strong winds.

The usual storm sails to be carried on any long distance voyage are a trysail, which can be set as a mainsail, and a storm jib.

Storm jib In very strong winds, there is little point in trying to beat close to windward. The aim should be to make good a course of 60 degrees or more to the wind without risking the boat being knocked flat in squalls. This calls for a comparatively small sail, preferably set low on the boat, although high enough to avoid being hit by rogue waves. Most boats can make to windward with just the trysail set, and the storm jib will usually tend to increase the leeway, but it very much comes into its own when the boat is put stern to the wind as its area alone, in the fore part of the boat, tends to keep the boat's head downwind.

On *Suhaili*, I had a 40-square foot Terylene storm jib, roped all around with large strong cringles in each corner. It survived five months in the Southern Ocean when gales appeared and

Storm Jib and Trysail

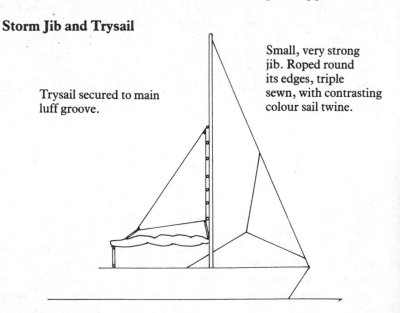

Trysail secured to main luff groove.

Small, very strong jib. Roped round its edges, triple sewn, with contrasting colour sail twine.

made its use advisable, on average, every five days. Sheeted hard amidships when running downwind, its area to the wind increased as the boat yawed, and this tended to keep the boat's head downwind. This sail, with a scrap of rolled mizzen, gave a moderate windward performance.

A storm jib should have larger than usual hanks for its attachment to the forestay, as they have to take a lot of wear, and it is not the sail you want to take in for repairs when it is used. If the boat has a luff groove, hanks would damage this, and should only be used in an emergency. Make sure the luff tape is the strongest available that will fit the groove, and that it is hand sewn to the sail, with plenty of knots in the sail twine so that if the twine breaks, the seam will not run far.

Swedish Storm Trysail

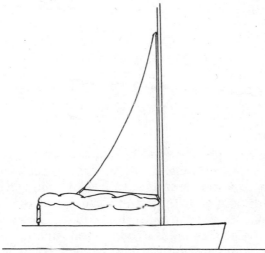

This is the tall, narrow, hollow-leeched sail, seldom seen outside Scandinavia. The sail is set up on the mainsail luff groove or track, with the clew taken to either a separate track on the boom, or, if slab reefing is fitted, to the last reefing pennant. To avoid the problem of removing the mainsail from the main track, a switch track can be fitted.

In the days of canvas sails, this sail often had a wire leech line, but with modern synthetic fibre sailcloth, this is not really necessary provided the leech is strengthened. Like all storm sails, a heavy cloth should be used.

This is the sail to set when wanting to make as little to leeward as possible in heavy weather. It replaces the mainsail if that does not have a fourth reef especially fitted for heavy weather use.

The simplest form of trysail has its head shackled to the main halyard, its tack to the gooseneck, and its clew lashed to the main boom or some convenient point on deck. It is not secured in any other way to the mast and boom. Sometimes it is possible to secure the luff, by slides or luff groove, to the mast, and this will give the sail more support and probably more pull. Some boats fit a special track on the mast for the trysail, so that it can be set quickly and easily without removing the mainsail first.

A trysail should be capable of being set quickly and easily. Use old fashioned and well tried techniques rather than experimental gimmicks. A wave-washed, windswept, heaving deck is not the place to have to tackle a flogging sail that has come loose somewhere.

RUNNING SAILS

Once the boat has the wind behind her, every part of the rig and sails is contributing directly to her progress. In a ten-knot wind, a boat beating to windward at eight knots will have a wind over the deck of 16½ knots, but if she is running downwind at eight knots, the wind over her deck will only be two knots. The weight of wind on a sail is lighter, when running, in any given wind conditions and this is why running sails can be made from lightweight material.

Running sails used to be lighter versions of the ordinary working sails, but next came large lightweight flying jibs that could be boomed out when running, and from this developed the spinnaker, which really came into its own with the introduction of nylon.

Running dead downwind is not particularly easy or profitable. In the first place the main boom has to be guyed out on one side of the boat, and the headsail poled out the other. This is known as goosewinging the sails. A yaw one way can back the headsail, and the other, the mainsail. Secondly, the sails are only giving the power from their surface area, and none from their aerodynamic shape, which is much more efficient. Most boats are hard to steer straight downwind, as a single spinnaker or headsail is unbalanced. Putting up another headsail the other side, i.e. so that it is sheeted on the same side as the main boom, such as another jib or blooper, greatly improves the steadiness of the boat. In light boats, such as multihulls, it is far more efficient to tack downwind than to run before the wind, as the boat's speed will bring the true wind forward, and enable a reasonable course to be held.

Twin running sails This provides the cruising boat with a sturdy, easily managed and balanced headsail arrangement for downwind sailing. The running sails will usually be longer and lighter versions of the jib, such as a reacher, the clew cut well up from the deck so that the sails will lift the bow and also give the helmsman a clear view of the horizon. Some boats fit twin forestays so that each sail can be hanked on separately. The sails can both be hanked onto one forestay but this means that neither can be lowered independently. When the boat has a double luff groove on its forestay, this is not a problem. The alternative to hanking both running sails to one forestay, is to hank on one and get it pulling, and then set the other unhanked or flying. Provided enough luff tension can be applied through the halyard, this will work, but handing a flying sail can be difficult. Ideally, both headsails should be poled out, as this pushes the clew further away from the boat, and steadies the sail.

Spinnakers Spinnakers are large, bright canopies of sail that are set forward of the forestay. There is no limit on their size, but there is a practical limit to what can be set, and what the boat will take. As a general rule they are two to three times the square area of the boat's largest genoa.

There are numerous special types of spinnaker available, and every sailmaker will have his favourite, but the most common type at the moment is the tri-radial, which can be set with the apparent wind from about 70 degrees on the bow to right astern.

The weight of cloth used for spinnakers varies with the wind range the sail should cover. As a general rule, lightweight spinnakers are of ¾ oz material and can be held up to ten knots of apparent wind. A 1½ oz material spinnaker will hold up to 15 knots of apparent wind, and a 3 oz up to 20 knots. Beyond that wind speed, spinnakers are usually only set by racing boats. On a cruising boat which is only going to have a single spinnaker, the 1½ oz is the most useful. I once set a special 5 oz spinnaker in a severe gale in the Southern Ocean, but the boat went as fast under twin headsails, one boomed out to weather, and was a great deal easier to steer.

Spinnaker gear The basic equipment required to set a spinnaker are a halyard, two sheets, two guys, a spinnaker pole and its gear. Because a spinnaker moves around on its halyard at the masthead, the halyard should always run through a swivel block on a crane at the masthead, so that it can lead comfortably in almost any direction. A spinnaker set on a genoa halyard, which has a fixed sheave at the top of the mast will either cut into the mast or chafe very quickly. On some racing boats, the spinnaker halyard comes out of the mast through a bell-mouthed opening. This is fine for coastal day racing where the halyard can be checked daily or renewed, but totally unsuited for anything longer.

The spinnaker pole is usually made of aluminium and as light as its strength allows. Its purpose is to provide a fixed point in space, which will vary with the trimming of the sail, to which the spinnaker can be secured. Together with the masthead, this is the only place where the spinnaker is held fixed, and if the pole were not there the sail would be very difficult to manage. The pole is always set out to windward, and its outer end becomes the effective tack of the spinnaker.

The pole secures, at its inner end, to a gooseneck fitting which runs on a track up and down the fore side of the mast. In some cases two tracks and goosenecks are provided, one on each fore side of the mast. The pole clips on to the gooseneck by means of a bayonet-type fitting with a quick release so that it can be removed fast if necessary. The purpose of the track is to allow the inner end of the pole to be raised and lowered so that, when in use, the pole will be as near horizontal as possible. As the normal length of a spinnaker pole is roughly the J measurement of the boat (the distance between the mast and the forestay at the deck) the pole end will be furthest from the mast when the

Spinnaker – Deck Layout

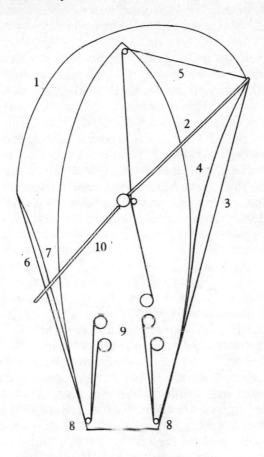

1 Spinnaker	6 Sheet
2 Spinnaker pole	7 Lazy guy
3 Guy	8 Double turning blocks
4 Lazy sheet	9 Winches
5 Fore guy	10 Main boom

pole is horizontal. A horizontal pole also means that the inward thrust of the pole is perpendicular to the mast and this avoids a tendency for the heel of the pole to want to push up or down the track on the mast. There must be some method of holding the gooseneck at a desired height on the track, and altering its height as necessary whilst the spinnaker is set, to allow the sail to be trimmed. This is usually done with an uphaul and a downhaul which can be led to the cockpit, or by tackles on the mast.

To set up the pole, attach a topping lift to the top of its outer end. Some boats have a special topping lift for this but it is usual to use the staysail halyard or weather spinnaker or genoa halyard if the latter is available. Attach a foreguy. This is a strong line leading from a block in the bows of the boat to the end of the pole. Its purpose is to enable the pole end to be hauled into the bow, and stop it rising up. Both the foreguy and the topping lift must be able to be adjusted whilst the spinnaker is set so that the sail can be trimmed. Slip the weather guy into the end fitting and snap it closed. Since this guy is going to be under a great deal of tension when the spinnaker is set, its splice will be hard up against the pole end fitting. To protect the splice, it is usual to put a disc or ball of hard-wearing material on the guy next to the splice so that, when set, this object will lie between the splice and the pole end. The weather sheet, which should be attached to the same snap shackle as the weather guy so that both can be released from the spinnaker together, is not going to be used, but is left clipped on, and lying above the end of the pole. The reason for putting the sheet above the pole is that if you want to gybe, the pole has to be dropped away from the guy, but if the sheet is beneath the guy the pole will drop onto the sheet and be impossible to swing forward.

Finally, clip on the sheet on the leeward side with its guy. The leeward guy is not going to be doing anything, and is usually known as the lazy guy as a result, but it is clipped into place so that it is ready for a gybe as the clew is difficult to reach once the spinnaker has been set.

Sometimes, the compression on the spinnaker pole can become very great, and this inward force at the pole's gooseneck can start to bend the mast. To relieve this loading on the mast, rig a tackle or line from the gooseneck, away from the mast in the direction the pole is pointing, to a block on deck, and heave tight.

Spinnaker setting   Being a large lightweight sail, with no fixed points of attachment except for the masthead and the pole, a spinnaker is very vulnerable when being hoisted. It has to be hoisted as quickly as possible because once the wind gets into it, it will billow downwind, possibly catching under the bow, but certainly increasing the load on the halyard and slowing the hoist.

With a large crew, extra hands can be put to haul on the halyard at the foot of the mast which speeds up a hoist, but even so, if the sail fills they may not make much progress.

It is best to prepare the spinnaker in advance. There are two usual methods, both of which involve laying out the sail with both sides together, and then tying a piece of rotten cotton or wool around the sail. The alternative is to pass the sail through a bottomless bucket, and at certain intervals release a rubber

Spinnaker Squeezer

Spinnaker halyard connects direct to head of spinnaker and to top of sock which includes bucket up-haul block.

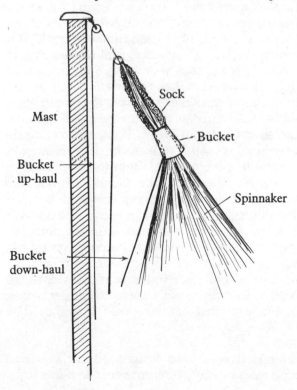

band around the bucket so that it is around the sail. Using either of these methods, the sail has to be split before reaching the foot, so that the tack and clew can be separately bound the same way. The sail is now held in together, and should not break out when being hoisted. When the sail is hoisted and the halyard made fast, pull on the sheet and the wool, cotton or rubber band will break allowing the sail to break out.

The worst mistake is to try and hoist a spinnaker without checking that it is not twisted. This leads to twists in the sail once it is up, which will probably not come out, and can lead to the sail tearing. The sail should always be checked by running down each luff tape to make sure it runs free to the clew.

Short-handed and cruising sailors quite often use a spinnaker squeezer to control the sail when setting or bringing it down. This consists of a bell-mouthed bottomless bucket, the base of which is attached to a long nylon sock, the same length as the spinnaker. A line goes from the bucket, the length of the sock to a strong fitting at the top end and back down again. The sock is then folded up on the bucket, until its head swivel fitting shows through the mouth and the head of the spinnaker shackled to this fitting. Holding the bucket in place, pull the head away, feeding the spinnaker into the sock at the same time through the bucket so that it is not twisted. When the sock is at full stretch, the clews of the spinnaker should just show at the mouth of the bucket. To hoist sail, clip the halyard onto the top of the sock, and the guys and sheets onto the clews. Hoist the sock to the masthead, and when all is ready, pull the bucket upwards by hauling down on the line which went from the bucket to the head of the sock and back again. As the bucket rises, the sock concertinas above it, and the sail comes out below.

To bring in the spinnaker, reverse the process. Pull down on the bucket, and the sail is forced in through the bell mouth. It is sometimes necessary to ease the sheet to help the spinnaker fold into the bucket.

The only snag with a spinnaker squeezer is that the bucket uphaul line, which usually runs inside the sock, can get twisted round the sail, but provided care is taken this should be avoided.

Spinnaker trimming Unlike a main or headsail, which are attached to a rigid mast or stay, a spinnaker is free-flying and relies on its own lift to stay set. Since this lift is governed by the trim of the sail, pole height, pole position, sheeting angle and tension, a spinnaker requires constant attention and its trim will vary with small changes of wind direction and force.

The old rule that if the luff of the spinnaker was curved in, and tended to luff about every ten seconds is a good guide, but does not necessarily indicate, that the spinnaker is properly set.

For the spinnaker to act like an aerofoil, the draught has to be moved towards the luff. This is achieved by setting the spinnaker pole so that it will apply tension to the luff. As a rough guide, if the pole is set too high, the top of the spinnaker luff will collapse, if it is too low, the collapse will occur at the bottom. When the pole is correctly set, the spinnaker should curl at the middle of its luff. When the spinnaker is difficult to set because of light winds or a sloppy sea, lower the pole a little to help settle the sail.

The best guide for obtaining the correct fore and aft position of the spinnaker pole is to get the luff vertical and at a right angle to the pole. It is the luff of the sail that must be kept square to the wind, not the pole, however, so this may mean adjustment of the pole. In light weather, when sailing on a beam reach, the pole will need to be brought aft from the forestay to keep the sail square to the wind. In heavy weather, easing the pole forward will decrease the efficiency of the luff and lose power.

On most boats, the spinnaker sheets are taken to a lead at the stern. In light weather moving the sheeting position forward, to move the clew closer to the tack, decreases twist and gives the sail a deeper shape which is more powerful. In medium winds the sheet should be taken further aft to open the leech. In heavy weather the sheet needs to go even further aft, but as this may not be possible owing to the length of the boat, take the sheet over the main boom to give the effect of taking the sheet further aft. This will lift the clew and open the leech, and helps to spill air from the sail which is probably becoming over-powerful and in this condition can cause broaching.

Broaching is usually caused by an increase in the wind, or a wave heaving the boat to give the same effect. The broach starts when the boat heels over, giving more weather helm. The main sheet and vang and spinnaker sheets should be eased immediately as the effect of the increased wind is to bring the apparent wind angle aft. Easing the main sheet luffs the sail, and easing the spinnaker sheet keeps the sail from overpowering the boat.

In light weather, the weight of the sheet and lazy guy can pull down the clew and leech of the spinnaker and prevent it from holding its shape. In these circumstances, rig a strong lightweight spinnaker sheet to the clew, take the weight, and then remove the heavy sheet and guy. Always put the lightweight sheet on with a long bowline, i.e. pull plenty of rope through the clew before knotting the line. The reason for doing this is that if the wind increases and it is necessary to re-rig the heavy sheet and guy, the clew is likely to be flying clear of the boat, and a short knot could not be reached from the deck. By putting in a long bowline, the knot can be easily undone however far out the clew is.

Handing a spinnaker   If the boat is not fitted with a spinnaker squeezer, the best method of bringing the spinnaker in is to let go the snap shackle on the guy at the end of the boom, and then pull in the clew by means of the sheet whilst rapidly letting down the head on the halyard. The sail is bundled in on deck, and subsequently packed away.

The pole must be brought to a position where its end can be easily reached from the foredeck, by easing the aft guy and hauling in on the foreguy. It may be necessary to ease the pole topping lift as well, but remember to make it fast again as otherwise the pole will drop once the spinnaker has been released from the guy. I was once given delayed concussion and a slipped disc in my neck because the topping lift was not resecured before I released the snap shackle on the guy. At least one member of the crew should be sitting ready on the foredeck with the lazy guy in his hands, and the moment the sail is released he should start to gather the sail in. The halyard should be allowed to run out in time with the gathering of the sail, and so that the sail does not fall into the water.

It often pays to run off downwind a little when bringing down a spinnaker, as this keeps the sail away from the mast where it might get torn or become entangled. If the wind is strong, it will certainly help if the helmsman bears away, and setting a headsail will increase the boat speed thereby reducing the apparent wind speed, as well as creating a lee for the spinnaker as it comes in.

When a guy, sheet or halyard breaks whilst the spinnaker is set, reduce the boat's speed by running off downwind. If the sheet breaks, it is usually possible to take up on the lazy guy and carry on sailing. If the guy breaks, and the usual cause is likely to be that it has chafed through where it passes through the pole end, either gybe and then rig another guy, or put the pole onto the sheet and haul the pole forward until the clew of the sail can be reached so that a new guy can be rigged. The latter system is much harder to achieve, and it is always safer to gybe, as the sail is brought under control more quickly. Remember that in most cases it is going to be almost impossible to reach the clew of the sail to release the snap shackle to get the spinnaker down until a pole is rigged.

When the halyard breaks, the sail will fall into the water to leeward, or if you are unlucky, under the bow. This is one of those times when all the crew are required in a hurry, as the longer the sail is in the water the less chance there is of getting it back on board untorn. If the sail falls over the bow it is most unlikely that it will not tear on the keel or log, but there is a small chance if the snap shackle on the guy can be let go quickly allowing the sail to stream astern secured only by the sheet. Haul it inboard, a task harder than you think, especially if there is a fair amount of wind. If the sail falls overboard clear of the hull to leeward, the chance of a tear is reduced but there is still a risk that the sheer weight of the water in the sail will rip the fabric, especially if the sail 'bellies' in the water. Again, let go the clew at the pole end so that the sail can stream out avoiding bellying, and then heave inboard, trying to pull on each side of the sail, as well as the middle at the same time.

Gybing a spinnaker There are two methods of gybing a spinnaker, the single pole and the two pole systems. The single pole system is the more difficult, but is practised by racing boats because the IOR forbids using two poles at a time.

Single pole method The spinnaker is set with a sheet and guy to each clew, the guy on one side going through the pole end. Start by running off downwind and squaring the pole so that the guys and sheets are out the same amount each side. Once the order is given to trip the catch at the pole end and release the guy, the helmsman must hold the boat steady downwind until the guy is clipped into the pole on the other side, and heaved in to the required angle. Station one man right in the bows of the boat with the lazy guy, which will become the guy on the weather side, in his hands. His job is to snap the guy into the pole end fitting and clear the pole through inside the forestay. If the pole has to be carried aft in the course of the operation, he will be responsible for releasing and, later, re-fastening the pole foreguy and topping lift as well.

Haul in on the pole foreguy the moment the spinnaker guy is released, and lower on the topping lift to bring the pole down to the bows of the boat. If the boat does not have an intermediate forestay, or has one that can be removed, the crewman in the bow will snap the new weather guy into the pole end catch, making sure he has placed it so that it will lead out forward when the pole is hauled out. Then take the tension on this guy, easing the pole foreguy at the same time, to bring the pole out on the other side. Adjust the topping lift to get the correct height, and the spinnaker is ready to be trimmed to its new working angle to the wind.

Where the boat has a fixed intermediate forestay, once the pole has been swung into the bow, it will have to be removed from its mast gooseneck, and the foreguy and topping lift let go. Run the pole aft until it can be pushed out forward between the mast and the intermediate forestay on the other side of the boat. It is then re-clipped into its gooseneck, the foreguy and topping lift re-connected, the weather spinnaker guy snapped into place, and then it can be hauled out ready for trimming.

The double pole method   The spinnaker is set as before, but before the boat is run off downwind, the other pole is set up with a topping lift and foreguy. As the boat is squared to the wind, and the sheets equalled on each side of the boat, the lazy guy is clipped into the end of the pole, and the pole hauled aft, and the weight of the spinnaker transferred from the sheet to the guy. The boat is now sailing with both spinnaker clews held by spinnaker poles. Now pull the spring catch on the end of the pole which was to weather, and drop the pole down and haul it in onto the deck.

If the pole does not release the guy easily, try easing out on its topping lift so that it can drop away from the guy. If that does not work, a quick ease of the guy, about a couple of feet, will often do the trick.

Jockey pole When the boat is close-reaching under a spinnaker, the pole will be swung right forward so that it almost
touches the forestay. This means that the angle the guy makes
with the end of the pole is very acute, putting added strain on
the guy, and it is also likely that the guy will be hard against the
shrouds, which could damage the shrouds, and will almost
certainly chafe the guy. To widen the angle made by the guy to
the pole end, and keep the guy off the shrouds, a short spar,
usually half the beam of the boat in length, is clipped on to a
padeye on the mast, and the guy run over a sheave in the outer
end. This spar, known as a jockey pole, is then swung right
outboard until it is forcing the guy away from the shrouds. To
hold this pole in position, either it may be lashed to the shrouds
with a sail tie, or better, put a couple of lashings from the pole,
one leading forward and one aft, to the toerail. The pole should
hold itself up with the guy tension.

Bloopers These are large, unboomed sails, the same weight as
the spinnaker, which set to leeward forward of the forestay.
They complement the spinnaker, and are usually filled by the
wind coming off the spinnaker's leech. The actual increase in
speed gained by setting a blooper is small, but they steady the
boat, and it is rare that a boat with spinnaker and blooper set
will start to roll and yaw out of control.

Gennickers This is one name for a cross between a genoa and
a spinnaker, a sail that is primarily used for reaching. It is a
single luffed sail that tacks into the gammon plate, or on the
weather hull in a multihull. Being securely tacked down, it is an
easy sail to steer to, and is easy to handle with a small crew. Put
on a pole, it can be used in place of the spinnaker. A useful
weight is 3 to 4½ ounces, the heavier weight being quite capable
of taking strong winds on a broad reach.

Squaresail Although only occasionally seen on cruising
yachts and of course on the square-rigged sail training vessels,
squaresails are one of the simplest to make and handle, and
provide an easily arranged downwind sail.
  The sail is lashed to a horizontal yard, which should be hung
from a metal swivel at the fore side of the mast. This swivel
should be long enough to allow the yard to swing round from

The Square Sail

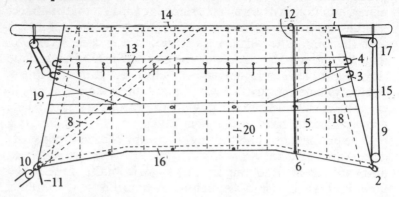

1	Head earing	10	Sheet
2	Clew spectacle	11	Tack
3	Reef tack cringles	12	Buntline
4	Reef-earing cringle	13	Reefpoints
5	Bull's eyes	14	Head tabling 4½"
6	Buntline cringle or	15	Leech lining
	hole with thimble	16	Foot band
7	Reef tackle	17	Reef band
8	Clew garnet on aft	18	Belly band
	side of sail	19	Reef tackle band
9	Clew garnet to yardarm	20	Buntline cloths

athwartships to as near fore-and-aft as possible to enable the sail to be used close-hauled. The weight of the yard should be taken on halyards led from above the yard onto the deck so that they can be adjusted. Guys should be led from each end of the yard to the deck for trimming. From each clew, a sheet will also lead to the deck. For most small boats, it is far easier to use a tackle instead of the swivel at the centre of the yard, as this will enable the yard to be dropped onto the deck when the sail is to be furled. The alternative is to fit ratlines to the shrouds, and footropes on the yard, so that the sail can be furled aloft. The practice of furling sails aloft is a comparatively recent introduction in the squaresails' 4000-year history.

A squaresail can be trimmed efficiently to within about six points (67 degrees) off the wind by boarding the luff with a bowline led down and forward from the leading clew. Squaresails can be reefed by slacking the sheets and then hauling the sail into the yard and tying the line of reefing points around the yard. Squaresails, whatever material is used in their construction, should be roped around their edges, and the earrings and cringles set into the rope rather than the sail cloth.

Rigging a squaresail   The four sides of a squaresail are the head, secured by robands to the yard, the sides known as leeches, and the bottom known as the foot. The two top corners are fitted with head earrings, used to stretch the head taut between the two yardarms.

The two bottom corners are known as the clews, to which the sheets are attached. Also attached to the clews are the two clew lines, which lift the clews upwards and inwards when the sail is being furled. Leech lines pull the leeches inwards, and buntlines lift the foot up to the yard when gathering in the bunt or centre of the sail. All these lines are led through blocks and down to the deck, so that the sail can be half-furled from the deck before the crew go aloft.

When furling the sail aloft, the crew spread themselves out along the yard, their stomachs on the yard itself, and their feet on footropes which are slung down below the yard and suspended from it by stirrups. The place of honour is at the yardarm, and this position is usually taken by the senior, or most experienced hand. These days, when most crews are inexperienced with squaresails, it is sensible to ensure that all the crew have safety harnesses on when going aloft, and clip

Raffee

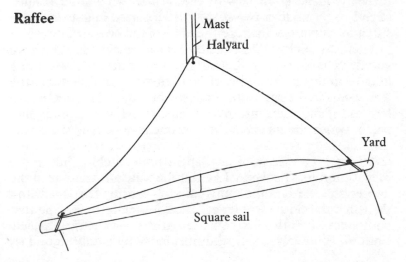

Mast

Halyard

Yard

Square sail

these onto the yard. Once aloft, the crew gather in the sail and roll it tight up against the yard. It is then secured to the yard by means of gaskets, which run round the yard and the rolled up sail.

When a boat is running under a squaresail, an extra sail can be set above the yard of the squaresail, known as a raffee. The diagram (*p 209*) shows the usual design of this sail; however, it can come in two parts, one on each side of the mast, or it may be rectangular, with a short light spar along its head. It is hoisted on a masthead halyard, and its clews are secured to the yardarms.

SAIL REPAIRS

Although most sail repairs are carried out by sailmakers, the ability to carry out effective sail repairs whilst at sea should be mastered by every sailor. Man-made fibres do not have the softness of natural fibres such as flax or cotton, and the main failure of modern sails usually results from the stitching standing out from the cloth instead of bedding into it; this makes the stitching more susceptible to chafe. Whenever a stitch is seen to part, repair it immediately, as otherwise the whole seam will split, meaning far more work in the end. Always use twine of the same material as the sail, so that the two will have equal stretch. When one or two stitches have parted in a seam, overstitch for about two inches either side of the broken stitches.

There are sticky tapes available for sail repairs, and these are very effective for quick first aid to a torn stitch or cloth. For a long-term repair, however, always stitch around the tape. If a tear occurs in the sail cloth, heat-seal the edges of the tear with a hot knife, and then turn over the edge before stitching on a patch, which should extend at least one inch beyond the tear.

Stitching The secret of neat and strong stitching lies in the preparation for the work. Lay out the sailcloth and cut to the desired shape. Mark the seams carefully with a blue pencil, and then tack the cloth together at 18-inch intervals, ensuring that both sides of cloth have equal length between tacks. In new cloth, the blue selvedge thread, just in from the selvedge edge, indicates the overlap of cloth to allow. Place the seam across your knees, with the upper cloth closest to you. Fasten the sail hook to your right if you are right-handed, and vice versa. Push the needle down through the lower cloth with a palm, and then twist it back, and up, through the two cloths. Pull the twine tight through the stitch just made by pulling against the sail hook. The stitch should come out of the cloth about ³⁄₁₆ of an inch from the edge. A rough guide as to the stitching intervals is to have between five and seven in the same length as the needle. With practice, even and neat stitching is not difficult, and this has the greatest strength. When one seam has been completed, turn the cloth over, and sew the other edge to the cloth in the same manner. Thus each seam will have two lines of stitching.

When starting a seam, put a knot in the end of the twine, and sew it into the cloth so that it will be hidden under the material once the seam is finished. When coming to the end of a length of twine, after pulling the stitch tight, knot the twine underneath the upper cloth. Then start the new length of twine one stitch back, so that the last stitch of the old twine, and the first of the new, overlap. With good stitching, it should be hard to see where one length of twine starts and another finishes.

Sewing leather   Leather contracts when it dries, and this can be used to advantage when sewing leather onto the rim of a steering wheel. If the leather is soaked first, and then sewn, it will shrink onto the rim, and provide a firmer grip.

Most leather available these days is calf hide, which is a soft material, and the thread should not be pulled too tight or it will rip the leather. Calf hide provides excellent patching material over areas that suffer from chafe.

The tools used in sailmaking are:

Palm   A stiff leather strap that fits around the hand and over the palm. It has a small indented plate set into the leather, which presses against the end of the needle to force it through the material. They can be bought for either left- or right-handed people.

Needles   Come in various sizes from 8 to 19, 8 being the largest. Sizes 12 and 14 are the most useful on a boat. Made from steel, they are chromed over, but will rust, and so should be kept in a watertight container, and left lightly rubbed with vaseline or oil. Sail needles are three-cornered, and the edges should not be sharp or they will cut the cloth when they are pushed through. Always use the smallest convenient needle for sail repairs.

Sail hook　A sharp hook on a lanyard. The lanyard is hitched around a convenient point, and the hook put through the material in line with the seam being sewn. It provides the sewer with something to pull the stitch tight against.

Sailtwine　Comes in convenient spools of flax, Terylene, nylon or cotton. For all but the lightest work, sailtwine is used doubled. Cut off sufficient for a convenient pulling length, usually half the arm's span, thread through the needle, and pull the ends equal. If the twine has not come waxed, pull it round a ball of beeswax before sewing.

Beeswax　Most twine comes pre-waxed, but a small ball of beeswax should be carried on board for coating unwaxed twine, and twine that loses its waxiness in use.

Pricker　A kind of fine marlinespike, with a sharp point set in a wood handle, for piercing holes in sailcloth.

Creasing stick　A piece of split hardwood or steel used for creasing seams to hold them in place whilst sewing. The seams crease better if they have first been rubbed with beeswax.

Fids　Tapered hardwood or steel spikes in various sizes used for making eyelet holes and stretching cringles as well as for splicing.

Knife　Preferably of the cobbler's variety of steel, as these are more easily sharpened.

The action of sewing a rope around the edge of a sail is called roping. Use roping twine, or heavy Terylene twine to do this. Great care has to be taken to ensure that the rope is sewn to the sailcloth, and not the sailcloth to the rope, otherwise wrinkles will appear. An allowance must be made for slack sailcloth, so that when set, the sail is not overstretched or pleated. It helps if a blunt needle is used, as it will pick its way through the rope strands more easily.

Tabling is the part of the sail turned down at the edge onto which the roping is attached. The roping is called the bolt rope, but may in fact be wire. It gives the sail more strength.

Lining cloths are extra pieces of cloth sewn onto the sail in the way of any chafing. They are sewn onto the sail where it might chafe on the spreaders or rigging screws. They are also used to assist in distributing the strains on a sail, at the clew for instance.

SAILCLOTH

The material used for making sails comes in rolls, called bolts, and varies in width and weight. The threads that run along the cloth lengthwise are called the warp, and those that run across the cloth are called the weft. The edges along the length of the cloth are called selvedge edges, and there is often a thin coloured line about an inch inside the selvedge edge which is known as the selvedge stripe. The selvedge edge will not fray unless it is cut, and because it is more tightly woven, does not stretch as much as the rest of the cloth. Sailcloth should, whenever possible, be cut along the line of thread. Where it is cut diagonally, it can stretch out of shape more easily.

Sailcloth is measured by weight in ounces per square yard in Britain, but the unit area for weight of cloth in America measures 36 × 28½ inches. Thus, a 2-oz American cloth is roughly equivalent to a 2½-oz British cloth.

The cloths that used to be used for sails were flax and cotton, but these have now been replaced by polyester cloth ('Terylene/Dacron'), nylon and, in a few specialised cases, Mylar. Of the natural fibres, flax is the stronger material, but stretches more than cotton, which holds its shape better as a result. The new man-made fibre materials are, on the whole, about twice as strong as the natural fibres weight for weight, do not absorb water to the same extent, dry more quickly, and are less susceptible to mildew. Working sails are usually made from Terylene, which has very little stretch, and light weather sails, such as spinnakers, are usually made from nylon.

All sailcloth can be damaged by exposure to the ultra-violet radiation from the sun. Most synthetic fibre cloths can have ultra-violet protection added to them, but a sail should not be made completely of current ultra-violet resistant cloths, as these do not breathe and quickly rot. Nylon rots about twice as quickly as Terylene, but a lot less speedily than flax or cotton.

The weight of the sailcloth used for a particular sail depends upon the weight and size of a boat, and the sail's purpose. As a general rule, the lighter the sailcloth the better, but obviously a lightweight sail is not going to be as strong or long lasting as a heavier one. Before having a sail made, consult the sailmaker, and tell him what you want the sail to do.

Mylar   Mylar is a fairly recently developed material. In its raw form it is a film of polyester, but in its sailcloth form it comes laminated to polyester cloth. Its main property is its lightness for its strength, and its lack of stretch. It is favoured on racing boats, but its use is limited for other purposes because of cost, and its inability to take hard wear. Repairs to Mylar are made by putting a contact adhesive on the sail and sticking a strip of similar Mylar material across the tear. If no other Mylar is available, almost any polyester cloth can be used.

CARE OF SAILS

There are four main causes of deterioration of sails; chafe damage, ultra-violet light, dampness, and general usage. This applies to modern synthetic sailcloth as well as the old natural fibres.

The most important factor with a new sail is to work it in gently. Do not set it first time in strong winds because it will stretch permanently out of shape and never give the power that the sailmaker has cut into it. Set new sails in light conditions, and let the material and sewing settle in.

Never overstrain a sail. If the sailmaker says that a particular sail has a range up to 20 knots of wind, then do not keep that sail set when the apparent wind, or the wind over the deck, exceeds that. At best you will stretch the sail permanently out of shape, at worst it will split. If the number of sails to be carried on board is limited, make sure that the sailmaker knows this, so that he can help you to select a range of sails with the correct weight to suit what you can afford and what you want the sails to do.

Sails should always be folded after use, and stowed neatly into a sailbag. Do not cram them any-old-how into a sailbag and forget about them.

Flax and cotton sails can be protected by various special preparations. Perhaps the most infamous of these is that used on Thames barge sails which consists of fish oil, red and yellow ochre powder, mixed into a paste and thinned out with river or fresh water.

Dampness   The principle cause of rot in sails is dampness, even in those made from man-made fibres. Salt water gets on to sails and soaks into the fabric. When it dries off, it leaves behind salt crystals. Unless washed away with fresh water, these salt crystals will absorb moisture whenever the atmosphere is damp, and transfer this dampness to the surrounding fibres. In flax and cotton, this dampness will eventually rot the material; in man-made fibre, it will encourage the growth of mould.

Washing sails   Some sailmakers offer a laundering service for sails, which involves washing the sails in soap or a soft detergent. You can do this yourself if you have a large clean area to lay out the sail, but be sure that the detergent you use does not remove the resin which is put into some sail cloths. Where possible, use liquid detergents, as they usually contain less alkali than powder detergents. Alkali makes polyester more sensitive to ultra-violet radiation.

Sails should be hosed off in fresh water whenever possible, and then allowed to dry out before being carefully folded and stowed. It's a bit of an effort at times but will greatly extend the life of the sail. In periods of lay-up, sails should be stowed in a dry place where they can be spread out to air.

Chafe   The main cause of chafe is the sail rubbing against the mast or rigging. The prevention lies in reinforcing the sail, or padding the mast and rigging at the most likely points of contact.

With flax and cotton sails, the twine used to sew the panels together beds into the material. This is not the case with Terylene or nylon, where the stitching stays proud of the sails surface and is vulnerable. Thus, when a sail made from man-made fibres brushes against anything such as the shrouds, runner backstays, spreaders or halyards, it is the stitching that takes the worst of the chafe, and, after a time, will wear through. Breaks in stitching are much easier to see if the thread is of a contrasting colour to the sailcloth. The phrase 'a stitch in time saves nine' applies to sails more than anything else. Once the thread has broken, the seam is weakened and, unless it is quickly re-sewn, the whole seam will split. The moment the stitching is seen to go anywhere, it should be oversewn immediately, with the new stitching going at least a couple of inches either side of the break to lock the broken thread. Where possible, knot each broken end of thread as well.

Nowadays sailmakers are using glue and double sided sticky tape to hold seams together before sewing them as well. This helps to prevent a seam from splitting but, if the sailmaker thinks it is worth sewing a seam, then it is worth keeping the stitching intact. There are proprietary seam sealants available, and these are essential for any long distance voyages.

On cruising boats, and boats that are to race over long distances, it is well worth putting self-adhesive tape over all the seams in the working sails. The tape protects the stitching, and also gives increased longitudinal strength to the sail. Where tape is unavailable, or considered undesirable, it is worth putting an inch or so of hand stitching at about metre intervals along all the seams, as this will reduce the distance a seam can split if the main stitching goes.

The other method of reducing chafe is to 'soften' any hard spots with which the sail is likely to come into contact. The ends of the spreaders are an obvious example, but any piece of rigging, or part of the structure that a sail might touch should be padded. The spreader ends can be bandaged with cloth or plastic tape to prevent the sail from tearing on a jagged piece of metal or a bolt.

Any sharp ends on the rigging, such as split pins, should be similarly taped. Do not just cover the obvious snags, think of where a collapsed spinnaker might catch on the mast, and tape everything that might act as a snag. The split pins in the rigging screws should be taped over for the same reason.

On some boats, standing rigging wires, such as the inner forestays and the shrouds, that do not have sails set on them, have been threaded through plastic piping before being swaged or spliced. The idea is that the piping should revolve as the sail or its sheet is pulled round it and thus prevent wear. Where you wish to add this protection after the rigging has been made up, take a length of polythene pipe and cut it with a sharp knife as if you were following the line of one strand in a three-strand rope. Then wind the pipe around the wire, and tape it at intervals with plastic tape. Piping on the rigging increases the windage, but this is not usually a problem in a cruising boat.

The old solution to the problems of sail chafe on the rigging was baggywrinkle. This is a soft fender, made up from short lengths of rope hitched around two lengths of marline. When the ropes have been hitched the full length, knot the marline at each end, tease out the rope, and then serve the marline around the rigging. Baggywrinkle is effective and cheap, except in time, and can be easily put on any piece of rigging that is touching a sail. If necessary more than one piece of baggywrinkle can be served onto a wire at short intervals from each other.

Ultra-violet damage　Just as ultra-violet radiation from the sun will fade curtains over a window, it will also fade sails. The fading of the colour, or the loss of sheen on a white sail, indicates that the sail is weakening. This can happen very quickly, even in a month or two in the hot sun. If sails are not in use, they should be stowed away clear of sunlight, or covered over with a sail cover. There is no ultimate protection against ultra-violet radiation as, if sails are made completely from ultra-violet-resistant material, they are much more susceptible to rot caused by dampness.

AWNINGS

An awning that covers the cockpit can be a very functional asset to a boat, keeping the sun out in hot climates and the rain out in temperate zones. Nowadays awnings are usually made of synthetic cloth, and not canvas, which obviates the necessity of slackening the lashings to allow for material shrinkage in the event of dew or rain. An awning should be set up over a central ridge line or the boom so that any water falling on it has a natural run-off. The material for the awning should be doubled where it will be in contact with the line or boom as protection against chafe. The sides of the awning should have eyelets at regular intervals to take lashings to hold it out, and it needs to be secured fore-and-aft as well. When properly set, an awning should not flap about except in fresh breezes. For further protection, side curtains can be fitted which will keep out slanting rain or sunlight.

A simple form of sun shade can be made from a square or rectangular piece of cloth with wood battens at each end. Lashings on the four corners are sufficient to hold it in place, and the awning can be placed over the boom, a ridge line, or suspended from a halyard.

In boats kept in hot climates, permanent metal frameworks to support an awning are often fitted, such as the Bimini top. This can be folded down like a pram hood when not required. They are usually set up so that they can be left erected when sailing to provide protection against extreme sunlight.

SAIL NUMBERS

Sail numbers are issued by national authorities so that yachts can be readily identified. Where no sail number has been issued, it is usual to put the first and last letters of the boat's name on either side of the sail.

The International Yacht Racing Union specifies the following sizes for sail numbers:

Height: 1/10th of the length of the foot of the mainsail, rounded up to the nearest 50mm.

Width: (excluding number 1, and letter I) 66 per cent of the height.

Thickness: 15 per cent of the height.

Spaces (between letters or numbers): 20 per cent of the height.

It is usual to put sail numbers as high up on the mainsail as possible, but the rules state that they must be at least higher than one third of the length of the luff. Sail numbers should be at different heights on either side of the sail, the starboard numbers being the higher. This is to avoid confusion if the sails are translucent. Sail numbers must be put on all headsails and the mainsail; they do not have to be put on spinnakers. The numbers on spinnakers should be placed at approximately half height.

Each country has been allocated a nationality identification letter, which should be placed above the sail numbers. The internationally agreed letter markings are:

A	Argentina	H	Holland	OM	Oman
AE	Dubai	I	Italy	P	Portugal
AN	Angola	IL	Iceland	PH	Philippines
ANU	Antigua	IND	India	PK	Pakistan
AR	Egypt	IR	Ireland	PR	Puerto Rico
B	Belgium	IS	Israel	PU	Peru
BA	Bahamas	J	Japan	PY	Paraguay
BL	Brazil	K	United	PZ	Poland
BN	Brunei		Kingdom	Q	Kuwait
BR	Burma	KA	Australia	RB	Botswana
BU	Bulgaria	KB	Bermuda	RC	Cuba
CB	Colombia	KBA	Barbados	RI	Indonesia
CH	China	KC	Canada	RM	Rumania
CI	Grand Cayman	KF	Fiji	S	Sweden
CP	Cyprus	KH	Hong Kong	SA	South Africa
CR	Costa Rica	KJ	Jamaica	SE	Senegal
CY	Sri Lanka	KK	Kenya	SK	Republic of
CZ	Czechoslovakia	KP	Papua New		Korea
D	Denmark		Guinea	SM	San Marino
DDR	German	KS	Singapore	3R	Union of
	Democratic	KT	Trinidad		Soviet Socialist
	Republic		and Tobago		Republics
DK	Democratic	KV	British	TA	Taipei
	People's Republic		Virgin Is.	TH	Thailand
	of Korea	KZ	New Zealand	TK	Turkey
DR	Dominican	L	Finland	U	Uruguay
	Republic	LX	Luxembourg	US	United States
E	Spain	M	Hungary		of America
EC	Ecuador	MA	Morocco	V	Venezuela
F	France	MO	Monaco	VI	US Virgin Is.
FL	Liechtenstein	MT	Malta	X	Chile
G	Federal Republic	MX	Mexico	Y	Yugoslavia
	of Germany	MY	Malaysia	Z	Switzerland
GR	Greece	N	Norway	ZB	Zimbabwe
GU	Guatemala	OE	Austria		

In certain places, letters are used for local identification, for instance, a sail number with the letter M after it in the UK denotes a multihull, and with Y after it denotes a Royal Yachting Association sail number.

7 MASTS, SPARS AND RIGGING

MAST MATERIALS

Wood A wood mast requires a straight grain throughout its length and to be free of knots. It should be as light as possible, as extra weight aloft will make the boat less stable. The traditional woods used were fir or spruce, of which spruce was preferred because of its strength and lightness; however it is now difficult to obtain and therefore very expensive. Oregon pine, also known as Douglas fir, is commonly used these days, but it is second best to spruce.

Very few boats, unless gaff-rigged, have solid wood masts, mainly because of the weight, and the difficulty of obtaining the length free of knots. The usual wood mast is built of sections or planks. Water-mixed glues used to be used, but are not as good as epoxy or resorcinol formaldehyde glues which are now available, as they tend to lose their grip, particularly in extremes of climate, causing the mast to split.

The traditional wood mast is made in two halves, the baulk of timber being sawn down the middle, and then the two halves reversed against each other so that the two outer faces then come together as the inside faces. This balances out any tendency to warp in one direction. The wood is then shaped on the outside, and hollowed out on the inside, and glued together. It provides a strong and elegant mast, but requires good craftsmen. Where insufficient length of timber is available, sections of wood can be scarfed on to give a greater length. Lloyd's usually accepts a one-in-seven scarf, but one-in-twelve is better.

The other, and in many ways simpler, method of building a wood mast is by making up a box as illustrated. If properly glued, this provides a very strong, light and sensitive mast.

Hollow wood masts must be reinforced at the heel, deck, spreaders and cap. The usual method is to make them solid at these points so that they will not tend to be distorted by compression, particularly from through bolts.

Sections Through a Hollow Wooden Mast

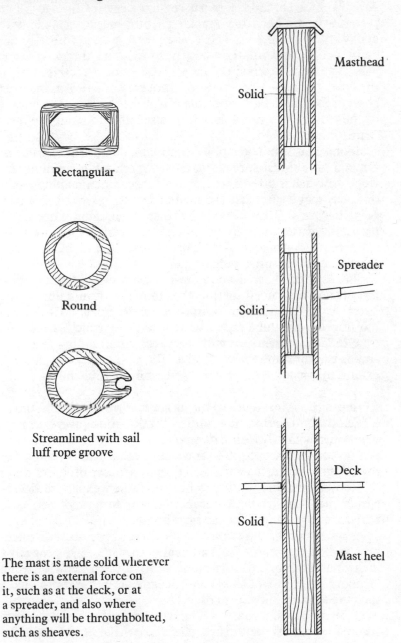

Rectangular

Round

Streamlined with sail
luff rope groove

Masthead

Solid

Spreader

Solid

Deck

Solid

Mast heel

The mast is made solid wherever
there is an external force on
it, such as at the deck, or at
a spreader, and also where
anything will be throughbolted,
such as sheaves.

All wood masts require regular inspections and maintenance. A solid mast should be given regular coats of linseed oil to prevent the timber from cracking. Built masts, if made with epoxy glue, should be well soaked with epoxy whilst under construction, and will then only need painting at regular intervals. The natural wood colour always looks attractive, but, if the boat is going to a hot climate, is not very practical as the mast absorbs too much heat, and this can affect the glue. If a voyage to the tropics is contemplated, it is sensible to paint the mast white first.

Booms and spinnaker poles can be made up from spruce or Oregon pine. Mast spreaders, however, should be of a harder wood, and ash is often chosen. In all cases when making a spar or mast, make sure that the timber is well seasoned and dry. New timber will be heavier because it contains more of its natural moisture, and as this moisture slowly evaporates, the timber can warp or crack. The timber should be carefully selected *after* this process has taken place.

Shakes or cracks in a wood mast indicate either that the mast has been overstrained or that the timber is drying out. If the latter, coat the mast with linseed oil to replace its natural moisture. Never fill a shake with a hard substance as the next time the wood shrinks it will compress around this substance, and as the substance will not give, the wood will, and this will extend the shake. Always use a soft, compressible filler.

Aluminium Most modern masts are made from aluminium as it is both light and strong, and will take quite severe stresses before permanently losing its shape.

The size of mast required for a particular boat is best left to the designer or the mast maker. There are many different types of section available, and it is best left to an expert to decide which has the right combination of fore and aft, and athwartships strength for the boat in question.

The strength of the section will depend upon its wall thickness and its diameter. Thus an oval mast with major axis of 10 inches, and minor axis of 5 inches, might be extremely strong fore and aft, but would require dozens of spreaders to give a sensible athwartships strength.

In many cases, a mast maker will try and persuade you to accept a particular section because it is one that he has available, or for which he owns the production dies. Always ask around, and get more than one quotation before placing an order.

Aluminium masts should always be anodised to protect them against salt-water corrosion. They can be painted, but this usually only protects the outside surfaces and leaves the inside, if unanodised, to fester away until the mast breaks. All fittings on a mast should be insulated from the mast. Stainless steel fittings cause electrolysis, and wood pads for fittings such as halyard winches can, unless properly sealed, create a water trap which will cause corrosion. A layer of a polysulphide sealant, or a sealant having similar insulating properties, should always be applied before fittings are riveted or bolted into place.

If an aluminium mast is rigged with external halyards, water can collect in the mast which causes corrosion and increases its weight. There should be an opening just above deck level to allow this water to escape. If the mast is keel stepped, the deck level opening should be able to be plugged, and it will also be necessary to have another, plugged opening, at the foot of the mast.

Aluminium masts and spars should be washed down with fresh water whenever possible to remove salt and other atmospheric sources of corrosion. Where corrosion is discovered, the metal should be sanded down to bare metal and then painted with etch primer, followed by a good two-pot epoxy paint.

It is important that the wall of the mast should be punctured as infrequently as possible, and that any such openings should be kept as small as possible. Never accept a mast where all the exits of internally-led halyards are cut in the same area. Halyard exits should be staggered down the length of the mast. If they have to exit in the same area, insist that the mast be doubled in that area, and the doubler bolted and riveted into place with good sealant between the layers.

GRP   Glassfibre would seem to be an ideal material for masts in that it is strong and light, and has no problems from salt water corrosion. There is not a great deal of experience with GRP masts at the moment, but it is likely to develop. The technology of carbon fibre in combination with GRP is being pioneered by racing boats, and perhaps such exotic materials will ultimately become more widely available.

FIDDED TOPMASTS

These are not part of a bermudian rig, but are often found on gaff and sprit rigs, where it may be desirable to reduce top weight, height or windage quickly.

The topmast is set up so that its weight is held by a fid, a short

Fidded Topmast

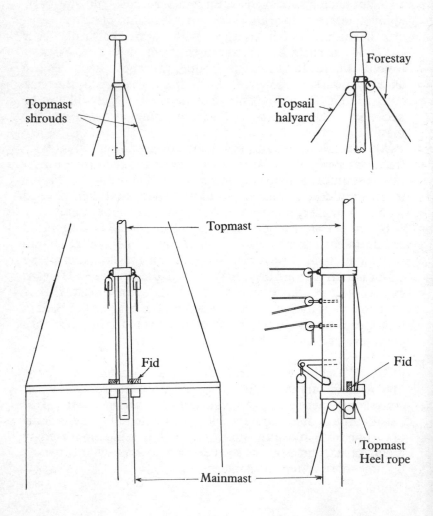

length of hard wood or metal, which passes through a slot cut in the heel of the topmast, and rests on trestle trees, or in a slot near the top of the lower mast. The topmast is held in place when set up by its rigging and brackets secured to the top of the lower mast, through which it will slide.

To set up the topmast, it is hoisted vertically in front of the lower mast and the heel pennant which is to be used to hoist the mast into place is led from the trestle trees of the mainmast, down through a sheave set in the heel of the top mast, back up and through a block at the trestle trees and back down to the deck. Now by taking the weight on the pennant, the heel of the topmast will be lifted, and the cap can be led between the trestle trees which will provide temporary support before the rigging is set up. Once the cap is above the trestle trees the topmast shrouds and stays can be attached, but left to run slack for the time being. The heel pennant is now hauled again until the heel of the topmast is just short of the trestle trees, and the fid hole is just above. The fid is then inserted, then the heel pennant eased so that the weight of the topmast is now taken by the fid on the trestle trees. The fid is then lashed in place so that it cannot shake loose and then the topmast rigging set up.

Sometimes the fid is secured into a special hole in the top of the mainmast, but in time, this hole will wear, and it is better to let the fid rest either side of the topmast on the trestle trees.

To strike, or send down, a fidded topmast, the rigging is slacked off, and the weight taken on the heel pennant and the mast lifted until the fid can be released. The topmast is then lowered to the deck in a reversal of the hoisting procedure.

RIGGING

The rigging of a boat comprises all the wires, rods, chains and ropes that support the masts. There are two categories: standing rigging, which are the parts set up permanently, and running rigging, which are the parts adjusted each time the boat tacks or the sails are trimmed.

If a mast were to be short and heavy enough, and well stepped at the keel with support at the deck, it would probably take the pull or thrust of the sails without having to be further supported. The modern Chinese Junk rig is thus arranged with an entirely unstayed mast. However, because most yacht masts are designed thin and long, to reduce weight and windage, they are dependent upon their rigging for support.

In its simplest form, the rigging supporting a mast may consist of only four wires; the forestay, the backstay, and on either side a shroud. If the mast is long, then further support is required, and additional stays and shrouds will have to be fitted, but in such a way that they interfere as little as possible with the working of the sails.

Shrouds   Shrouds provide the athwartship support for the mast. Theoretically the best support would be a horizontal wire, but of course the shrouds have to lead down to the deck. The narrower the angle between the wire and the mast, the less lateral support the wire will give, and the greater compression it will put on the mast. The two factors that control this angle are the beam of the boat abreast the mast, and the height above deck that the shrouds are attached. If the boat is very wide, or the sheeting angle of the headsail is small, it is possible to put the chain plates, to which the shrouds fasten at the deck, inside the gunwale. In practice, the usual shroud angle at the masthead is between 10 and 15 degrees, racing boats going for the smaller angles, cruising boats giving their mast as much support as possible by going for the larger. Now, unless this angle is intolerably reduced, it is obvious that the boat would have to be impossibly wide for a very tall mast, and this is why spreaders are used. These push the shroud away from the mast and widen the angle at the point of attachment. When tight, the wire will force the spreader in towards the mast, and to counteract this inward force, another, lower shroud is fitted, leading from the root of the spreader. If the mast is even taller, a further spreader can be fitted, so that the mast has two spreaders each side, spaced roughly equidistantly between the deck and the masthead. Some modern rigs even have three sets of spreaders, but this is mainly because the masts have been made very light to reduce weight, and need the extra support.

Shrouds are named according to the position they occupy supporting the mast. The uppermost shroud, provided it goes to the masthead, is known as the cap shroud. If it connects short

Shrouds

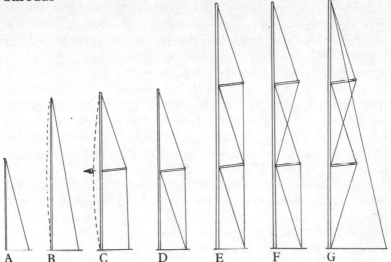

A Simple support for a small dinghy mast.

B Longer mast, shroud angle at masthead too small to provide sufficient support, and mast bending in the middle.

C Spreader inserted to widen shroud angle at the masthead, but mast still bends to leeward in the middle.

D Mast properly supported, with spreader to widen the masthead shroud angle, and lower shroud to prevent sagging to leeward.

E Longer mast, with additional spreader to keep masthead shroud angle sufficient for support, and an intermediate shroud fitted to base of the upper spreader to prevent the upper part of the mast sagging to leeward.

F An alternative system of rigging shrouds on a two-spreader rig.

G A shroud system sometimes used in multi-hulls, where there is sufficient space at the mast base to rig a cap shroud to provide the only support for the sideways force on the mast. This system allows the genoa to be given a much narrower sheeting angle.

More than two spreaders may be fitted, where the mast is taller still, or it is desired to give the same support but with narrower spreaders. The usual system is a continuation of E.

of the head, it is known as the upper shroud. The lowest of the shrouds is called the lower shroud. Where there are two sets of spreaders, there will be another shroud in between the lower and cap shrouds, and this is called the intermediate shroud. If the rig has three sets of spreaders, there will be an upper and a lower intermediate shroud on each side.

Spreaders should always be set at an angle to the mast so that they bisect the angle that the shroud turns through at the spreader end. This means that they are always angled upwards. On some masts the spreader socket is set for this angle, on others, the spreader is hinged at the mast, and is held in the desired position, either by a small lift that holds it at the right angle, or by a secure seizing at the spreader end. The shroud should always be secured at the spreader end in any case, as in a choppy sea it could be shaken loose. Once the shroud has been firmly secured, the end of the spreader should be covered to prevent the sails from catching and tearing on any sharp obstructions. Special plastic spreader end fittings can be bought for this purpose, but, if they are not available, the end can be well bound with plastic tape. Alternatively, for a better job, bandage the end with strips of cloth, and then sew leather round and over the bandage.

The strain on shrouds varies with height, and although in theory the higher the mast the stronger the shroud needed to support it, in practice the lower shrouds take the greatest strain, particularly when the boat is working in a heavy sea. The lower shrouds should be of a stronger wire than the others. In cruising boats, and long-distance racing boats, double lower shrouds are to be preferred, one leading forward and one aft of the upper shrouds on each side of the deck. Apart from giving the mast extra support both athwartships and fore and aft, and avoiding the need for babystays or runner backstays from the lower spreaders, four lower shrouds allow the mast to be quickly held in place when it is being stepped.

A simple formula for calculating the strength of shrouds, and their attachments, is to say that the main lower shrouds on either side of the mast should be equal in strength to the displacement of the boat. Thus, a boat of ten tons displacement should have lower shrouds made from wire that has a breaking strain of ten tons, or two wires of five tons breaking strain each, on either side of the boat. The cap shrouds should be of the same strength as one third of the boat's displacement. If the mast has two sets of spreaders, the intermediate shrouds should be equal in strength to two thirds of the displacement.

Many modern racing craft have shrouds which are not as strong as the figures given above, as the owners are prepared to sacrifice safety for less topweight and windage, and a better racing performance. A light rig may be acceptable for coastal racing, where there are usually other craft close by, but is not to be recommended for ocean racing and cruising.

Wire will stretch under tension, and the longer the wire, the more stretch there will be. On a tall mast, with a continuous cap shroud, the cap shroud will stretch a small amount when the mast is under pressure, which will allow the mast head to sag a little to leeward. The rigging screws will have to be tightened until this stretch is minimised. Rod rigging hardly stretches at all, and the amount can be ignored for all practical purposes.

It is possible to reduce the number of shrouds running down to the deck, and reduce windage at the same time, by using diamond shrouds or linking plates at the end of each spreader. With linking plates, each shroud is made up in sections, the first running from the mast connection to the linking plate at the spreader end. The spreader ends are connected by another, different, wire, and so on down to the deck. The vertical sections of wire will have to be made stronger as they near the deck, because each is progressively replacing more wires, and therefore must take more loading. The spreaders should still be set to bisect the angle made by the two parts of the shroud at the spreader end. The disadvantage of this arrangement is that each wire must be individually adjusted and tensioned, and this means going aloft.

Shrouds should be tensioned so that the mast is straight and there is no slack in the wires. The best way of checking the straightness of the mast is by looking up the sail track. When setting up the shrouds, the wires opposite to each other on either side should be taken up evenly, and then the final adjustment can be made by taking half or full turns at a time on each side. Start with the lower shrouds, and then work up the mast to the cap shrouds. If conditions are calm, a form of plumb bob can be made from the main or burgee halyard to ensure that the mast is vertical to the deck. (See below, *Tuning the mast*.) Once the mast is straight and the rigging taut, secure the rigging screws with seizing wire or split pins, and then cover them with tape to prevent sails or sheets catching on them. If the rigging screws have lock-nuts, use Loctite to ensure that they do not move.

New rigging wire will always stretch a bit, so once the shrouds have been set up, they will probably need tightening again once they come under tension. Do not try to tighten the rigging screws on the weather side whilst under way. If, under tension, the mast bends from the straight, put the boat onto the other tack, and take up or undo the rigging screws to straighten it again. It may take a number of tacks to get the mast absolutely right.

It is a thoroughly bad practice to have the leeward rigging slack when sailing, and this indicates that the shrouds have not yet been set up properly. In a choppy sea, slack shrouds can jump out of their spreaders, or jerk against their clevis pins, and these snatching loads are far greater than the normal loads on the rigging and likely to cause the wire or a pin to break unexpectedly, particularly if it is stainless steel.

Diamond shrouds Diamond shrouds provide a system of support for a mast that does not require the wire to come right down to the deck. Because the length is reduced, the stretch will also be lessened, and this means that the wires can be slightly smaller which reduces weight and windage.

The wire leads from its securing point on the mast, down round a spreader, and then back to the mast at the root of the next spreader, where its rigging screw will be. Their disadvantage is that they cannot be adjusted from the deck level, and so any adjustment involves sending a hand aloft. This can be avoided by passing the wire through a sleeve at its lower screwing point and then leading it down to its rigging screw at the base of the mast. However, since this just puts the weight, windage and stretch back, the mast might as well have a normal shroud in the first place.

Diamond shrouds are often used on fractional rigs, and when placed so that their spreader points out at 45 degrees on each bow, can supply a combined forward and athwartships, support for the top of the mast, where the stays and shrouds terminate below the masthead.

It is possible to hold a mast straight using nothing but

diamond shrouds, but this system will require a substantial cap shroud to prevent the mast toppling sideways. To be effective, this cap shroud would have to lead to a point well away from the mast, and the system is only practical on boats with a very large beam, like catamarans or trimarans.

Forestays The forestay is the main forward support for the mast, and usually leads from the masthead to the gammon plate, the fitting at the stemhead. If the boat has a bowsprit, it will run down to the cranse iron. Any other forward leading stay will be named according to the position it occupies, e.g. fore topstay, inner forestay, or the sail it supports, as in jib-stay. On multi-masted boats, there will need to be a number of stays between the masts to provide fore and aft support. The most famous of these is the main brace, the mainmast forestay.

The basic objective of forestays is to prevent the mast from sagging back under strain. The most important stay is the outermost and top one. This stay, the foretopstay, holds the masthead in position, provides support (on all but some fractional rigs) for the main headsail, and must be strong enough to check the whipping effect on the mast of a boat pushing into a head sea. It has also to be strong enough to hold the mast against the considerable aft pull exerted by sheeting in hard on the mainsail.

On most masts, and certainly if they are above 30 feet in length, the middle section of the mast will tend to be bent by the pressure of the mainsail. This puts a strain on the mast, and also tends to make the main sail more full. A second, inner, forestay needs to be rigged to compensate. On a single spreader rig, this forestay will lead from the spreaders. On a two spreader rig, this stay would lead from the upper of the two sets of spreaders. Another stay, a baby-stay, can be led from the lower spreaders but this will not be necessary if there are four lower shrouds and the forward pair are led well forward of the mast. However, these forward lower shrouds should not be too far forward, as if so, they can prevent the spinnaker pole being guyed back abeam.

It is quite useful to be able to adjust the tension in the intermediate forestay so that the mast can be curved forward when going to windward. This tends to flatten the mainsail which gives a better shape for fresh or strong winds, and the

Stays

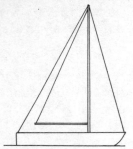

Mainsail pulls centre of
mast backwards.

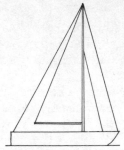

Intermediate forestay
reduces backward pull
of mainsail, but with
staysail set, pulls
mast forward.

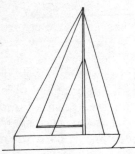

Runner backstay counters
forward pull of intermediate
forestay when a staysail
is set.

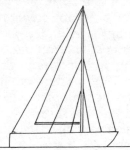

Lower shrouds set fore
and aft of mast to
prevent mast bending in
its lower section.

Fractional rig, fitted with a
jumper strut to counter the
pulls of the forestay.

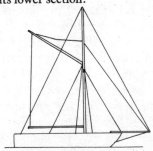

Gaff rig, the backstays are
runners. The lower and
intermediate forestays
counter the pulls of the
rig.

stay can be eased in light weather, when a fuller shape to the mainsail is more efficient. This adjustment can be made by tightening or undoing the rigging screws, but where frequent adjustments are necessary, it is probably better to fit a hydraulic ram in place of the rigging screw.

On many boats the forestay is also a roller furling system for the genoa. The safer systems revolve around a fixed reel or wire forestay, but in some the whole stay revolves on bearings at the top and bottom. These bearings take the full strain on the forestay and, if not well designed, are a permanent threat to the security of the mast.

Backstays This is the stay that prevents the mast toppling forward, and which provides support when running. It will usually run from the masthead down to the stern of the boat on a sloop or cutter. On a ketch, yawl, schooner or multi-masted boat, it will usually run to the foot of the mast immediately behind. The backstay does not have to be a single wire; it can be divided into two separate stays which come down on either side of the stern. An alternative system, which reduces the windage, is to have a single wire from the masthead to a plate about halfway down to which two other wires are connected; these continue down to each side of the deck. This bridle arrange ment is particularly appropriate for catamarans, as any working of the two hulls re-adjusts the bridle rather than slackening one of the backstays.

The backstay is often used as a convenient aerial for the radio. However, the section which is going to act as an aerial must be insulated from the remainder. The insulators used must be as strong as the wire, and, in addition, as a precaution the wires should loop round each other within the insulator so that if the insulator breaks, the backstay will increase a few inches in length but not break completely.

The backstay is the one piece of standing rigging that may, with advantage, be adjusted whilst the boat is under way. When hard on the wind, the backstay tension needs to be increased to keep the forestay from sagging. When the boat is running before the wind, the backstay tension can be eased off. This can be achieved by adjusting the rigging screw. On most medium size yachts, and above, a hydraulic ram is fitted to the stay at the deck, and pumped up when tension is required. A cheap

A Modern Large Boat Rig

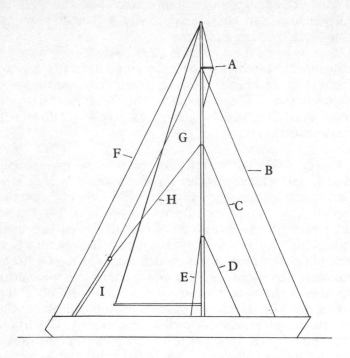

A Jumper strut to support topmast, and counter the bending caused by the forestay.

B Forestay.

C Intermediate forestay.

D Baby forestay.

E Lower shrouds set abaft mast. The lower shrouds and the baby forestay ideally are set at 120° to each other round the mast.

F Backstay. With a large roach mainsail, this would have to be a runner.

G Upper runner.

H Lower runner.

I Runner whip. In this case, it takes both the upper and the lower runners' pendants, reducing the number of ropes that need to be handled when tacking or gybing. The two runners could be set on independant whips.

method of applying tension to a backstay is to fit a bridle, and put a travelling block on each side. Any arrangement which draws the blocks together and downwards, will now pull each arm of the bridle towards the other, which tensions the whole arrangement.

Triatic stays This stay is only required on boats with more than one mast. In a fore and aft rig, the after mast cannot be set up with a forestay as it would interfere with the sail set from the forward mast. To provide support, a triatic stay connects the two mastheads. Normally, this is a standing wire, spliced to the exact length required and shackled or pinned at each masthead. If the triatic is going to require adjustment from time to time, it can be led through a block on one of the masts, usually the lower of the two, and then led down to a tackle at the deck.

Jumper stays Where the uppermost of the forestays is not attached to the masthead, but to some point below, the section of mast above will need support. This is provided by a jumper stay, which is basically the same as a diamond shroud, but in a fore and aft line forward of the mast. A spreader, known as a jumper strut, extends forward of the mast from the attachment point of the forestay. The jumper stay runs from the masthead, over the end of the strut, and down to an attachment point on the mast, which will be the same distance below the strut as the masthead is above.

If a mast is to have no running backstays, it can be supported by a series of jumper stays on its fore part, each one based upon its own strut, which will be supported forward by a forestay.

Running backstays Although 'runners' are adjusted each time the boat tacks or gybes, they provide a part of the necessary support of the mast, and it is usual to count them as a part of the standing rigging.

Running backstays perform the same task behind the mast as the intermediate forestays do in front. However, since the mainsail has to be able to swing easily from side to side, a permanent intermediate backstay is not possible, and runners provide temporary intermediate support in its place. They are rigged in pairs, one to each side of the boat, and the weather runner is always set up tight. The lee runner is slacked off, and carried forward to the mast so that it will not chafe or interfere with the mainsail.

When tacking or gybing, the lee runner must first be set up, and then the weather runner may be slacked off as the boat passes through the wind so that it will not be in the way on the other tack.

Unless a jump stay has been fitted, there should be a runner for each intermediate forestay. However, this would mean a large number of tackles or levers on deck, and so all the runner pennants are led to one tackle, which tightens them all together. This will require fine tuning to ensure that all the pennants have the right amount of strain when the tackle is taut. The best way to achieve this is to make one pennant the desired length, and any others slightly shorter, the difference being made up with a lashing of Terylene rope which can be adjusted until the required tension is reached.

Runners should lead as far aft as possible, and at least as far behind the mast as the forestay leads in front. The simplest system of setting up runners is to put a block on the end of the pennant or pennants, and then run a rope from the deck lead point, up through this block, and then down to a deck lead block before being taken to a winch. The alternative method is to use a Highfield lever on each side of the deck. The runner pennant leads from the mast, through a strong deck lead block, and then clips or shackles onto the lever. With a Highfield lever, the tension on the runners will always be the same, and so a deliberate bend cannot be put into the mast by easing the tension.

On some racing boats and day boats, the main backstay is a runner. This is not a seamanlike practice, as it is all too easy for someone to accidentally let go this runner and deprive the mast of all its aft support.

Since one runner will always be set up and the other slack, a simple method of automatically drawing the slackened runner forward out of the way of the mainsail is to rig a length of elastic rope from one runner, round the front of the mast, and onto the other. The elastic stretches when both runners are set up, but the moment one is released the elastic draws it forward to the mast. This saves having to go forward and lash the lee runner after each tack.

There are few items of rigging more awkward than the

leeward running backstay. They need to be slacked off to clear the sail so that they will not chafe it and, at the same time left sufficiently taut so that they cannot wander behind the spreaders, or bang against the mast and spreaders. Quite a few boats have lost their masts because the runners, in being set up, have caught behind the spreaders and broken them off. The elastic system will do on its own for small boats, but with large boats with heavier wire for the runners, a stronger method is required.

The ideal method of securing the leeward runner is to place an eyebolt, or use the toerail as a securing point. Choose a convenient point a short distance abaft the chain plates. The position should be chosen so that the runner is not in the way if the main or mizzen is sheeted right out when running before the wind, and also so that it will not hit the spreaders. Either move the lower runner block to this position once it has been eased, or take a whip from the runner pennant, through a block at this point and then back to a winch. The whole purpose is to set the runner up as taut as possible in this new position, not so that it will support the mast, but so that it is firmly under control.

For cruising boats, and short-handed sailing, the whip has distinct advantages as it can be operated from the cockpit without the need to go forward. On multihulls, the leeward runners can be set up well outboard and the whip system is much to be preferred.

Gaff standing rigging   The support which can be given to the mast on a gaff rig is governed by the need of the gaff jaw to slide up and down the mast. This means that no shrouds or stays can be fitted below the position the jaw occupies when the mainsail is set. As a result, gaff masts are usually thicker and stronger than bermudian masts.

Four lower shrouds are fitted to a gaff mast, fastened to chainplates set just forward and aft of the mast on each side. The forestay usually secures to the stemhead, and is made of the same strength of wire as the shrouds. Running backstays provide the only method of supporting the mast from aft, as any permanent backstay would get in the way of the gaff.

Where a topmast is fitted, or the mast extends well above the lower shroud securing point so that a flying jib or a topsail can be set, cross-trees are fitted to the mast level with the lower shrouds, to act as spreaders for the cap shrouds. A topstay, usually led to the cranse iron on the outer end of the bowsprit, provides the forward support, and a running backstay must be fitted. If the boat is two-masted, it may be possible to set a triatic stay between the mastheads which will provide the aft support for the fore topmast, instead of rigging up runners.

TUNING A MAST

When a mast is stepped, the first task is to take its weight with the stays and shrouds so that it is supported, and the crane or derrick can be released. Then set up the shrouds over their spreaders so that the tension is equal on each side of the mast, and the mast itself is straight. Start by setting up the cap shrouds, and tension them by hand. Next tighten the intermediates a little more than the caps. Finally, put slightly more tension on the lower shrouds. If there are two lower shrouds each side, tighten the forward ones until the mast is slightly bowed forward. Or, if only lateral lower shrouds are fitted, tension the intermediate or baby stay to give a slight forward bend to the mast. This task is greatly helped if the shrouds on each side are exactly the same length, as then a simple way of checking that the mast is straight is to ensure that the rigging screws on each side are taken up by an equal number of turns.

There are two methods of checking whether the mast is straight. The first is to look up the mainsail track, and adjust tension on the shrouds until the track is straight. To check whether the mast is exactly perpendicular, take a central fixed halyard, such as the mainsail halyard, and cleat it when its shackle is level with one of the chain plates. Then take it across the boat and check if it is level with the chain plate on the other side.

Next, set the forestay to about the required length, assuming that it is the type that can be adjusted, and tighten the backstay or stays. If the shrouds have not been set up properly, the masthead will tend to cant over to one side or another. Tension the shrouds again until the mast is, once again, perpendicular.

The mast is now set up straight, but there is no tension on it from the sails, so the next part of the operation must be carried out under sail. Choose a day with light to moderate winds, as you will want to tune the mast with full mainsail and the No 1 headsail set.

Find a clear stretch of sheltered water, and put the boat close-hauled. The mast will probably lean to leeward. Go about, and tighten the shroud the amount you think is necessary and then go about again and check. The object of this is to tighten the shrouds whilst they have no weight on them. Repeat this process, tightening each side as necessary until the mast is straight on both tacks. You will probably find that the leeward shrouds will be slightly slack when you have finished. This is perfectly all right, so long as they are not so slack that the spreaders are jumping about.

Once the mast has been tuned laterally, check that it has a slight curve aft by adjusting the intermediate and baby stays. Sometimes, as tension from the headsail tightens the forestay, the masthead can bend forward. This tightens the leech of the mainsail, and makes the sail too full, which increases the side force, causing the boat to heel more and reduces the sail's drive. The forestay should always be made as tight as possible when close-hauled, so that the headsail does not sag and lose power. This is done by tightening the backstay, or using a special tensioner on the backstay when close-hauled.

New rigging wires or rods will stretch slightly at first, necessitating further adjustment at regular intervals.

The mast should not be left under tension when the boat is at rest, as it will tend to lose its shape. Always ease the backstay tensioner at the end of a voyage, and, if one is fitted, the intermediate forestay tensioner. If the boat is to be left for some time, then all the rigging screws can be eased by one or two turns, so that the tension is reduced.

There are no absolute rules for tuning a boat, as each boat is different, and will sail better with a different rigging adjustment. Experimentation and experience are the best guides.

LAZY JACKS

Lazy jacks are lines which go from each side of the mast down to each side of the main boom, so that when the mainsail is lowered, it is contained, and cannot blow off to leeward. I believe the idea originates from the Chinese junks, which rigged lines each side of their sails so that when they reefed, or furled, the sail was under control and easy to tie down.

In their simplest form, lazy jacks are lines, led from a convenient point on the mast, such as a spreader roots, down to the main boom to be tied off on the same side of the boom. Thus, they would lead from the port spreader to the port side of the boom and vice-versa. When the mainsail is lowered, it will drop between these lines instead of spilling out over the deck. They are not normally seen on ocean racers where there are plenty of crew available, but they make life much easier for the cruising or short-handed sailor.

The usual method of rigging lazy jacks is to have a single line, secured to an eye or a spreader on the mast, that extends downwards halfway to the deck. On the lower end is shackled a single block. A line is then taken from a point towards the fore end of the boom up and through this block, and back down to the boom again about one third of the way from its other end. One of these ends should be adjustable so that the length may be altered to suit the varying foot heights of the sail. To do this, the end should be led to an eye where it can be tied off, or through a block fitted to the boom and then to a clam cleat.

More than one set of lazy jacks can be fitted to each side of the boom, and sometimes they consist just of three or four lines led from various heights on the mast to differing points on the boom, but this will mean a lot of adjustment if the height of the boom varies.

The lines should be made fairly strong, certainly strong enough to support the weight of the boom and sail, as there will be times when the topping lift, if fitted, will be left off, and the weight will fall entirely on the lazy jacks. Stainless steel wire, plastic-coated, is as good as anything for the standing part down from the spreader, as the plastic helps to protect the stitching of the sails.

RATTLING DOWN

Rattling down is the task of putting ratlines on the shrouds, and although not many vessels have ratlines these days, a knowledge of how to set them up can be useful if it becomes necessary to climb the mast and there is no alternative means available.

Start by setting up the shrouds evenly, but not too taut, taking care that no turns are left in the wires as the rigging screws are tensioned, because the shrouds may then revolve on some subsequent occasion and wind up the ratlines.

The proper method is to first seize a sheer pole into position. This is a horizontal length of wood or metal, seized onto the shrouds about 5 feet above the deck. The next step is to stand on the sheer pole, and seize on a wood batten roughly at breast height, and parallel to the first one. Before putting on the end seizings, if there are more than two shrouds, bowse the end shrouds slightly in towards each other. Continue seizing battens onto the shrouds in the same manner, and at the same intervals, until the hounds are reached.

Once all the battens are in place, make up the ratlines, which should be at approximately 14 inch (35 centimetres) intervals. The ratlines have an eye-splice at each end, and are secured by means of a clove hitch to the middle shrouds. The eyes are seized to the two outer shrouds in the following manner. Splice the seizing stuff to the eye in the ratline. Then take the seizing round the shroud, back through the eye, and then back round the shroud in the reverse direction. Repeat this seven times, and finish off with a clove hitch over the seizing between the shroud and the eye.

When all the ratlines are in place, remove the battens and if they are still in position, the bowsing lines, and the released tension on the shrouds should pull all the ratlines out straight. When completed, the shrouds and ratlines should be straight and evenly spread.

DERRICKS

Although derricks are usually associated with the older type merchant ships, where they were used for loading cargo, they provide a simple and quite quickly rigged method of heaving heavy weights about a boat, or from the boat into the water or onto a quay.

The main boom makes a ready-made derrick of sorts as it has a gooseneck at the mast which allows it to swivel through a wide angle in two planes. However the normal fittings on a boom will not usually be strong enough to take anything but light weights, and if a heavy weight, such as an engine, is to be lifted, greater support will be required.

The actual maximum weight that can be lifted will depend upon the size of the boom and the strength of the gooseneck. Calculating the loads on the various parts of the derrick is not difficult, and, in its simplest form, involves the resolution of a number of parallelograms of force.

Sketch out the derrick, with accurate measurements for the length of the boom, the angle it makes with the mast, and the height of the topping lift lead on the mast. Then draw off a convenient number of units from A to B, representing the load to be lifted, and create parallelograms as shown. The loads and stresses on the various parts of the derrick can be found by scaling off from the various parallelograms (see diagram).

Take any strain on the gear very gently, and if in doubt as to whether the boom or gooseneck are strong enough, do not take the risk, wait until a crane, or a boat with a stronger boom is available.

When using the boom as a derrick, strops should be fitted around the boom to take the topping lift and runner rather than using fittings on the boom.

Topping lift   This should be led from a braced part of the mast, a spreader level with a forestay is ideal, and a strop should be taken right round the mast. If there is no intermediate forestay, rig one up to the stemhead to compensate for the loading on the mast. If the plumb position of the runner is going to change whilst the load is in suspension, then a running topping lift will

Calculating the Loads on a Derrick

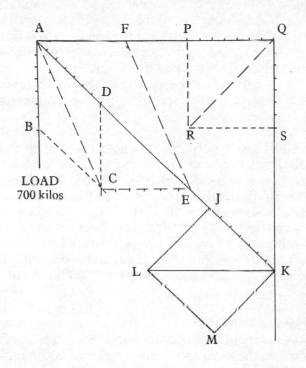

AB = DC = AD = BC = JK = MK = 700 kg
AF = CE = PQ = QS = 730 kg

The thrust on the derrick is AE = 1940 kg
The load on the topping lift head block is QR = 1000 kg
The load on the runner block A is AC = 1300 kg
The load on the topping lift is CE = 730 kg
The load on the runner heel block is KL = 1000 kg
The load on the topping lift head block is FM
The thrust on the derrick is AP

have to be rigged, and the tail led to a winch. It is always better to put a tackle on the topping lift rather than a single whip.

Runner The runner is the rope or wire that is connected to the load. It is led through a runner head block, down to a foot block, and via the other blocks if necessary, to obtain a clear lead to a winch. The runner can be rigged as a single whip, or if it is desired to reduce the load on the runner rope, as a purchase. A purchase will reduce the loading on the runner rope, but not reduce the load on the topping lift or the weight the derrick must take.

Guys The guy's purpose is to hold the derrick in position laterally, and stop it swinging about. There are two, one led from each side of the derrick head. They can take the form of a single line on a small derrick, but should have a tackle on them if the derrick is large, or the load a heavy one. The guys should be led to a firm point on deck and be cleated or tied off firmly. If the load has to be swung round, then this will be done by hauling gently but firmly on one guy and easing out the other at the same time. Avoid jerks, as this will jerk the load or start it swinging.

Rigging and using derricks Always ensure that the rope and blocks used are in good condition. Never use a piece of old rope just because the load or working conditions are dirty. Never ask the equipment to take a load greater than the safe working load of the weakest item.

When a derrick is in use, the topping lift and runner winches should be manned, and the tails cleated when the winch is not actually in use.

Never have less than five turns around a winch, and when lowering either the derrick on its topping lift, or the load on the runner, ease the rope gently round the winch drum to avoid jerks.

Make sure the topping lift and runner have clear leads to the winch, and in such a way that riding turns are avoided. If a riding turn occurs, say, on a winch for the topping lift, lower the load on the deck on the runner before trying to clear the trouble, and vice-versa.

Make sure that the load is securely fastened to the runner and taken at its point of balance. Take the weight of the load gently, and when it is an inch or so up, stop heaving and check that all the gear is in order and accepting the load comfortably. This way the load can only fall an inch if something fails.

Finally, do not allow anyone to pass underneath the derrick or the load whilst the load is in suspension.

8   COMMUNICATIONS

Signalling at sea is an outstanding example of international co-operation, commencing in 1855. The codes, flags, frequencies and procedures are international, and designed so that vessels from different countries and with different languages can communicate easily and quickly with one another. The procedures should be learned, as their misuse can cause confusion and interfere with other, perhaps more important, communications.

THE INTERNATIONAL CODE OF SIGNALS

This code, consisting of 1, 2 and 3 letter or numerical groups, is the basis of communications at sea. It enables a boat to compose a message and then encode it into the groups from the book. The receiving boat or station can then look up the groups and obtain the meaning in its own language.

The single-letter signals may be made by any method of signalling, with certain exceptions, and should be learned.

A   I have a diver down; keep well clear at slow speed.

B★ I am taking in, or discharging, or carrying dangerous goods.

C   Yes (affirmative or 'The significance of the previous group should be read in the affirmative').

D★ Keep clear of me; I am manoeuvring with difficulty.

E★ I am altering my course to starboard.

F   I am disabled; communicate with me.

G   I require a pilot. When made by fishing vessels operating in close proximity on the fishing grounds it means: 'I am hauling nets.'

H★ I have a pilot on board.

I★ I am altering my course to port.

J   I am on fire and have dangerous cargo on board: keep well clear of me.

K   I wish to communicate with you.

L   You should stop your vessel instantly.

M   My vessel is stopped and making no way through the water.

N   No (Negative or 'The significance of the previous group should be read in the negative'). This signal may be given only visually or by sound. For voice or radio transmission the signal should be 'N O'.

O   Man overboard.

P   *In harbour.* All persons should report on board as the vessel is about to proceed to sea.
    At sea. It may be used by fishing vessels to mean: 'My nets have come fast upon an obstruction.'

Q   My vessel is 'healthy' and I request free pratique.

R   No meaning in the International Code, but used by vessels at anchor to warn of danger of collision in fog.

S★ My engines are going astern.

T★ Keep clear of me; I am engaged in pair trawling.

U   You are running into danger.

V   I require assistance.

W   I require medical assistance.

X   Stop carrying out your intentions and watch for my signals.

Y   I am dragging my anchor.

Z   I require a tug. When made by fishing vessels operating in close proximity on the fishing grounds it means: 'I am shooting nets.'

NOTES

1. Signals of letters marked ★ when made by sound may only be made in compliance with the requirements of the International Regulations for Preventing Collisions at Sea, Rules 15 and 28.

2. Signals 'K' and 'S' have special meanings as landing signals for small boats with crews or persons in distress. (International Convention for the Safety of Life at Sea, 1960, Chapter V, Regulation 16.)

RADIO TELEPHONE

The most commonly used form of communication between boats nowadays is by means of the radio; VHF for short ranges up to about 40 miles, and single side band (SSB) medium and high frequency for longer distances. Semaphore, flags, and Morse lamps are hardly ever used, but, since a radio can break down, their procedures are set out in this section.

VHF RADIO

The range of a VHF set is governed largely by the height of the aerial, and by the power in watts of the transmitter. Aerials should be placed as high as possible on the boat, the top of the mast is the usual position, and connected to the radio set by screened cable to prevent loss of power and interference. The only disadvantage with placing the VHF aerial at the masthead is that if the mast breaks, the boat will lose her main form of communication. A small emergency antenna with a length of screened cable, fitted with a connecting plug for the radio, is therefore a useful piece of equipment to carry. Alternatively, the boat should have a small hand-held VHF set.

Before using the VHF set, switch on and listen on the desired frequency channel to find out if anyone else is using the frequency. This avoids interfering with their traffic, and avoids garbling one's own. When a break occurs in the traffic, commence your own call.

Calling procedure   Speak clearly and slowly at all times.
1. Repeat the name of the boat you are calling three times.
2. Follow this by saying 'This is' and then repeating your own boat's name or call sign three times.
3. Finish by saying 'Come in please, over'.
4. Wait and listen for a response.
    There is a tendency for people to call again much too quickly if no response is received to the first call. Wait a good minute before calling again as the other station may be

temporarily unmanned, or a person may have to come to the set from some distance, and your repeat call might drown out their response.

5. Once contact has been established, messages can be passed, and when traffic is complete, finish by saying 'This is (your name or call sign) listening channel – – Out.' This indicates to others that you have finished so that they can commence their own calls. It also tells anyone else who might wish to call you which channel you are listening to.

6. 'Roger' is used to indicate that an instruction has been received and understood.

Keep your messages short and clear. Remember that someone else may be waiting to use their radio, and their messages may be more important.

Phonetic alphabet   Where there is interference on the radio, or the radio is being operated at its maximum range and the signal may be weak, or where it is necessary to pass over a word which can be confused, it is best to spell out the word or words concerned. To do this the International Phonetic Alphabet is used. The italicised syllables should be emphasised.

Alfa	*Al* fah
Bravo	*Brah* voh
Charlie	*Char* lee
Delta	*Del* tah
Echo	*Eck* oh
Foxtrot	*Foks* trot
Golf	Golf
Hotel	Hoh *tell*
India	*In* dee ah
Juliett	*Jew* lee *ett*
Kilo	*Key* loh
Lima	*Lee* mah
Mike	Mike
November	No *vem* ber
Oscar	*Oss* cah
Papa	Pah *pah*
Quebec	Kweh *beck*
Romeo	*Row* me oh
Sierra	See *air* rah

Tango	*Tan* go
Uniform	*You* nee form
Victor	*Vik* tah
Whiskey	*Wiss* key
X-ray	*Ecks* ray
Yankee	*Yang* key
Zulu	*Zoo* loo

Safety messages   There are five safety prefixes, and whenever these are heard, transmissions should cease on the frequency being used. In each case, the prefix is repeated three times before the message.

MAYDAY   This is the distress prefix and is only used in emergencies. It is used to indicate that a vessel or aircraft is in grave or imminent danger, and requests immediate assistance.

MAYDAY RELAY   Indicates that a vessel or aircraft is transmitting on behalf of a vessel in imminent danger, and requires immediate assistance.

PAN   The prefix used to indicate that a very urgent signal is about to be transmitted concerning the safety of a vessel, aircraft or person.

SECURITE   Used to prefix messages concerning the safety of navigation or important weather warnings.

C.Q.   This is the general call to all stations, used when calling on an unidentified boat, or when there is information of general interest to transmit.

Mayday procedure   A mayday message should be transmitted on the International Distress Frequencies which are VHF Channel 16 and 2182 Mhz.

1. Repeat MAYDAY three times.
2. 'This is (type of vessel and name or call sign)' repeated three times.

3. 'In position . . .' (Give the position as a latitude and longitude whenever possible as it is less likely to be misunderstood).
4. Give the nature of the problem.
5. Give the number of people on board.
6. Say 'Over' and listen for a response.

Carry on transmitting the same message at one to two minute intervals until a response is obtained. If power is in short supply because the batteries are low, and time permits, wait until the silent period and then transmit.

Once contact has been established, the receiving ship or shore station will want to know more details, such as the nature of the problem, whether the boat is in imminent danger of sinking, or any of the crew injured etc.

LIGHT SIGNALLING

The use of the Morse Code with signalling lamp is a well-proven and reliable method of passing messages, and although it has been largely replaced by the universal use of VHF radio, it is still required knowledge for watchkeepers on merchant and warships.

The basis of light signalling is the Morse Code, developed by the American Samuel Morse, and generally adopted by about 1850. It uses a system of dots and dashes in different orders to represent each letter of the alphabet and each single number.

Using the Morse Code   It is important to transmit in a uniform manner, and the duration of each unit should follow the following pattern:
  A dot is one unit.
  A dash is three units.
  The space between units making up a letter or number is one unit.
  The space between complete letters or numbers is three units.
  The space between words or groups is seven units.

The Morse Code

A · −	J · − − −	S · · ·
B − · · ·	K − · −	T −
C − · − ·	L · − · ·	U · · −
D − · ·	M − −	V · · · −
E ·	N − ·	W · − −
F · · − ·	O − − −	X − · · −
G − − ·	P · − − ·	Y − · − −
H · · · ·	Q − − · −	Z − − · ·
I · ·	R · − ·	

Numerals

1 · − − − −	6 − · · · ·
2 · · − − −	7 − − · · ·
3 · · · − −	8 − − − · ·
4 · · · · −	9 − − − − ·
5 · · · · ·	0 − − − − −

Light signalling procedure

To call another vessel	ZZZZ
Response	A series of 'T's.
Message from	DE followed by the name or call sign of the transmitting vessel.
Word acknowledgment	Upon receipt of each word the receiving vessel sends a 'T'.
Erase signal	EEEEE is used to indicate that the last group or word was signalled incorrectly. It is acknowledged with the erase signal, and then the transmitting vessel will transmit the last correctly sent word or group and continue the message.
Repeat signal	RPT is used to indicate that a message is going to be repeated, should be repeated back, or to ask for a signal to be repeated.

Repetition signals	Made after RPT.
	AA – Repeat all after –
	AB – Repeat all before –
	WA – Repeat word after –
	WB – Repeat word before –
	BN – Repeat all between – and –

Acknowledgment of repeat   OK.

Ending signal	AR used to indicate that the message is complete.
Received signal	R used after AR by the receiving vessel to indicate that the message has been received and understood.

Interrogative vessel's name   CS used when requesting the name or call sign of the receiving vessel.

Waiting signal	AS used to indicate, at the end of a message, that a further message will follow shortly. It is also used between groups to separate them as a period signal
Affirmative	C used on its own to indicate an affirmative statement or reply.
Interrogative signal	RQ – used to indicate a question.
Negative signal	N used to indicate a negative statement.

FLAG SIGNALLING

The basis of flag signalling is the International Code Flags and Pendants (or pennants, either spelling is correct, it is always pronounced pennant).

Flags will normally be hoisted on a flag halyard leading from the yardarm. It is rare to see more than one hoist of flags at a time, but if a vessel wishes to send a long message, the order would be: masthead halyard, starboard yardarm, port yardarm, triatic halyard. This is a rare occurrence, and usually the order of the halyards is immaterial as each group of flags is a message in itself. When using flag hoists, merchant ships will normally hoist the flags in their groups directly onto the halyards. Naval vessels precede their groups with the code pendant (answering pendant) to indicate that they are using the International Code and not a code of their own.

Flag signals are left flying until acknowledged, or the signal has been overtaken by events.

Signalling procedure A vessel wishing to signal another will hoist that vessel's sign before sending the message. Where a general message is being sent, the flag or group will be hoisted where it can best be seen and need not be acknowledged.

On seeing her call sign hoisted, the addressee vessel will hoist the answering pendant at the dip (halfway) to indicate that she has noticed and is ready to receive the signal. The answering pendant should be hoisted on a halyard where its position, either at the dip, or fully hoisted, is obvious. The triatic halyard should be avoided for this reason.

Once the signal has been made by the transmitting vessel, and received, decoded and understood by the receiving vessel, the answering pendant should be fully hoisted. If further messages are to be sent, the transmitting vessel will then haul down the signal and prepare the next one, and the receiving vessel will haul down her answering pendant to the dip once more.

When the transmitting vessel has finished her message, she should fully hoist her own answering pendant to indicate that the message is complete, and this will be acknowledged in the same manner by the receiving vessel.

Substitutes Because few vessels carry more than one set of flags, there are three substitute flags, which are used in places where the same letter appears more than once.

These flags are the first, second and third substitute. The first substitute is used to repeat the uppermost signal flag in a group. The second substitute repeats the second signal flag and the third substitute the third signal flag.

Thus if a flag signal comprising GBA – FBG – NCA were to

be joisted, the flags used would be: GBA – F 2nd Sub, 1st Sub – NC 3rd Sub.

Calling an unknown vessel   The following 2-flag hoists can be used to address an unknown vessel:

CQ = This is the general call signal.
VF = You should hoist your identity signal.
CS = What is the name or identity of your vessel.
YQ = I wish to communicate by (method) with the vessel
bearing – – – – from me.

There are three other useful groups:
ZQ = Your signal appears incorrectly coded. You should
check and repeat the whole.
ZL = Your signal has been received but not understood.
YZ = The words that follow are in plain language.

SEMAPHORE

Semaphore is very seldom used nowadays, but could come into use if no flags are carried, and the batteries used to power the radio or signalling lamp are flat.

Semaphore procedure   The transmitting vessel will make the attention signal which will be answered by hoisting the answering pendant or making the letter C in semaphore.

The International Code is not used in semaphore. The message and numbers are fully spelled out.

At the end of each word, the arms are dropped to the 'break' position. The break position is also used between letters when double letters occur in the text.

The erase signal is a series of Es.

The acknowledgment of each word is indicated by the receiving vessel with the letter C. If C is not made, the last word transmitted is to be repeated.

All signals are ended with AR.

Semaphore

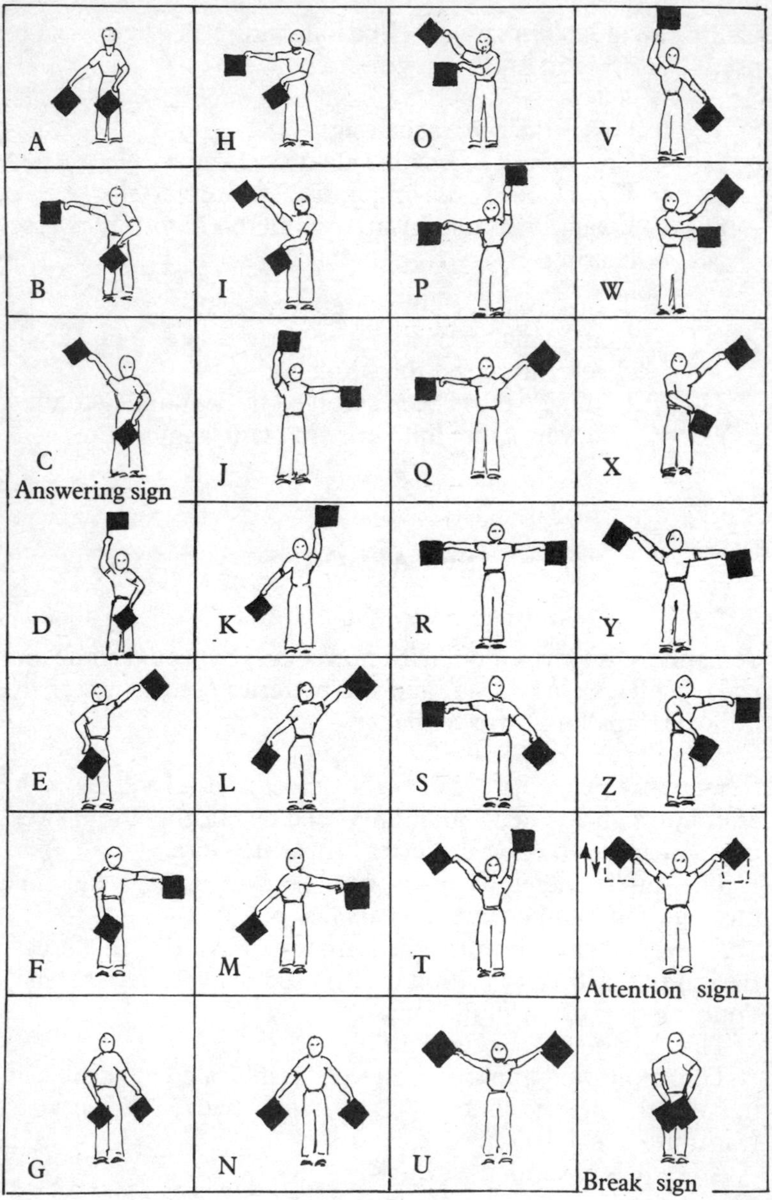

A

H

O

V

B

I

P

W

C
Answering sign

J

Q

X

D

K

R

Y

E

L

S

Z

F

M

T

Attention sign

G

N

U

Break sign

Morse Signalling by Hand-flags or Arms

Dot

Dash

Break sign between dots
and/or dashes.

Break sign between letter,
groups or words.

Erase signals, if made by
the transmitting station.
Request for repetition if
by the receiving station.

DISTRESS SIGNALS

The following signals, used or exhibited either together or separately, indicate distress and need of assistance:

1. A gun or other explosive signal fired at intervals of about a minute.
2. A continuous sounding with any fog signalling apparatus.
3. Rockets or shells, throwing red stars fired one at a time at short intervals.
4. A signal made by radiotelegraphy or by any other signalling method consisting of the group $\cdots - - - \cdots$ (SOS) in the Morse Code.
5. A signal sent by radiotelephony consisting of the spoken word 'Mayday'.
6. The International Code Signal of distress indicated by NC.
7. A signal consisting of a square flag having above or below it a ball or anything resembling a ball.
8. Flames on the vessel (as from a burning tar barrel, oil barrel etc.).
9. A rocket parachute flare or a hand flare showing a red light.
10. A smoke signal giving off orange-coloured smoke.
11. Slowly and repeatedly raising and lowering arms outstretched to each side.
12. The radiotelegraph alarm signal.
13. The radiotelephone alarm signal.
14. Signals transmitted by emergency position-indicating radio beacons (EPIRBS).
15. A piece of orange-coloured canvas with either a black square and circle or other appropriate symbol (for identification from the air).
16. A dye marker.

The use of any of these signals except for the purpose of indicating distress is prohibited, as is the use of any signal that might be confused for them.

9 METEOROLOGY

The atmosphere, pressure, wind and waves, cloud and pre-
cipitation, depressions, anti-cyclones, tropical revolving
storms, ocean currents, land/sea breezes should all be studied
by anyone going afloat.

THE ATMOSPHERE

What we know as the atmosphere is divided into three layers.

Troposphere – Varies from 0–10 miles at the equator, and 0–5
miles at the Poles.

Stratosphere – 5–10 miles to 50 miles, and includes the Ozon-
osphere which extends from 20–50 miles.

Ionosphere – 50–150 miles and contains the radio-reflecting
layers, the Kennelly Heaviside at 55 miles and
the Appleton Layer at about 150 miles.

The atmosphere, which decreases in density with height is
made up of a number of gases. The approximate proportions are
nitrogen 78%, oxygen 21%, Argon just under 1%, and traces of
carbon dioxide, hydrogen, helium and other gases.

Most weather changes take place in the troposphere, which is
the area of most concern to seafarers, and are caused by the
sun's heat varying the temperature of the air in this layer.

The sun, 93,000,000 miles from the earth and at a temperature of about 6,000° centigrade, sends out heat as short wave
radiation. This heat passes through the atmosphere with little
appreciable effect, and strikes the earth's surface causing the
surface to warm up. The amount of heat absorbed by the earth
depends upon latitude, the most being received at the equator,
and the least at the poles.

When the sun strikes the sea, the heat is dissipated into the
oceans, and causes little change in temperature. Because it is

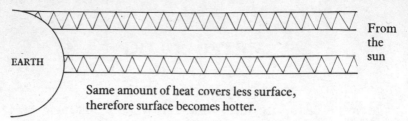

Same amount of heat covers less surface,
therefore surface becomes hotter.

able to store this heat, the sea surface temperature hardly changes between day and night. The heat striking a land surface is not absorbed so deeply, with the result that land heats up more during the day, and cools down again at night. The air in close contact with the earth's surface is warmed and cooled by conduction from the surface.

There is a time lag between the heat striking the earth and some of this heat being emitted, in the form of long wave radiation into the atmosphere, which causes a time lag between the moment when the sun is having its greatest heating effect and when the lower air reaches its maximum temperature.

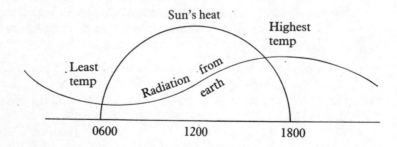

The distribution of land and sea over the earth's surface causes the atmospheric temperature to vary considerably. Other major factors are cloud cover, the temperature of ocean currents, and the dynamic effect of the earth's rotation on its axis. The variation of the sun's elevation due to the tilt of the earth's axis causes a fundamental change in temperature, and is responsible for the seasonal changes.

PRESSURE

The weight of all the gases in the atmosphere exerts an average pressure at sea level of 14.7 lbs/sq in, or about 1013 millibars. The millibar is a measurement of pressure equal to 1,000,000 dynes/sq cm.

The atmospheric pressure is not the same over the earth's surface; it varies according to latitude and from place to place in the same latitudes. In the tropics the pressure remains reasonably constant, but in temperate areas it is normally undergoing continual change. The temperature variations between the surfaces of land and sea also create pressure differences.

Knowledge of the atmospheric pressure is important to the seaman as it indicates the weather that he is likely to experience. As a generalisation, high pressure is associated with fair, but not necessarily sunny, weather, and low pressure with strong winds and rain.

Isobars Isobars are lines joining places of equal pressure, similar to contours on a map. Since the wind direction and speed depend upon differences in pressure between areas, the isobars, normally drawn at 4 millibar (mb) intervals on a synoptic chart, give the seaman a great deal of information.

Pressure gradient The pressure gradient is the fall in pressure relative to the distance between isobars. It is measured in millibars and nautical miles. The pressure gradient is greatest where the isobars are close together and vice versa. The steeper the gradient, the stronger will be the winds in that area. However, wind velocity varies with latitude for identical pressure gradients.

WIND

Where an imbalance in pressure occurs, wind will be generated, blowing from the area of high pressure towards the area of low pressure at the earth's surface.

If we consider two columns of air of equal height and temperature, AB and XY, the atmospheric pressure will be the same at the bases of both columns A and X. Suppose now that column AB is heated, it will expand to C. The pressure at A and X will be the same, but the pressure at B will be greater than at Y. This causes a transfer of air from B to Y, which will reduce the pressure at A and increase it at X causing a transfer of air from X to A. The greater the difference in pressure (the pressure gradient) the faster air will be transferred.

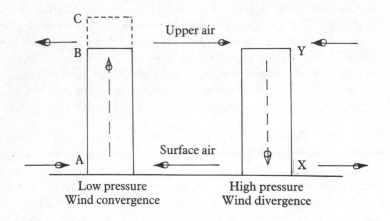

Low pressure
Wind convergence

High pressure
Wind divergence

Air is very rarely transferred straight between areas of high and low pressure due to the effect of the earth's rotation or the geostrophic force. This causes masses of air to be deflected to the right in the northern hemisphere and left in the southern hemisphere. On a planet entirely covered by water, the winds would follow the directions shown in the diagram below. In fact, the winds do tend to follow these directions over large oceans, but there are major changes close to land masses. The diagram shows the names given to various regions. These regions move north and south with the seasons by about 5 degrees of latitude.

ISOBARIC SYSTEMS

Anti-cyclones An anti-cyclone or 'high' is a high pressure system where the air is subsiding from upper levels. The wind circulates round them in a clockwise direction in the northern hemisphere and anti-clockwise in the southern hemisphere. As the air is subsiding rainfall is uncommon.

Anti-cyclones are divided into four basic types, warm and cold, and temporary and long lasting. A cold anti-cyclone is formed when the air over an area is more dense than that close by. A warm anti-cyclone forms when there are larger than usual amounts of warm air over an area.

Most anti-cyclones move in an easterly direction, but in eastern parts of oceans, their movement is usually slow, and can be erratic. The 'Azores High' is an example, and this may remain almost stationary for quite long periods.

Winds are generally light, but it is as well to keep an eye on the pressure gradient, particularly when a depression is moving towards an anti-cyclone.

Isobaric Systems

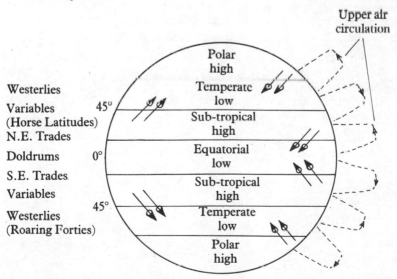

Depressions   Also known as 'lows', depressions are areas of low pressure, with the lowest pressure being in the centre of a circle of closed isobars. The wind circulates around a low in the anti-clockwise direction in the northern hemisphere, and clockwise in the southern hemisphere.

Depressions form when large masses of warm and cold air meet, such as in the western North Atlantic, western North Pacific, and the Southern Ocean. The boundary between the two masses of air is known as a front. A depression starts life as a small ripple in this front, which grows and develops a wind circulation.

There are two types of front. A warm front occurs when warm air replaces cold air, and a cold front is when cold air replaces warm air. The slope of the frontal surface is about 1 in 150.

Life of a Frontal Depression

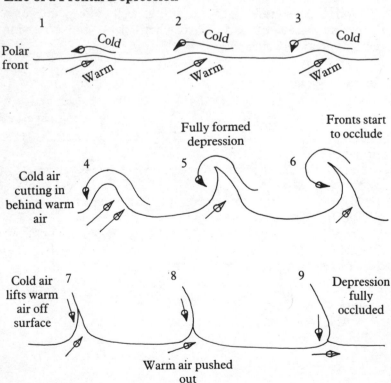

General points about depressions

1. Depressions generally move in a direction parallel to the warm sector isobars.
2. Warm fronts move slower than cold fronts.
3. An occluded depression moves very slowly and is often stationary.
4. A depression with the same pressure gradient all round it is stationary.
5. A depression usually moves in the same direction as the strongest winds around it.
6. A depression tends to move towards where the pressure is falling most quickly.
7. The greater the angle between the front and the warm sector isobars, the faster a depression will move.
8. Small depressions move quickly in approximately the same direction as the air stream in which they formed.
9. When secondary depressions form, they tend to move cyclonically (anti-clockwise) round the primary depression.
10. When the secondary and primary depressions are of the same size, they will revolve cyclonically round each other.
11. Depressions with lower than normal winds tend to deepen.
12. Depressions with greater than normal winds tend to fill.

Buys Ballot's Law   This states that if an observer puts his back square to the wind in the northern hemisphere, the *L*ow pressure will be on his *L*eft.

In fact, because of the geostrophic force, or spiralling effect of the wind in towards the centre of low pressure, the centre will lie about two points forward of his outstretched arm if it is placed at right angles to the wind.

From this, it is easy to work out that a low in the southern hemisphere would lie two points forward of the right arm of an observer with his back square to the wind.

Weather through a Frontal Depression

	Warm front		Warm sector	Cold front	
	Approaching	Passing		Passing	At the rear
Pressure	Steady fall	Stops falling	Little change	Sudden rise	Rising steadily
Wind	Veers from S to SW, and increases	Veers with possible increase in velocity	Steady, possibly backing as cold front approaches	Sudden veer from SW to W or NW, with squalls	Velocity tends to decrease, steady in direction
Temperature	Rising slowly	Slight rise	Little change with relatively high temperatures	Sudden drop	Little change but tendency to fall
Sky	Becoming overcast Ci, Cs, As, Ns	Ns and Fs	Overcast with St turning to Sc	Cb	Cb, Ac, Cu with blue sky

Precipitation	Continuous from drizzle to heavy rain or snow	Rain stops but may be slight drizzle	Intermittent slight rain or drizzle possibly fog	Heavy rain, thunder and possibly hail	There may be a narrow belt of continuous heavy rain, turning to heavy showers later
Visibility	Deteriorating	Poor	Poor	Great improvement	Excellent except in showers

Key to cloud type abbreviations

Ac = Altocumulus	Ci = Cirrus	Fs = Fractostratus	St = Stratus
As = Altostratus	Cs = Cirostratus	Ns = Nimbostratus	
Cb = Cumulonimbus	C = Cumulus	Sc = Stratocumulus	

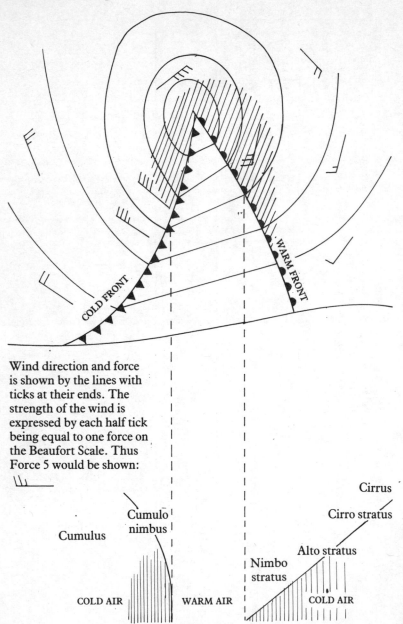

Wind direction and force
is shown by the lines with
ticks at their ends. The
strength of the wind is
expressed by each half tick
being equal to one force on
the Beaufort Scale. Thus
Force 5 would be shown:

COLD FRONT

WARM FRONT

Cumulus

Cumulo
nimbus

Cirrus

Cirro stratus

Alto stratus

Nimbo
stratus

COLD AIR   WARM AIR   COLD AIR

The Beaufort wind scale

Beaufort scale number	Description and limit of wind speed in knots	Sea criterion
0	Calm, less than 1	Sea like a mirror.
1	Light air 1–3	Ripples with the appearance of scales are formed but without foam crests.
2	Light breeze 4–6	Small wavelets, still short but more pronounced, crests have a glassy appearance and do not break.
3	Gentle breeze 7–10	Large wavelets. Crests begin to break. Foam of glassy appearance. Perhaps scattered white horses.
4	Moderate breeze 11–16	Small waves, becoming longer; fairly frequent white horses.
5	Fresh breeze 17–21	Moderate waves, taking a more pronounced long form; many white horses are formed. (Chance of some spray).
6	Strong breeze 22–27	Large waves begin to form; the white foam crests are more extensive everywhere. (Probably some spray).
7	Near gale 28–33	Sea heaps up and white foam from breaking waves begins to be blown in streaks along the direction of the wind. (Spindrift begins to be seen).
8	Gale 34–40	Moderately high waves of greater length; edges of crests break into spindrift. The foam is blown in well marked streaks along the direction of the wind.
9	Strong gale 41–47	High waves. Dense streaks of foam along the direction of the wind. Sea begins to roll. Spray may affect visibility.
10	Storm 48–55	Very high waves with long overhanging crests. The resulting foam in great patches is blown in dense white streaks along the direction of the wind. On the whole the surface of the sea takes a white appearance. The rolling of the sea becomes heavy and shocklike. Visibility affected.

| 11 | Violent storm 56–63 | Exceptionally high waves. (Small and medium-sized ships might be for a time lost to view behind the waves). The sea is completely covered with long white patches of foam lying along the direction of the wind. Everywhere the edges of the wave crests are blown into froth. Visibility affected. |
| 12 | Hurricane 64–71 | The air is filled with foam and spray. Sea completely white with driving spray; visibility seriously affected. |

There is an extended scale for exceptional winds as follows:

Force	*Knots*
13	72–80
14	81–89
15	90–99
16	100–109
17	110–118

Winds are named for the direction from which they are blowing; a westerly thus blows from west to east.

Land and sea breezes As land heats during the day, it heats up the air over it by conduction. The heated air becomes less dense and the pressure will fall. The sea temperature, however, remains almost constant, and the pressure over it is relatively high in comparison with the land. Thus a pressure gradient is formed, and air flows from the sea to the land creating a *sea breeze*. This will normally set in during the late morning and reach its maximum strength at about 1400 hours local time, and then die away towards sunset.

After sunset, the land will cool rapidly, also cooling the air above it which becomes more dense and increases the atmospheric pressure over the land. Once this pressure is greater than the pressure over the sea, a *land breeze* starts to blow from the land out to sea. This breeze will normally commence shortly after sunset and continue until dawn.

Land and sea breezes will usually extend a couple of miles off the coast, but may extend further if the temperature difference is greater. The sea breeze is usually the stronger of the two, and can reach Force 3 to 4. They usually blow at right angles to the coast, so if there is a prevailing wind blowing along a coastline, it will tend to be bent in towards the coast once the sea breeze develops, and away from the coast with the land breeze.

Local winds

Monsoon   Monsoons are winds created by the effect of large land masses over areas of oceans, which are sufficiently strong to replace the normal planetary wind circulation. The best known example is the Indian Ocean monsoon, which is caused by high and low pressure over Siberia. In winter the land cools, and creates a fairly stable area of high pressure. The winds, blowing clockwise round this anti-cyclone, cause strong and steady north-easterly winds to blow over the Indian Ocean. It becomes established in December and dies away in April. In the summer, the Asian continent is heated, creating an area of low pressure, and the anti-clockwise winds blow towards this cyclone. This creates a south-westerly wind in the Indian Ocean, stronger than the NE monsoon, which blows from June until October.

The same pressure system causes the China Sea monsoon which gives strong, north-west to northerly winds from December until April, and lighter south-easterly winds from June to October. Similar monsoon winds are found on the north coast of Australia and in the Bight of Benin, off Nigeria.

Katabatic winds   These are strong winds formed usually at night which blow out over the sea from high ground. As air is cooled at night, it becomes dense, and heavier than air lower down a hill or cliff. This denser air moves downhill at considerable speed, and can create winds up to Force 6 to 7.

Anabatic winds   When low-lying air is heated, it becomes less dense and expands and moves upwards to replace cooler more dense air above. The wind created is usually light.

Tropical Revolving Storms (TRS)   These form when the equatorial convergence zone is well north or south of the equator, and the change in direction of the Trade Wind which crosses the equator causes strong convergence wind currents.

The proximity of other disturbances, such as local surface heating from islands, provides unstable weather conditions which, with a strong convergence current, increase the chances of a cyclonic disturbance.

In general, tropical revolving storms do not form closer than 5 degrees latitude to the equator, and they cannot cross over from one hemisphere to another. They usually form between June and November in the northern hemisphere, and December to April in the southern hemisphere.

After forming between 5 and 10 degrees of latitude, a TRS will move just north of west at about 12 knots until it reaches the tropic. At this point it will usually slow, before starting to curve north or east at a speed of between 15 and 20 knots. Wind velocities can build up to 130 knots, with the strongest winds being found behind the trough line in the dangerous quadrant. Seas can build up quite quickly to a very dangerous size, and every effort should be made to avoid a tropical revolving storm.

The illustration shows the plan of a tropical revolving storm. The rule is to head away from a cone drawn 40 degrees either side of the storm's probable path, and to the left, if possible, in the northern hemisphere, as this is probably away from the path of the storm. Generally TRSs tend to follow a path curving to the right in the northern hemisphere, but by no means always. It is essential to obtain good weather information. If this is not available by radio, the following rough rules apply:

1. Watch for a swell which develops for no apparent reason. The swell waves can be felt up to 1000 miles from the storm centre.
2. Watch the barometer. If it varies more than 3mb from the normal reading for the time and place, be wary.
3. Clouds will change from cirrus, with bands leading towards the storm centre, which will be followed by cirrostratus, cirrocumulus and altocumulus. A band of black nimbostratus marks the bar of the storm, and with it comes torrential rain.
4. The atmosphere starts to feel oppressive.
5. Changes in the direction or velocity of the wind. If these are accompanied by fluctuations in the barometer, a tropical revolving storm is not far away.

To find the direction of the storm centre, observe the wind direction as the barometer starts to fall. Draw a line on the chart from your position on a bearing 12 points (135 degrees) to the right of the wind's direction. When the barometer has fallen 10mbs, draw another line from your position, 10 points (112½ degrees) to the right of the wind's direction. After it has fallen a further 10mb, draw another line 8 points (90 degrees) to the right of the wind's direction. These lines all point to the storm's centre in the northern hemisphere; in the southern hemisphere, substitute left for right.

Tropical Revolving Storm

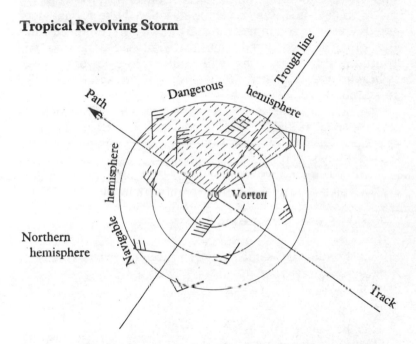

A tropical revolving storm is not something any small boat wants to be caught in, as heaving-to is dangerous, particularly once the waves start to change direction. It is best to get clear if possible, and the further one can put oneself from the centre the better. Where there is sea room, a boat in the dangerous semi-circle should proceed at her best speed with the wind on her starboard bow. If the boat is in the path of the storm, she should reach with the wind just abaft the starboard beam, and if in the navigable semi-circle, she should run with the wind on the starboard quarter. In the southern hemisphere, read port for starboard in this paragraph.

WAVES

Waves are set up by the friction of the wind on the sea's surface, and they will take the same direction. The longer the wind blows in the same direction, and the stronger it is, the larger the waves will become. Waves can be considered like a train which builds up in size and moves out and away from the area in which they are generated. Even when the wind eases, the train will continue to run, although it will gradually lose power.

Seas are waves created directly by the wind, and are referred to as smooth, rough or high.

Swell refers to waves outside the generation area, which can usually be identified by their oily unbroken surface. They are described as low, moderate or heavy depending upon their height. Only seas break at the crests.

There are a number of approximate formulae that apply to waves which can be useful to the seaman, where:

C is the speed, measured in knots.

L is the length, measured in feet.
(The horizontal distance between successive wave crests.)

T is the wave period measured in seconds.
(The interval between the passage of successive crests past a point.)

H is the wave height measured in feet.
(Vertical distance between the crest and trough.)

$$C = 3.1 \times T$$
$$L = 5.1 \times T^2$$

Breakers will form when the depth of water is less than $\dfrac{L}{2}$.

Waves will break if $\dfrac{H}{L} > \dfrac{1}{13}$.

These formulae must be treated cautiously, as although waves exceeding a height of 50 feet are extremely rare, the combination of a large swell with a large sea wave can create waves of double this height, as has been known in the Southern Ocean.

CURRENTS

The water in the oceans of the world is continually moving, and the great ocean currents are formed where the wind blows constantly in the same direction, such as in the Trades and the Southern Ocean. The main surface currents form closed systems, which circulate round the permanent anti-cyclones centred at about 30 degrees latitude north and south. The Southern Ocean current forms a part of the circulatory systems of the South Atlantic, South Pacific and Indian Oceans, but also flows continuously around the world.

Since these currents can run at up to three knots, and in places at even higher speeds, the seaman making an ocean crossing must take them into account when planning his voyage.

Currents are named, either with a local name, or by the direction in which they are setting.

Very often it is possible to tell whether or not the boat is in a current by changes in sea temperature. A cold current from the north entering an area of warmer seas will often have a quite well defined border. By taking frequent sea water temperatures, it would be possible to know almost exactly when the boat had entered the current. A particularly good example of this is the Gulf Stream, which is a warm current emanating from the Gulf of Mexico, and heading out in a clockwise direction into the cooler Atlantic waters. The interface between the Gulf Stream and the cold Labrador Current in the North Atlantic is known as the Cold Wall, and besides a temperature difference there is a colour difference which may be noticed – the Labrador Current's green hues contrasting with the deep blue of the Gulf Stream.

CLOUDS AND PRECIPITATION

Clouds are made up of minute water particles which have been absorbed by the atmosphere, and condense when the air temperature falls. All air carries some water vapour; the amount depends upon whether the air has been flowing over water or land, and on its temperature. Air of a higher temperature can absorb more water vapour than air of a lower temperature. As air cools, it reaches dewpoint, the temperature at which the water vapour condenses, forming clouds.

The factors that cause air to cool and cause clouds to form are:
When warm air is forced to rise at a warm front.
When warm air is forced to rise at a cold front.
When air rises in a convection current.
When air is forced to rise by high ground.
When there is turbulence in the atmosphere which will cause warm and cold air to mix.

Clouds are classed as high (above 20,000 ft), medium (8000 –20,000 ft), and low (below 8000 ft). There are several types in each category. Clouds can be divided into six main types:

Cirrus.   Detached delicate fibrous or feathery clouds. Usually white without shading. It is a high cloud.
Cumulus.   A dome-shaped cloud, usually with protuberances, and a horizontal base. It has a dense appearance with sharp edges. It may vary in height from a few feet to 35,000 ft, although its usual base is from 1500 to 5000 ft.
Alto.   A medium height cloud.
Stratus.   A more or less continuous layer of low cloud.
Nimbus.   Heavy dark threatening cloud, which usually indicates rain.
Fractus.   Any broken cloud, for example, stratus that has been broken up by air currents.

All clouds can be described using one of the terms above or a combination. Thus cirrostratus is a high thin layer of cloud, and cumulonimbus is a towering cauliflower-shaped mass, which is dark at its lower levels.

Category	Stable air conditions	Unstable air conditions	Tending to be unstable air conditions
Low	Stratus (St) Nimbostratus (Ns)	Cumulus (Cu)	Stratocumulus (Sc)
Medium	Altostratus (As)	Cumulonimbus (Cb)	Altocumulus (Ac)
High	Cirrostratus (Cs)	Cirrus (Ci)	Cirrocumulus (Cc)

Orographic cloud   This is formed when air is forced upwards, and thus cooled, by a mountain. It is usually stratus type at the base. The most famous examples are the Levanter cloud over Gibraltar and the Table Mountain's 'tablecloth' at Cape Town, South Africa. Orographic cloud does not have to be in contact with the mountain; it can form some way above, and this patch of cloud, which does not move with the air flow, is a useful indication to the seaman that land lies below it.

Fog   Fog is effectively cloud on the surface, formed when air is cooled by conduction from a cool surface. There are four main types of fog:

1. Radiation fog. Formed by radiation from the ground cooling the air immediately above the surface.
2. Advection fog. Formed rapidly when warm moist air moves over a colder land or sea surface.
3. Mixing fog. Also known as frontal fog. Forms when two different air masses meet.
4. Sea smoke. Forms when very cold air flows over relatively warm water.

Mist and haze   Mist is basically thin fog and is defined as existing where visibility is reduced by water particles to between 1000 and 2000 metres. Where visibility is reduced by dust, smoke or sand to the same limits, it is known as haze.

FORECASTING

Since weather forecasts are now available for offshore and inshore waters, and facsimiles (which produce an automatically printed synoptic chart) available at sea when crossing oceans, there is no excuse for going to sea without some advance knowledge of the weather to be expected.

Weather forecasting in the equatorial low and sub-tropical high zones is comparatively simple. Except for tropical revolving storms, the winds in these areas are fairly predictable. It is in the temperate low zones that a knowledge of depressions, and the weather associated with them, can indicate the winds and rain to be expected.

Weather lore, mostly stemming from the days of sail, provides a very useful guide, and some of the old sayings are worth remembering. Local weather sayings are just that, local, and although they may apply to the area concerned, local factors may be the cause, and they should not be relied upon elsewhere.

1. When seabirds fly out early, and go far out to sea, it indicates fair weather and light to moderate winds. This only applies to land-based seabirds, such as gulls and gannets, and obviously would be misleading if albatrosses or petrels were observed, as they spend the greater part of their lives at sea.
2. Seabirds over land indicate stormy weather on its way.
3. Fog and dew forming overland at night indicates fine weather as neither forms under an overcast sky or when there is a lot of wind.
4. Soft, delicate looking clouds indicate light to moderate breezes.
5. Hard-edged, oily-looking clouds indicate stronger winds on their way.
6. Small, dark coloured clouds indicate rain.
7. The sun setting on a clear horizon indicates fair weather.
8. The sun setting high above the horizon because of cloud obscuring it indicates rain and/or wind. This applies particularly in the temperate zones, where depressions come from the west. The cloud is the first sign of the approach of a front.
9. Red sky at night, sailor's delight – Fair weather.
   Pale yellow sunset – rain.
   Bright yellow sunset – wind.
   Grey sky at morning – fine weather.

Dark blue sky – wind.

Light blue sky – fine weather.

10. A veering wind – Fair weather.

A backing wind – Foul weather.

If one thinks of the winds associated with a depression, the wind backs as the depression approaches bringing with it stronger winds and rain. As the warm front passes, the wind veers, and it veers again with the passage of the cold front, after which, conditions improve. The only thing wrong with this expression is that when the wind veers with the passing of the warm front, there is still the cold front to come.

11. 'When the wind is before the rain, soon you can make sail again.'

'When the rain is before the wind, topsail halyards you must mind.'

As a depression approaches, the first sign is likely to be rain, and the wind will increase with the arrival of the depression. If a strong wind comes first, it will probably have been caused by the depression, and the later rain by the passing of the cold front, and the wind will then moderate.

10   STABILITY AND BUOYANCY

CENTRE OF EFFORT

The centre of effort of a yacht is the combined geometrical centre of the sails set. When calculating the centre of effort, the fully set mainsail and largest working headsail or headsails are used.

To calculate the centre of effort of a sail, draw lines from each corner of the sail to the midpoint of the opposite sides, and where the lines meet is the centre of effort. Unless the sail has a very large roach, the roach can be ignored. When the centre of effort for every sail has been plotted on the sail plan it is necessary to resolve these individual efforts to find the centre of effort for the boat as a whole.

If the boat has only two sails this is a simple matter. Draw a line between the centres of effort of the two sails, AB. From A drop a perpendicular AX measured off in some convenient unit and proportional to the area of the headsail. From B raise a perpendicular BY, measured off in the same units and proportional to the area of the mainsail. Connect XY, and where it crosses the line AB will be the centre of effort.

Example

Mainsail = 300 sq ft   Distance between centre of efforts
Genoa   = 350 sq ft   of the two sails is 13 inches
Sum   650 sq ft

$$\frac{650}{13} \quad \frac{\text{square feet of total sail area}}{\text{Length of line between C of E's}} = 50 \,(\text{sq ft/unit})$$

Thus the centre of effort of the boat will be along the line from the centre of effort of the smaller sail. $\dfrac{350}{50} = 7$ inches

Centre of Effort

A   = Centre of effort of mainsail
B   = Centre of effort of headsail
BY = Ratio of mainsail area
AX = Ratio of headsail area

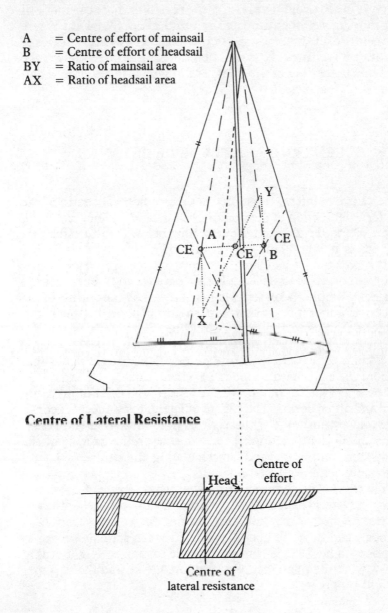

Centre of Lateral Resistance

If the boat has more than two sails, resolve the centre of effort of pairs of sails, and then, using the results of these calculations as a new centre, work the calculations through. Knowing where the centre of effort is for a particular boat, and where it moves to in different settings of the sails helps to enlarge one's knowledge and understanding of the boat, and is vital if the best performance is to be achieved.

CENTRE OF LATERAL RESISTANCE

The centre of lateral resistance is the geometrical centre of the underwater section of the boat in the fore and aft line, including keel, skeg and rudder. It is everything below the waterline that would resist lateral movement of the boat.

It is possible to calculate the centre of lateral resistance using a formula such as Simpson's Rules (*see page 293*), but there is a perfectly simple and practical alternative. Lay the outline of the boat over a sheet of cardboard, with carbon paper between, and draw the shape of the boat below the waterline. Cut out the underwater shape from the cardboard. Then balance this shape on a knife-edge, with the knife perpendicular to the waterline. Where the cardboard shape is balanced, mark each end of the shape where it is in contact with the knife, and this line gives the fore and aft position of the centre of lateral resistance. Since the fore and aft positions of the centres of effort and lateral resistance are all that is required for working on the balance of the boat, this simple method of calculating the centre of lateral resistance is quite effective.

There is no absolute relation between the centre of effort and centre of lateral resistance. It is usual for the centre of effort to be slightly nearer the bow, but the amount will vary from boat to boat, and how the boat is trimmed when actually sailing as opposed to how she is trimmed on the drawings. It is useful to know what the relationship is supposed to be and the designer should supply it.

BUOYANCY

A boat displaces its own weight of water. This is Archimedes' Principle. If weight is added to the boat it will sink to accommodate the weight, and the water displaced by this additional sinking will, equal the weight added to the boat.

The buoyant volume of a boat is the watertight part of the hull. It divides into two at the waterline. That below the waterline is known as her buoyancy, and that above, as her reserve buoyancy.

The position of the waterline will, therefore, depend upon the weight of the boat and the density of the liquid in which it is floating. One cubic metre of water weighs 1000 kilogrammes or one metric tonne. However sea water is more dense, and a cubic metre of sea water weighs approximately 1025 kilogrammes. Thus a boat of the same weight will float higher in sea water than in fresh water.

Waterplane coefficient This is the ratio between the waterplane area of the boat, and a rectangle having the same length and breadth.

Block coefficient Also known as the Coefficient of Fineness, this is the ratio between the underwater volume of the boat, and a block which has the same length, breadth and height.

Prismatic coefficient This is the ratio between the underwater volume of the boat and a block with the same length and the same cross-section as the midship section of the boat. If the boat has her greatest beam abaft the midship point, then the cross section would be taken at the widest point.

STABILITY

Most small boat seamen take the stability of their boats for granted. It is assumed that the designer took care to see that the boat would be stable and safe at sea, and since a yacht never

Buoyancy and Stability

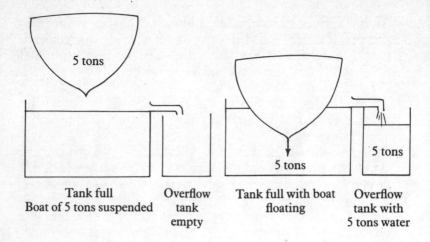

Tank full
Boat of 5 tons suspended

Overflow
tank
empty

Tank full with boat
floating

Overflow
tank with
5 tons water

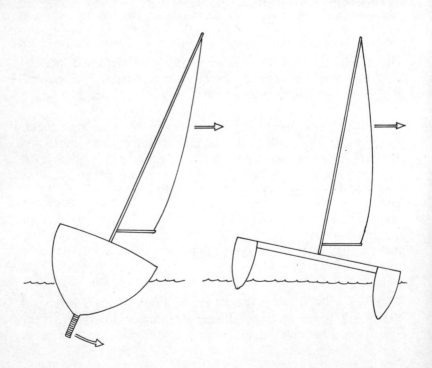

adds or subtracts large loads like a merchant ship, the stability of the boat is not going to change unless major alterations are made. However, the stability of a boat has a considerable effect upon how comfortable she will be in a seaway, and, in the case of a sailing boat, how well she will stand up to the wind under sail. It is generally known that if a sailing boat heels over rather easily when under sail, the solution lies in adding weight low down, or reducing weight high up, but it is not so obvious that if a power boat rolls quickly, the solution may be to add weight high up to give the boat an easier motion. Too much weight added high up, however, would make the boat capsize the moment she put to sea. When a boat takes on a large quantity of fuel or stores, or uses up either, the stability of the boat will be altered and this will affect how she rolls, pitches and heels to external pressures. The boat's whole handling characteristics might change, making her a better sea boat or a crank.

TRANSVERSE STABILITY

The factors that govern the transverse stability of a boat are its beam, displacement and the positions of the centres of buoyancy and gravity above the keel and their relationship with each other. We will begin by defining each of these factors:

Displacement 'W' This is the total weight of the boat, and by Archimedes' Principle, equal to the weight of water displaced by the boat.

Centre of buoyancy 'B' This is the geometrical centre of the underwater part of the boat, or to put it another way, the centre of gravity of the water displaced by the boat. The transverse and longitudinal positions of 'B' are always considered separately, and we shall only concern ourselves with the transverse. 'B' is always on the centre-line when a boat is upright, but will move from side to side as she rolls. The force of buoyancy acts vertically upwards through whatever position 'B' occupies at any one time. KB is the distance from the bottom of the keel to the centre of buoyancy.

Beam   The beam of a vessel plays a large part in its stability. The wider the boat, the greater the external force required to heel it over. Thus, a wide monohull will require less keel weight to give it the same angle of heel under a given wind than a narrow monohull; whilst multihulls have large enough effective beam to remove all need for a ballast keel to provide stability.

Centre of gravity 'G'   The centre of gravity of a boat is the point through which all the boat's weight acts vertically downwards. Its position does not move as the boat rolls. KG is the distance from the bottom of the keel to the centre of gravity.

Metacentre 'M'   This is the imaginary point on the boat's vertical centre-line, where a line drawn vertically upwards from the position of the centre of buoyancy at any time cuts the vertical centre-line. Its position hardly moves for angles of heel up to about 15 degrees and is therefore taken to be a fixed point based upon its position at lesser angles.

The righting lever 'GZ'   As a boat heels over, the downward force of G and upward force of B create a couple which tends to push a stable boat back on an even keel. Looking at the diagrams, it can be seen that provided the metacentre M is above G, the boat will be stable. If G and M are in the same position, the boat will have no righting moment, and there will be no force trying to push the boat back on to an even keel. If, however, M is below G, the boat is unstable, and as the boat heels, a force is created which is pushing the boat over even further.

The actual moment created which is working to right the boat when she has been heeled by some external force is the displacement of the boat (W) times the distance between the centre of gravity (G) and a point on the vertical line drawn down through the metacentre (M) which subtends an angle of 90 degrees to the centre of gravity. Conventionally, this point is known as 'Z'.

Finding the metacentric height (GM) by means of the inclining test   The test should be carried out in calm water, on a calm day with all lines slacked so that there is no exterior force affecting the boat. The materials required for the test are a

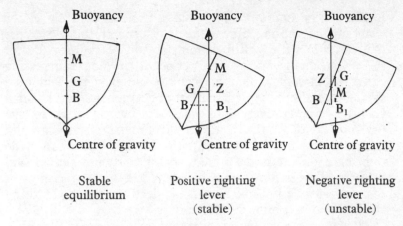

Buoyancy	Buoyancy	Buoyancy
Centre of gravity	Centre of gravity	Centre of gravity
Stable equilibrium	Positive righting lever (stable)	Negative righting lever (unstable)

weight or weights of about 1/500th of the boat's displacement, a plumb bob, and an accurate rule.

Suspend the plumb bob from a high point in the cabin down to the cabin sole, where it can point at the rule which is laid athwartships on the sole, and measure the length of the plumb line from its suspension point to the tip of the bob. Place the weight amidships and note the position of the plumb bob on the rule. Then move the weight outboard a known distance, and then re-measure the position of the plumb bob.

Make sure that if anyone else is on board at the time, they have not moved, and that when taking the measurements of the plumb bob, you are occupying exactly the same position.

The calculation to find the GM is as follows:

$$\frac{GM}{\text{Shift in boat's centre of gravity (GG)}} = \frac{\text{Length of the plumbline}}{\text{Deflection of the plumbline}}$$

But, as we know that the shift of boat's centre of gravity (GG) is equal to:

$$\frac{\text{Weight used in the test} \times \text{Distance it was moved}}{\text{Displacement of the boat}}$$

$$\text{The GM} = \frac{\text{Test weight} \times \text{Distance moved} \times \text{Length of plumbline}}{\text{Boat's displacement} \times \text{Deflection of plumbline}}$$

Rolling   The stability of a boat can be altered by either changing the righting lever or the displacement, the two factors that can affect the righting moment, and changing either of these will change the rolling period of the boat. Increasing either will increase the statical stability and make the boat more stiff. Decreasing either will make the boat more tender. In small boats it is comparatively simple to change the rolling period (the time in seconds for the boat to roll from port to starboard and back to port again, or vice versa). Move weight upwards and the righting moment is decreased, and the rolling period will increase. This is something that should be tackled with great caution, as a miscalculation could lead to the boat losing stability and becoming dangerous.

When at sea, a dangerous situation can arise when the ship's rolling period, and the apparent period of the waves are equal. This is known as synchronism, and if unchecked, can lead to the boat capsizing. One or other of the periods must be altered quickly, and the easiest way to do this is to change course either into the waves, which will reduce their period, or away from them, which will increase it. Alternatively, the boat's speed can be increased or decreased. The apparent wave period is the time, in seconds, between the passage of successive wave crests or troughs, past a fixed point on the boat.

Curves of statical stability   This is a graph of the righting moment (GZ) plotted against the angle of heel. It is required for any vessel which wishes to have a load line, but is very useful to the seaman as it tells him:

1. The range of stability. This is the number of degrees of heel for which the boat has positive stability.
2. The angle of vanishing stability, i.e. the angle of heel at which the boat ceases to have a moment pushing it back upright.
3. The maximum righting moment, and the angle at which it occurs.
4. The point of contraflexure, which is the angle of heel at which the deck edge submerges.
5. The dynamical stability. Found by multiplying the boat's displacement by the area under the curve on the graph.
6. An approximate metacentric height can be found by draw-

ing a vertical line on the graph upwards from the angle of heel of 57.3 degrees, and drawing on the tangent to the curve at its origin. Where the lines intersect is the approximate GM measured on the GZ side of the graph.

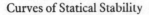

Curves of Statical Stability

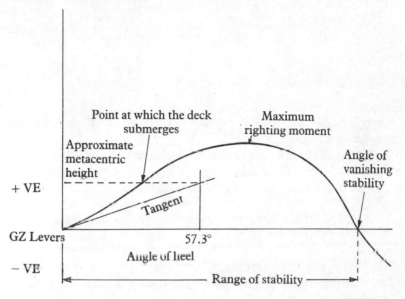

Loll When a boat is unstable in the upright position, but achieves stability at an angle of heel, she is said to loll. Loll is different to list, as the boat will have positive stability at the same angle either side of upright, whereas when a boat is listed, due to unequal stowage of stores, she will come back to the same angle of heel after being moved by wind or waves.

The usual cause of loll is flooding. A large quantity of water inside the boat will rush from side to side as the boat is heeled by wind or wave, and this moves the centre of gravity of the boat to one side, and may move it beyond the position of the centre of buoyancy. This creates a negative righting lever, which will force the boat to heel further until the centres of buoyancy and gravity are in a vertical line with each other once more. If the boat is pushed the other way, it will flop over, and the water inside will rush across to the other side, forcing the boat to heel

Loll

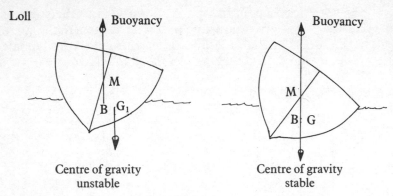

Centre of gravity
unstable

Centre of gravity
stable

until equilibrium is reached again at an equal angle of heel, but to the other side.

Loll can also be caused by the addition of weight high up in the boat, or the removal of weight low down, but whatever the cause, the boat is unstable and should be made stable as quickly as possible.

There are four basic methods of reducing loll, all of which will lower the centre of gravity of the boat:

1. Removing top weight.
2. Moving weight from high on the boat to a lower position.
3. Adding weight low down.
4. Reducing the free surface effect.

The removal of top weight is obvious, as is moving weight from a high to a low point. The only method of adding weight low down at sea is likely to be by flooding an empty tank low in the boat. This will lower the centre of gravity, but it will also lower the freeboard which might not be desirable if the boat is holed.

Free surface Water or fuel in the bilges or a half filled tank will move across the boat or the tank as it rolls from side to side. The centre of gravity of this body of liquid will similarly move from side to side. If the tank is less than half full, the liquid's movement will be greater, and the move of the centre of gravity of the fluid greater as well. Whereas if the tank is more than half full the movement is less.

Free Surface

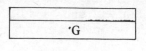 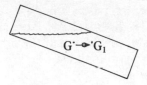

The effect of this movement of the centre of gravity of the liquid in a tank is to reduce the effective metacentric height, and therefore the righting moment, of the boat.

The loss of GM can be calculated using the formula:

$$\frac{\text{Length} \times (\text{Breadth of the tank})^3}{12 \times \text{Displacement of the boat in cubic feet}}$$

The loss of metacentric height due to free surface can be reduced by fitting longitudinal divisions to the tank, as this will reduce the movement of the liquid and, therefore, the movement of its centre of gravity. The loss of GM varies inversely as the square of the number of compartments into which the tank is subdivided longitudinally.

In general, the free surface in half filled tanks will not have a huge effect upon the stability of the boat, and, in any case, it might be inadvisable to contaminate drinking water and fuel tanks with salt water to fill them up. If the boat is holed, the crew will be concentrating on sealing the hole and pumping out the water inside as quickly as possible, and this will remove the free surface of the flooding water.

Even a partial longitudinal bulkhead will reduce the free surface effect if it prevents the liquid from moving across the tank. A barrier descending halfway down the tank in its centre line will restrict the movement of liquid if the tank is more than half full, and this will slow down the shift of its centre of gravity so that not all the liquid has moved across the tank before the boat starts to roll back, and move the liquid back the other way across the tank.

Thus, a boat starting a long voyage with full tanks can expect to lose a proportion of her righting moment as the voyage progresses and the contents of the tanks are used, through free surface in the tanks. If the boat starts the voyage in a tender state, i.e. with a small righting moment, this could be dangerous. If the boat had a large righting moment, and was stiff at the outset, the rolling of the boat should become less abrupt as the voyage progresses.

LONGITUDINAL STABILITY

In a normal yacht, there is a large reserve of longitudinal stability, and never any danger of the boat pitch poling in calm conditions. In very large seas the effect of moving weights about in the boat is going to make so little difference that it is hardly worth worrying about. The main interest in the longitudinal stability from the seaman's point of view lies in the trim of the boat and the pitching moment.

Trim   The trim of a boat is the difference between the draft at the forward perpendicular and the aft perpendicular. In each case, the perpendiculars are the points furthest forward and furthest aft of the keel before it starts to slope upwards at each end. However, this definition really applies to a boat with a straight keel, and for sailing yachts, where there is quite possibly a continuous curve from the bow to the stern, the forward perpendicular is normally level with the collision bulkhead, and the aft perpendicular at the sternpost. The keel can be ignored, the body of the boat is all that concerns the seaman.

The performance of the boat can change dramatically for quite small changes in trim, and it is well worth experimenting to see if the performance can be improved by moving weights about. Power boats will always rise at the bow when underway, but sailing boats may not necessarily do so due to the pressure of the sails and rig.

To calculate the weight required to change the trim of a boat, it is necessary to find the Centre of Flotation or the Tipping Centre which is the geometrical centre of the waterplane and the point about which the boat trims. Any weight placed a distance forward of the Tipping Centre will put the bow down by the same amount as it would put the stern down if placed the same distance aft of the Tipping Centre.

The formula to calculate the moment to change trim by 1 cm is:

$$\frac{\text{Displacement} \times \text{Longitudinal GM}}{100 \times \text{Length between Perpendiculars}}$$

The longitudinal metacentric height can be found by using the inclining test in the fore and aft line if necessary, but it would be easier to obtain the information from the designer.

In practice, it is far simpler, having found the Tipping Centre, to take a known weight and place it a known distance forward of the Tipping Centre, and have someone else in a dinghy to measure the draft forward when the weight was at the Tipping Centre and in its new position.

Pitching   A boat's pitching is governed by the waves, its waterplane shape, the weight of the hull and where that weight is located, and the weight and centre of gravity of the mast and rigging. The naval architect will always work out the pitching moment when designing the boat.

It is generally accepted that a short swift pitching period is advantageous in a sailing boat as it gives more speed. Stores and weights are stowed as near the centre as possible to reduce the period. Moving weights to the ends of the boat will increase the pitching period. Modern racing boats have 'U' rather than 'V' shaped forefoots for this reason as the 'U' shape does not sink into the water as easily. It might be preferable for a cruising boat, however, to have a longer pitching period as it is more comfortable, and weight can be put into the ends of the boat to achieve this.

In power boats, especially slow to medium speed displacement craft, an easy pitching motion is desirable, and weights can be moved from the middle to the ends to give this. Excessive weights in the ends, however, could cause the boat to hog, i.e. the ends to drop in relation to the middle of the boat.

Simpson's Rules   Simpson's Rules provide an accurate method of finding the area of a waterplane, assuming the curves around the area are parabolic. There are three rules, and in each case, the waterplane is divided down its middle from the bow to the stern, and then subdivided into sections from forward to aft. The rule chosen for a particular waterplane depends upon the number of intervals between athwartship measurements, the ordinates.

Simpson's first rule   This is used when the number of intervals is divisible by 2, and the interval is the same between ordinates. Measure off the distance from the centre-line to the outside curve for each ordinate. Starting from one end of the waterplane, multiply each ordinate in sequence by 1, then 4 then 1. If the number of intervals was four, then the five ordinates would be multiplied by 1.4.2.4.1. Add together all these products and multiply them by one third of the common interval. The formula for the figure would be:

Area = ⅓l × (x + 4x1 + 2x2 + 4x3 + 2x4 + 4x5 + x6)

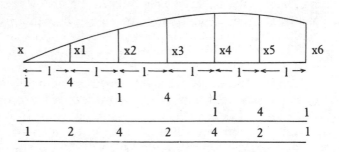

Simpson's second rule   The second rule is used in exactly the same way as the first except that the number of intervals is divisible by 3. The multipliers in the second rule are 1.3.3.1.

Area = ⅜l × (x + 3x1 + 3x2 + 2x3 + 3x4 + 3x5 + x6)

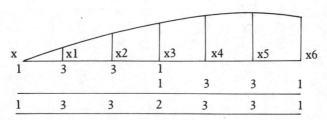

Simpson's third rule The third rule is used when the area between two adjacent ordinates is required. The multipliers are 5.8.-1. The formula for the above figure would be:

Area = ¹⁄₁₂l × (5x + 8x1 − x2)

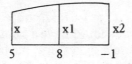

Where the number of intervals is not divisible by either 2 or 3, then the waterplane would have to be divided up into two parts that would fit the rules, and then the two parts added together.

Volumes may also be calculated using Simpson's Rules. First it is necessary to calculate a series of waterplanes at equal intervals, or a series of vertical cross sections. Then apply the appropriate rule to the series of areas of waterplane or cross section. To calculate the displacement of a boat, it is then only necessary to convert the volume into cubic metres and multiply by the density of the water. This would give the displacement in metric tonnes.

11   MAINTENANCE

No seaman would put to sea in an unsound boat, and anyone who goes out in a boat should have a knowledge of its construction, so that if it becomes necessary, they can carry out essential repairs. These repairs may have to be made at sea or in a port where there are no facilities available.

HULLS

A boat's hull may be constructed from a wide range of materials and differing techniques. The main ones, and how to effect repairs, are described below.

Wood
Carvel, or plank on plank   This is the most common method of planked construction where each plank butts onto its neigh-

Carvel or Plank on Plank

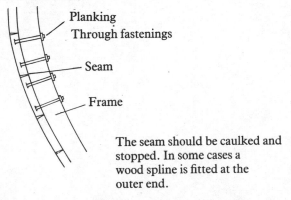

Planking
Through fastenings

Seam

Frame

The seam should be caulked and stopped. In some cases a wood spline is fitted at the outer end.

In many cases the holes in the planking for the through bolts will have dowels fitted into them.

bour. The system depends upon tight caulking for its water-tightness.

All wood hulls should have regular inspections for rot or damage, and this is usually done when the boat is hauled out for its annual refit.

The most likely problem at sea is the caulking coming loose or impact damage. Caulking is dealt with later, but repairs to impact damage usually involve nailing a patch over the damage until the boat gets to port. There the damage can be properly assessed and planking replaced if necessary. Sections of plank should be replaced from points midway between frames, and then an internal doubler screwed or bolted over the butt where the ends of the planks join.

Clinker A clinker hull depends for watertightness upon its copper rivets, and is affected by the dryness of its timber. If the boat is left ashore for a long time, or is in a hot climate and not regularly washed down, the timber will shrink, which loosens the rivets, allowing in the sea. The solution is to keep the hull well wetted; before re-launching after a long period ashore, fill the bilges with water so that the planks can swell before the boat goes into water. Even then, the hull will let in a little water for a few days whilst the wood swells.

An ideal, but expensive, long-term solution to the problem of constantly expanding and contracting hull strakes is to clean down the hull to bare wood and then coat the hull with raw linseed oil. Keep coating the hull, preferably in dry conditions,

Clinker

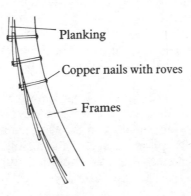

Planking

Copper nails with roves

Frames

until the wood will absorb no more. Then paint or varnish the hull. The linseed oil replaces the moisture in the timber and does not evaporate so the wood does not shrink as much.

When a clinker hull is damaged or holed, the damaged timber has to be removed. This involves removing carefully the rivets either side so as not to bruise or damage the wood in the strakes to be retained. Square off either side of the damaged area, and cut out a piece of timber that exactly fits the gap. Place the new piece of timber in position and carefully drill it so that the rivet holes align exactly with the existing holes in the strakes above and below and then insert and hammer home the new rivets. At the butts between the new piece of timber and the old, it is usual to put a butt piece inside the hull and rivet it into place. This helps to provide longitudinal strength in the damaged strake and make the butt joint more watertight.

In small clinker boats such as dinghies, where the boat is often hauled ashore, the landings on the strakes become damaged. To prevent this, fillets are often fitted over the landings. Where the boat is constantly hauled over an abrasive surface such as shingle, it is worth doubling the planking from the keel to the turn of the bilge over the centre part of the hull.

Cold moulded   Cold moulded hulls are made of a series of thin veneers glued together. The veneers are laid at an angle to each other, and the final outer layer is laid horizontally to give the impression of a planked yacht. With modern glues the veneers are very firmly fixed together and cannot move independently even if one layer becomes wet and its neighbour remains dry. Although a cold moulded hull is often very attractive when varnished, if the boat is going to a hot climate it is best to paint the topsides white, as this reflects the heat and prevents the outer veneer losing too much moisture which will lead to shrinking and, possibly, splitting of the planks. If the hull is to remain varnished then it will need to be washed over at least daily.

Some cold moulded hulls have splines, small narrow strips of wood, glued in between the outer veneer strakes. These are designed to be sacrificial in so far as the shrinking planks will unglue from the splines, instead of splitting from each other.

The maintenance of a cold moulded hull is similar to any other wooden hull. If the outer layer of planking can be well oiled, with raw linseed oil in dry conditions, before being varnished, the chances of the wood drying sufficiently to split are greatly reduced. Nevertheless, it is still advisable to paint the topsides for hot climates. When inspecting the hull, look for signs of dampness, usually shown by a discolouring of the timber, and rub back down to the bare wood. To remove the stains, coat the offending area with oxalic acid as this will clean the timber and enhance its natural colour. Then oil the area and re-varnish. If the hull is splined, and the splines are showing signs of cracking, remove the spline, clean out its channel and glue in a new one.

If the hull has been varnished, it will be necessary every two or three years to remove all the varnish and rub down to bare wood. When the wood is clean, coat with oxalic acid and then wash it clean again after a couple of hours. Then apply as many coats of raw linseed oil as the timber will take. The oil will darken the wood but it is worth it.

Where a cold moulded boat has received damage, it may be possible, if the damae is only on the surface, to remove just the outer layer of veneer and glue in a new piece. If the hull is varnished, care should be taken to match up the new timber with the existing timber so that the repaired area does not stand out when the job is finished. If the damage is a hole through the hull, then the veneers are going to have to be stripped away for a considerable area around the hole, so that a good overlap, and strong join to the existing hull can be achieved. Starting from the outside, where the greatest stripping of existing veneers is necessary, each layer will have less removed until one comes to the innermost skin which will just require squaring off before a new piece is fitted. Each layer should be well glued and stapled onto the previous layer, and when the glue has hardened, the staples removed, and the surface cleaned and faired before glueing in the next layer.

Repairs to a cold moulded boat require more time and a fair amount of skill. If the time is not available, a patch of glass fibre with epoxy glue will make an effective, if unsightly, temporary repair.

Diagonal The only real difference between a diagonal hull and a cold moulded hull is the way the layers of planking are secured to each other. Usually diagonal hulls have their layers of wood riveted or screwed together. Between each layer of timber is placed a membrane of canvas coated with white lead or paint to provide greater watertightness.

There is a trend towards using kevlar or glass cloth and epoxy as the membrane between layers of timber. The epoxy acts as a very strong bind between the layers, and this is a very strong and light method of construction.

Maintenance of diagonally built hulls is the same as for cold moulded hulls except that sometimes where the layers of planking are riveted together, it is necessary to caulk in between the strips of planking. The area to double check each time the boat is out of the water is the butts of the planking, particularly at the keel or at the chines, as this is where water can most easily get into the timber and lead to rot. Rivets on a diagonal hull should be checked, and tightened as necessary using the same method as for clinker hulls.

The timber   A glance at a hull will not always tell you the true state of the wood, and it is worth scraping back the paint to the bare wood to check. The wood should be firm, and digging a fingernail into it will tell you whether it is in good condition or not. A great deal depends upon the timber used in the boat's construction. Pine is soft in its natural state, whereas mahogany and teak are hard to the touch.

Be on the lookout for marine borers, such as gribble, and teredo worm. Their entry holes are usually quite small, but they will move along inside the planking for considerable distances, and once they are in the timber, they are hard to kill. A change of mooring from salt to fresh water is one simple way of killing them, and if this is not possible, scrape all the wood down to a bare surface and apply a strong and pungent wood preservative, preferably from inside as well as outside.

If the hull planking, keel stem or stern is soft, or shows signs of considerable boring, the damaged area is best removed and replaced.

Wooden boats going to the tropics where teredo is prevalent should seriously consider sheathing as a protection against this voracious pest. A simple form of sheathing is marine plywood, as the borers do not like the glue used in its manufacture. Glassfibre, epoxy and glass cloth will all do the job. Copper sheathing was the old method and it is very effective. Paint on its own will last a while as protection, but even the most ferocious anti-fouling can be penetrated by the teredo.

Fastenings Fastenings are often hidden behind dowels, but it is advisable to check one or two in each plank for condition. Ferrous metal fastenings are usually easy to check, the most obvious sign that they need to be renewed being the presence of rust. Brass and copper are not so easy. They may look perfectly healthy on the outside, but if you take one out you may find it has wasted away. If this is the case you may have a major renewing problem on your hands.

When putting in fastenings, ferrous fastenings should be well bedded down with white lead; brass and copper should be rubbed over with beeswax before being inserted.

When the fastenings have been re-secured, re-glue the dowels over them again, and when the glue has hardened, clean off the surplus dowel with a chisel, rub down, fill, and paint.

Steel The main disadvantage with steel is that when bared it is quickly attacked by salt water, and rusts. The purpose of paint is to seal off the surface of the steel to keep oxygen away from the bare metal and prevent rust being able to form. Painting of a steel hull has to be carried out very carefully and thoroughly, to ensure that no air can reach the hull's surface. Rust can spread very quickly, and it is important to treat it as soon as it is noticed, as it eats into the metal of the hull, reducing its thickness and its strength. Once a patch of rust appears on the hull it must be attacked as soon as possible by cleaning the paint and rust off the area affected, wire brushing it until nothing but clean metal is visible, and then applying a metal primer immediately. If the rust appears through the hull where the paint is quite thick, and is otherwise looking in good condition, chip off the paint around the rust mark and then chamfer down the edge of the paint around the patch before wire brushing. It is important to remove the paint back to good metal, do not trim too close around the rust patch itself as this will not give sufficient surface of metal for the paint to adhere to.

If the hull has a lot of rust patches, the time may have come to clean the whole hull down to bare metal and build up a complete new layer of protective covering. The old fashioned method of doing this is to scrape or chip the old paint and rust off and then wire brush the surface clean before applying primer. This is a long and laborious task, and it is far quicker, provided one is careful, to burn off the old paint using a blow lamp or gas torch. The flame should not be allowed to burn the paint black, but only soften it so that it will scrape off easily. If the paint is burned it is much harder to remove. The flame should be kept moving slowly and continuously over the surface, and never allowed to dwell on one spot, as this will overheat that area and possibly burn any paint or fitments on the other side of the surface. When all the paint has been burned off, any rust scale should be chipped off and then the whole surface wire brushed before applying a primer. The cleaned and wire brushed bare metal should be painted immediately, as the moment the bare metal is exposed it commences to oxidise.

The easiest method of cleaning off a metal surface, paint, rust and all, is to sand-blast it. This is a messy business, as sand and grit gets everywhere, so put a screen round the boat before starting and obtain a face mask and goggles to protect the eyes and mouth. Sand-blasting grit is not cheap, and an advantage of having a screen about the job is that the grit can be re-used thus saving costs. Once the hull has been cleaned, clean up the sand, and paint immediately. Use a zinc primer, or red lead as a base coat. Alternatively, lead shot-blast the cleaned hull, and then apply a coat of epoxy paint.

When the surface has been given two good coats of primer, apply two of undercoat, and then rub down with wet and dry sandpaper before applying top coat.

When checking over a steel hull look out for signs of pitting in the metal surface. This indicates either past rust or electrolysis. If the pitting is deep and widespread, it will be necessary to renew the plates affected. Alternatively they can be doubled which means welding a new plate over the badly pitted one. Before painting the new plate remove the mill scale from it. If you suspect electrolysis as being the cause of the metal wastage, check the anodes. If they have not dissolved at all they are not working and need to be wired up properly.

Pay particular attention to all fastenings in the hull and any reinforcing straps. It is around these that water can collect and is very difficult to dislodge. If any fastenings or skin fittings are of non-ferrous metals such as bronze, it is best to remove them and replace with steel. Ferrous and non-ferrous metals together only require water to act as an electrolyte, and they start an electric current between them.

Aluminium Aluminium is a light, strong and easily worked metal that would be the ideal building material except that when exposed to air it oxidises (corrodes). To prevent oxidisation the surface must be protected in such a way that it is sealed off from the air or water, and this protection must be complete.

On small sections of aluminium, such as spars, the most effective treatment is anodising. This is an electrolytic process, and the treatment is limited by the size of the baths to take the aluminium section. Anodising does not provide a protective layer like paint, it provides a protective layer within the surface of the metal, and to be effective, must penetrate to a depth of 25 microns.

On large sections such as a hull, the aluminium must be protected with paint. New aluminium plate does not provide a good surface for paint, and the surface must be either etched with acid, or abrased mechanically. Mechanical abrasion can be achieved by sandpaper, or by vibration sanding. Once the surface has been abraded it should be cleaned off to remove aluminium dust. The best method is a good scrub and rinse with hot water. Since oxidisation will commence immediately, the surface should be painted as soon as it is dry. The first coat of paint should be a special etch primer, but if the surface has been properly abraded, a zinc chromate paint can be used. The next coat should be a two-part epoxy zinc chromate, after which a polyurethane finishing coat can be applied. Ideally, spray on two coats of the finishing polyurethane paint.

In the event of damage or scratches, the affected area must be cleaned off, with an abrasive if necessary, cleaned with a special solvent, and repainted as quickly as possible.

Welding of aluminium, by far the most common method of joining, weakens the adjacent metal to about half its original strength. The only way to avoid this is by heat treatment which is not practical with a large structure.

Electrolytic action is set up between aluminium and stainless steel when oxygen is excluded. Whenever it is necessary to secure stainless steel fittings to aluminium, a barrier layer of zinc chromate paste should be used, and it is advisable to put a barrier of some inert material between all metal fittings and an aluminium surface. Where stainless steel bolts have to be used as opposed to an alloy or monel, the bolts should be coated with paste to reduce the surfaces in contact.

Glassfibre   Glass reinforced plastic (GRP) has been in use for some time now as a boat building material, and has the advantages of lightness for strength, elasticity, and the hull being moulded in one piece.

Various types of resin are used with a variety of combinations of lay-up. The resin on its own, when set off by the addition of a catalyst, is very hard and brittle and would make a most unsatisfactory hull material. Likewise glass, but when spun into very fine threads, it can be bent into almost any shape.

Glass for boatbuilding comes in two basic forms – woven rovings and chop strand mat. Glass cloth, which is what woven rovings really is, is a very strong and pliable material. Chop strand mat provides little strength on its own, but acts as a binding fibre for the resin.

GRP hulls are usually made up by a combination of layers of woven rovings and chop strand mat, each layer being applied onto a coat of resin, and then well 'wetted' in place with more resin either with a brush or a roller so that no voids exist within the layers of glass.

There are two basic types of GRP hulls, those constructed of solid GRP, and those made up on the sandwich principle with a layer of foam between two thinner layers of GRP. The method of construction varies. Usually hulls are laid up in a highly polished female mould, which is painted with a releasing agent and then has a gelcoat, a pigmented resin, painted on to it. This gelcoat is the outside surface of the hull, the equivalent of paint on a wood or steel hull. The gelcoat should be thick enough to take small scratches without going through to the glassfibre beneath. Laid over the gelcoat is a layer of fine chop strand mat, and then, usually, a layer or two of normal chop strand before a layer of woven rovings. The reason for the chop strand mat is that it provides a better, more even backing for the gelcoat. Where there are large flat panels, such as on decks, the lay-up is quite often supported by end-grain balsa, or sometimes foam.

The foam sandwich method can be used in a mould, or laid up on top of a male mould. If it is laid up on a male mould, the surface needs a great deal more work on it, rubbing down and polishing to get a surface as good as is usual from a female mould. However female moulds are very expensive to build, and are only worthwhile when a large number of similar hulls are wanted. For a one-off boat, the male mould and sandwich method is by far the cheapest method.

Glassfibre hulls should be cleaned, polished and waxed annually if the initial highly polished surface is to be maintained. Marks and scratches can be polished out with fine grinding paste, but must be waxed over immediately, as the paste removes the sealed surface and will allow the gelcoat to absorb water or dirt. Never allow a GRP hull to be cleaned by using any form of scouring liquid, as this will remove the protective wax. If a boat has been at sea for a time, the salt water will have dried out and left salt crystals on the hull and all exposed surfaces which will abrade the gelcoat, and give the boat a dull look. Washing the whole boat down with fresh water will get rid of the salt. Glassfibre hulls, however well they are made, will absorb water if they are not sealed by paint or waxed gelcoat. Very few GRP boats have anything on the inside surface of the hull, and water that gets into the bilge will slowly work its way into the material, and upwards by capillary action. In time this water can add quite a lot of weight to a hull, and the only way to lose it is to warm up the whole boat. Bear in mind that salt is deliquescent, and the salt left in the fibres will soon absorb moisture from the atmosphere and quickly restore the extra weight again. The only way to keep the water out for a while is to wash the inside down with fresh water and remove the salt first before drying the boat out.

Scratch repairs   When a deeper scratch has to be repaired, clean out the scratch with fresh water and wipe over with acetone. When the area to be repaired is dry, mix up some gelcoat, making sure to match exactly the colour used on the hull, and then paint it into the scratch and put tape, such as masking tape, over it. This holds the gelcoat in place whilst it goes off. Once the gelcoat has hardened it can be rubbed down with wet and dry paper or rubbing paste, until the patch is indistinguishable from the original gelcoat around it; then wax polish the whole area.

Penetration   When the hull has been pierced by collision or a severe knock, the damaged area should be cut away and ground down at the edges to provide a taper for the new resin and glass fibre to adhere to. If the hole is large, it may be necessary to place a piece of highly waxed and polished material over the hole to provide a mould against which the new GRP can be laid. If small, there may be sufficient material around to act as a base. Build up GRP in layers over the hole, allowing each layer to go off before applying the succeeding one. If GRP is laid up too heavily, it will exotherm, i.e. heat up itself, and this weakens the lay-up. Bring the layers up to surface and then grind down to line up with the existing hull. Then apply gelcoat over the repair and, when dry, rub this down so that it is flush with the existing hull; then polish and wax the outside surface. Ensure that there is a good overlap and bond with the existing hull, and clean off the hull around the hole with acetone before starting the repair.

Voids Voids are small air gaps in the lay-up, in the gelcoat layer or between the gelcoat and the lay-up. The first thing to do if there is a suspicion of a void is tap the hull with the handle of a screwdriver, the sound is lighter if a void exists, and establish the exact position and size of the void. Mark the position with a crayon. Take a small drill and drill carefully through the hull into the void. Then inject resin mixed with catalyst into the void until it is filled. Cover the hole with a piece of tape and leave it to harden. The resin can be injected using a hypodermic syringe.

If the void is a deep one, or spread over a large area, it may be necessary to cut the hull back to the void and build it up with chop strand mat and resin and finally with gelcoat.

When voids are found they should be filled as soon as possible as the void is a point of weakness.

Osmosis This shows as small bubbles or blisters in the gelcoat. It is usually to be found below or near the waterline, and if not treated can eventually affect the structural strength of the hull. One way of avoiding osmosis is to paint a new glassfibre hull with two-pack polyurethane paint before applying the usual underwater protective paints. It may be a little extra weight, but polyurethane paint will prevent the hull absorbing any moisture and save weight that way in the long run.

There are various theories as to the cause, one being that an orthophalic gelcoat allows moisture to pass through more easily than through the laminating resin. This may be so, and certainly since the introduction of isophalic gelcoats as opposed to orthophalic, osmosis has been less prevalent.

Various methods of treatment are suggested, from removing all the existing gelcoat by sand-blasting or the use of heat and a scraper, (both of which methods require considerable care and expertise), to mechanically abrading the affected area and then painting with two-pack epoxy paint. Unless a boatyard is available with personnel experienced with removing gelcoat, the best method for the sailor is mechanical abrasion.

Rub down the gelcoat in particular areas where there are blisters, and if wet and dry abrasive paper is used, wash off the area and allow to dry. One method of discovering whether the area is dry is to tape a square of perspex onto the hull and watch to see if condensation forms underneath. If it does, the surface is still damp. When the surface is dry apply two-pack polyurethane paint carefully. Do not use the paint in very cold conditions as it will go on too thick and run, which will allow moisture into the hull lay-up.

Painting gelcoat When the gelcoat becomes badly scuffed or, after a few years, if the gelcoat topsides have not been polished and waxed regularly, the colour begins to fade; white gelcoat goes slightly cream in colour. There is currently no method of rejuvenating gelcoat colours, so the time has come to either have the hull re-sprayed with gelcoat or painted with two-pot polyurethane paint. If it is decided to re-spray with gelcoat, it is best to have it done professionally. When it is decided to paint the hull, the existing gelcoat must be rubbed down to give a good adhesive surface, and then either an epoxide or solvent etch primer applied. The length of time the primer is left is critical; check the instructions on the paint tin, but typically the top coat should be applied after not less than six hours and not more than 24 hours.

Two-pot polyurethane paint provides a very hard surface. If more than one coat is to be applied, it should be applied within 24 hours of the first. The first coat should be well rubbed down first to provide a smoother surface. Once the top coat has been applied and has hardened, it can be burnished. A well polished painted GRP hull is difficult to distinguish from a gelcoated hull, and has the advantage that the paint is impervious to water whereas gelcoat, if not waxed, is very slightly absorbent.

FERROCEMENT

The use of ferrocement as a boatbuilding material is not new, and provided the boat has been well built, the material has some considerable advantages. It is cheap, and the materials are readily available, the only skill required is that of plasterers, to make sure the mortar is applied properly and to obtain a good finish.

The basic principle of ferrocement boatbuilding is a framework made of high tensile steel rods, and to this frame is attached a mesh made of ½ to ¾ inch square pattern, and up to eight layers, depending upon the size of the final craft and the thickness of the hull required. A mixture of two sand to one of good quality Portland cement is used to plaster the boat, and a good plasticiser should be added to the mix. Ideally, the boat should be plastered in one continuous operation. Curing of the cement takes place over a period of seven to fourteen days, and the structure must not be allowed to dry out during this time. A spray system, which will deposit a fine mist over the entire surface is ideal, and should be started as soon as the surface of the cement is dry enough to take it. Portland cement likes a high temperature, and all cement is useless if the temperature during building falls to freezing point. Some recent work has shown that the use of steam for curing reduces the normal shrinkage of cement by 50 per cent, and greatly speeds the curing process.

One major advantage of ferrocement as a boatbuilding material is its resistance to damage and the ease with which repairs can be made. A ferrocement hull is remarkably resilient, and when hit hard, shatters only in the immediate vicinity of the blow. Once the reinforcing has been tidied up, the resulting hole can be easily plastered with cement again.

Once a hull is completed and cured, it can be painted with an epoxy resin coating which provides a good seal against water penetration, and also binds in any small slightly loose particles of sand. Fuel and water tanks should also be painted, as should the bilges, particularly in the engine area. Oils have a habit of seeping through cement.

Where rust marks show through the cement surface, the mesh is probably too close to the surface. Lightly drill out round the area, and push the mesh back into the void created, holding it in place with an epoxy filler which is also used to fill the void and provide a fair finished surface.

THROUGH HULL FITTINGS

An average boat may have as many as seven hull openings below the waterline, and each should be treated as if it is a potential leak. The engine will require a cooling water inlet and an exhaust which, even though it lies just above the waterline, should have a stopcock. The WC requires an inlet and outlet valve and a sink may require a drainage opening. The log transducer will require its own opening, as may the echo-sounder (although on some GRP boats it is possible to pass the signal through the hull). If the boat is large and has more WCs and perhaps uses salt water for washing or cooking, the number of openings becomes almost alarming.

There is one basic rule for all openings through the hull below or near the waterline; all should be fitted with a valve or stopcock known as a seacock, so that they can be closed if the pipe they connect to starts to leak. Any through hull openings close above the waterline should also be fitted with seacocks as boats heel over at sea, or if left unattended for some time, can take in water which will lower the waterline. This valve should be attached directly to the hull fitting and not connected to it by a piece of pipe. The reason for this precaution is obvious, as if any of the pipework inside the boat, or any of the equipment connected to the pipework, develops a leak, the boat can quickly fill with water. Apart from this emergency use of the valves, they also allow routine maintenance to equipment to be carried out without having to haul the boat out of the water. Never accept a non-return valve on its own as a substitute for a good shut-off valve; non-return valves have been known to fail. The only exceptions to this rule are those openings that allow access for instruments such as the log and echo-sounding transducers, where a stopcock cannot be fitted. However these openings are not attached to anything else that can leak, and are usually plugged by the transducer. Where possible, however, a cap that can be screwed on to the hull opening should be kept readily accessible.

Types of seacocks

Gate valves A simple valve which operates like a bathroom tap. You screw it down, and the gate closes the opening. The problem with these valves is that their threads can be corroded by electrolytic action, and then they are impossible to close. They can also give the impression that they are closed, when in fact something is jammed inside, and water can still pass through.

90-degree shut-off valve This valve, which usually has a tapered spigot, is the best type of seacock as you know whether it has closed properly, because if not, the handle will not turn fully. Over a period of time, the spigot may wear, in which case the valve will not close properly; however, signs of wear should show when making the annual check. If wear is observed, put some grinding compound in the valve and re-grind the taper, or fit a new valve.

Another type of 90-degree valve has a ball inside, drilled through so that water can pass through and, when turned through 90 degrees, the blank faces of the ball seal the valve. These valves seem to work quite efficiently.

Materials for hull valves A good quality bronze is the ideal material for most hull openings. It does not rust, and provided it is kept well greased, should give years of useful life. They should be stripped at each haul-out, cleaned and re-greased. Always check that the bronze itself is not being de-zinkified by electrolytic action, which will occur if the boat's cathodic protection is not working properly. The signs to look for are a reddening of the surface of the material. Verdigris, a greenish encrustation, is not particularly harmful, but should be cleaned away as it can spread and block the spindle.

When bronze or brass fittings are put on an aluminium hull, they should be insulated from the hull by a thin rubber gasket well coated with a sealant. Check the fastenings at frequent intervals, and the holes for these fastenings through the hull to make sure the aluminium is not corroding.

Steel fittings suffer from attacks of rust which will, in time, mean that a replacement is necessary. Cast iron is much less subject to rust, but is more brittle. Stainless steel is occasionally seen for hull fittings, but it can suffer from electrolytic action, and I have known it crumble away in less than six months.

Fittings from the plastic family would seem to be an ideal choice for any below-water use, but many of them harden and become brittle in time. Their use should be restricted to lightweight purposes, such as small log and echo-sounder transducers, and they should never be used where it is necessary to fit a valve or stop cock.

Where fittings are bolted to the hull that might be vulnerable to damage or fade away, as with a sacrificial anode, the bolts used to secure them should be secured to the boat, and then the fitting attached. This prevents the bolt coming loose and falling out of its hole when the fitting is removed.

Most race rules now require racing boats to carry wood plugs to fit all below-water hull openings. This is a good rule, and should be followed by all boats whether racing or cruising. Before I went around the world, I plugged all *Suhaili*'s hull openings and turned off all the valves, as it gave me one thing less to worry about. For those worried about sealing off the WC, do as I did, and take a bucket.

STERN GEAR

Almost inevitably, with the wear it receives, the stern gland and propeller shaft will need to be examined and tightened. The best way of checking to detect wear is to push the propeller from side to side and look for movement of the shaft at the stern gland. If it is slight, re-packing the glands will probably be sufficient, if it is more than 1/16th of an inch, however, the shaft should be withdrawn and checked, and the gland re-packed. If a cutlass-type bearing is fitted, renew the inserts.

A great deal depends upon where the boat has been operating. If it has been in muddy waters, more wear can be expected on the glands, and inspections should be made more frequently, because the sediments in the water will cause more abrasion.

Always check the propeller for de-zincifying. It shows in a coppery covered surface to the propeller, and small craters in the surface. The cause is electrolysis and indicates that the anodes have not been working properly (if the anodes have not been reduced they are certainly not doing their job). Check the wiring of the anodes. They should be connected to the engine and the shaft log. The propeller shaft should be connected to the engine, and if a flexible coupling is fitted, a wire should connect the tail shaft to the other side of the coupling.

Finally, make sure that the grease injector is clean, and not gummed up with old hardened grease, or if a cutlass type bearing is fitted, that the water supply to the bearing is working.

KEEL

If the keel bolts are not fully watertight, a certain amount of flexing will be noticeable where the keel joins the hull; it usually shows as cracks in the filler at the join. Chock the keel so that it is pressed as tight as possible to the boat, and then tighten the keel bolts, putting plenty of weight on the spanner. If there are rust marks around the join, then the time has come to undo the keel bolts and check them. If they have surface rust on them, this should be wire brushed and primed. If the rust has formed into scales it must be chipped off and then the bolts wire brushed and primed. If the diameter of the bolts has been reduced by rust by 10 per cent or more, seek advice on whether they should be renewed. A lot will depend upon how many bolts there are and how thick they were to start with.

If the join looks all right, but the keel has been in place for some time, it would be a wise precaution to draw one of the bolts just to make sure it is in good condition. Alternatively, have the keel bolts X-rayed.

If the keel has been removed, before offering it up, wire brush and prime the top surface. Try to get at least three coats of paint on the surface, and let them dry properly. Put plenty of sealant on the top surface of the keel and around the keel bolts. White lead is as good as anything, but there are many other good sealing compositions. If possible some form of gasket, such as canvas, should be put in between the keel and the hull, and this should be well soaked with a scalant, white lead or even paint.

Any rust marks on the keel itself should be cleaned down to bare metal, wirebrushed and primed. Build up several coats of good hard paint before anti-fouling.

RUDDER AND STEERING

There are many different designs of rudders, but they are all dependent upon their hinging device and so this is what should be checked first. Most rudders will have some form of well tried gudgeon and pintle system. Check that there is a good sacrificial washer between these bearings as they should not be allowed to wear against each other. The bearings should be checked for wear. If they are metal on metal, it may be necessary to rebush them.

There should be no movement in a rudder's bearing, and the rudder should turn smoothly but firmly between its stops, which should prevent it from turning more than 32–35 degrees either side of amidships.

Examine all fastenings on gudgeons and pintles, and replace or tighten them if necessary. Make sure that all metal parts are well painted before applying anti-fouling.

On all rudder stocks, the steering will be controlled by a tiller bolted to the stock. In some cases the tiller arm is the method used for steering, in which case everything will be visible and easily checked. Where the tiller is connected to some form of transmission system, be it wires, rods, hydraulic, or gears, the tiller should be a snug fit on the rudder head and the retaining bolt screwed up tight. Clean off any rust or corrosion and paint or grease the tiller.

With wire transmission systems, check the wires for any snags which indicate chafe, or rust. Wires can become quite

Rudder and Tiller

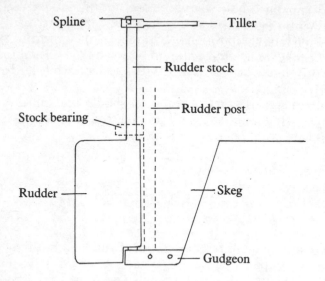

Spline — Tiller

Rudder stock

Rudder post

Stock bearing

Rudder — Skeg

Gudgeon

The tiller connects to the top of the rudder post, usually by means of a splined joint. The steering system will connect to the tiller arm, whether it be an hydraulic ram, rods, wires or chains. Most yachts have an emergency system that connects directly to the top of the rudder post.

rusty before they start to lose strength but then they lose strength fast. If there are any signs of wear or age, replace the wires with new, and, even if they are stainless, grease the wires. For preference do not use stainless steel wires for the steering as stainless steel can work harden. Far better to use galvanised flexible steel wire, and soak the wire in a tallow and white lead mix or boiled linseed oil. A wire system should have the wires led through protective pipes between turning points so that nothing can get tangled with them. At all turning points there should be a pulley, and the sheaves should be kept well oiled and free running. The wires will usually connect to a chain which runs on a sprocket on the steering wheel axle. This chain should be kept clean and well greased.

Rod systems are slightly less susceptible to wear and corrosion than wire systems. However, the rods will be bolted on to couplings and right-angle gears, and these bolts can work loose and jam the whole system. Tighten them and put a loctite washer on each. All the couplings should be kept well greased and the rods should be greased or painted. All gear boxes have some form of lubrication within them and this should be kept topped up.

Hydraulic systems have the advantage of a simple transmission system, but the pipes and their joins have to be regularly inspected. The most obvious signal that something is wrong with a hydraulic system is finding that the hydraulic oil reservoir level is dropping, or finding hydraulic oil on any part of the system. Usually this can be traced to a loose union which just needs tightening a little, never too much. The hydraulic rams must be kept clean. There is a small seal at the end of the ram cylinder which prevents fluid coming out of the cylinder when the ram moves. If the ram gets dirt on it, this dirt can damage the seal. Hydraulic systems must only be filled with clean hydraulic oil, and kept filled. The most usual cause of any difficulty is air in the system, and the best way to get rid of this is to turn the wheel from one side to the other and hold it hard over. A newly installed system will take a while to clear the small air bubbles, but the more it is used the better. Many hydraulic systems will creep a little, so do not be concerned if the wheel seems to move away from centre, even though the rudder is amidships. Avoid putting a mark on the wheel, though, as it will cause confusion, and it is worthwhile to fit some form of helm indicator.

CARE OF DECKS

Decks, of whatever material, should always be kept clean and free of oil or grease. Any rubbish left on the deck will get trodden in and cause damage to the surface. Anyone wearing yachting boots or shoes with a heavy gripping sole should clean them before stepping on board as grit can become wedged in the sole. Hard leather-soled shoes should only be worn on a painted steel deck, and it is customary to remove shoes of this sort before boarding.

The old fashioned custom of washing the decks every morning when the crew first turned to, became almost a ritual, but the early morning is the time to clean the decks as the morning dew lifts dust and dirt and makes it easier to wash overside.

Glassfibre decks The surface of glassfibre decks is highly polished when new from a mould, but this surface is fragile. Dust, grit and salt crystals, when trodden on the deck will abrade the surface. The decks then lose their shine and also the glassfibre becomes slightly porous. Glassfibre decks should be washed off with fresh water whenever dirt has gathered, or after a voyage when salt left on the deck will crystallise. If the dirt is difficult to move, as when the deck has been given a non-slip surface, use a liquid soap and a soft scrubber to clean it away. In the case of sticky substances a solvent will have to be used. On no account should a glassfibre deck be cleaned or scrubbed with an abrasive scouring powder such as Vim or Ajax, as these will remove the protective surface and the deck quickly becomes dull.

Steel decks Metal and salt water are not designed for each other as salt is very corrosive. The decks should be kept well protected by paint, and where rust appears, the offending patch should be wire brushed and then repainted, preferably on a hot dry day, so that moisture in the pores of the steel has evaporated. If rust patches are not treated immediately they will spread quickly. Although the rust will rise to a thickness of four times the plate before the plate is completely eroded, once rust has got a hold it will reappear more easily as moisture gets trapped in the minute holes in the metal. Any object that might penetrate the protective skin of paint should be removed from the deck, and if heavy items are being moved about, put wood runners beneath them. It does not hurt to wash steel decks down with fresh water when possible as although fresh water will cause rust, it is nothing like as corrosive as salt water.

Wood decks Nothing sets a boat off as well as clean wooden laid decks and they require only a little effort to achieve. Regular washing with a stiff broom and a detergent will keep the decks clean and smart. If the decks are of oak, use salt water for washing as it bleaches out the wood to give a white finish, whereas fresh water darkens the wood. With teak decks it does not matter so much except that the surface layer of the teak does not look so attractive when bleached by salt water, as after a long voyage.

Holystoning decks should only be done when the decks have got into a very bad state, and there is no other way to get back a clean even surface, as it wears the wood down. The best stone to use is a soft sandstone. Wet the deck and sprinkle sand over it. Then rub the stone up and down the deck. To obtain the best effect a slurry should form of sand, water and some of the stone. When finished, wash down the deck with water to get rid of the sand.

To remove stains from a wood deck, cover the affected parts with a mixture of lime and water and leave it to dry. The lime leeches out oil stains after a while.

Only when the deck timbers are old should a laid deck be painted and the only reason for painting a deck is to make it watertight if caulking the seams no longer works. On work boats, a wood deck is often treated with boiled linseed oil because dirt would continually stain the deck, and the oil seals the wood to prevent stains. The oil will darken the surface however.

Where the wood deck is of plywood, it should always be painted for protection. It is not a good idea to cover a plywood deck with canvas or something similar, as water will get through to the plywood, and because it cannot evaporate, the plywood will eventually rot. If a plywood deck is to be covered with anything it should be a man-made fibre epoxied to the deck.

The caulking on laid decks must be kept in a good condition, and should be renewed or repayed whenever it shows signs of cracking. This prevents water getting down between the seams, where it will eventually rot the deck planks. It also prevents drips coming through the deck onto whatever is below, unless the deck planks have been laid over a wood or steel deck.

Caulking When the seams between the hull or deck planking start to leak, it is usually because the caulking has come loose or rotted. In the case of modern compounds, it usually means that the compound has lost its adhesion to the wood.

Take an awl, or any thin sharp instrument, and push it

through the seam where it is leaking. If it passes through easily, the seam definitely needs hardening up or re-caulking.

Before caulking, remove all the old caulking material. Almost anything hook-shaped will do, but a bent over file or screwdriver is ideal. Make sure that it will fit easily into the seam, or the sides of the planking will be damaged. Put a fine, but not sharp edge on the instrument, insert it into the seam, and scrape out the old caulking.

There are two types of caulking material, oakum and cotton. Oakum is teased out rope strands which have been impregnated with tar. It is coarse, and only used on large seams such as those found on large vessels. It comes in large balls, and must be twisted up before it is used. Cotton also comes in large balls, and usually in four or five strands. This is very convenient for the small boat, as a number of strands can be selected according to the size of the seam.

Caulking may be driven in wet or dry. If wet, it is driven into a good oil paint which has been painted into the seam with a small brush. If dry, the caulking should be painted over after it has been driven. The paint helps to hold the caulking in place and prevents it from rotting.

Take a string of suitable thickness, cotton or oakum, and force its end into the beginning of the seam. Push it into the seam for a couple of inches, and then loop back over itself, and push into the seam for three to four inches before looping back again. This puts an average of three thicknesses of the caulking in the seam. When the caulking has been put into the seam for a couple of feet, force it down firmly with a caulking iron and mallet.

The number of layers and thickness of the caulking material will depend upon the size of the seam. The objective is to have an even finish, just below the surface of the planking, so that there is still room for the finishing compound to obtain a grip.

There are various types and sizes of caulking iron, but for small boat work, the smallest will do. Place the iron in the seam, and give it an exploratory tap with the mallet. The object is to hammer it home firmly into the seam, but not so hard that it will come out the other side. If the cotton or oakum comes out the other side of the seam too easily, it is probably not thick enough and should be removed. Add one or two more strands, well twisted together, and try again. Make sure that the caulking iron is straight in the seam, and does not catch on the side of the planking.

On thin planking, which would not take a great deal of force, a single strand of cotton should be used, and forced, not hammered into place. A useful tool for this is a wheel, the thickness of which is less than the seam. If a handle is put on the wheel, it is easy to run up and down inside the seam tightening the cotton.

When caulking a large area, caulk the butts of the planks first, and leave the caulking squared off at the ends, but so that the longitudinal caulking will go over it. When the end of a length of caulking material is reached, taper it off in the seam, and start the next length, similarly tapered, over it.

The most difficult seams to caulk are those between the keel and the garboard strake, and the outermost seam on the deck which is known as the Devil. (Hence the expression 'between the Devil and the deep blue sea', i.e. when one is perilously close to falling overside.) These seams are difficult to get at effectively, and in the case of the keel and the garboard, the keel is usually of a harder wood than the planking and will not swell as much when immersed so that there is less pressure on the caulking and the chances of a leak are greater.

Once the seams have been caulked, they are payed with a composition which fills up the rest of the seam to the surface of the planking. This helps to seal the seam, protect the caulking and provides a better finish.

In large vessels and workboats, marine glue is the usual paying compound. Its basic constituent is pitch, and it comes in solid chunks that must be heated up and melted down. Marine glue should not be overheated; if it starts to bubble, it is too hot. When liquid it is poured into the seam with a ladle. It is usual to overfill the seam and leave the surplus for a while so that the marine glue can settle into the seam. The surplus glue can be scraped off at a later date, but this is most easily done on a cold day when the glue is brittle. On a warm day, or in a hot climate, the glue sticks to the scraper and will come out of the seam. To remove the remains of marine glue, and restore the deck to its proper clean finish, the decks will finally need to be holystoned.

Hull seams are usually payed with a good white lead putty. However, putty will become hard over a period of time, and will not give as the planks expand and contract. This leads to the edges of the planks becoming damaged. A compound which never fully hardens, or remains slightly elastic, is kinder to the planking. If such a compound is to be used, and there are a number available, they sometimes require a special primer paint, so decide upon the choice of material for paying the seams before the caulking material is put in.

When paying of the seams is complete, leave the surface slightly concave, so that as the paying material is squeezed by the expansion of the planks, it does not get forced out proud of them.

ENGINES

Petrol engines   The choice is between a petrol (gasoline) or a diesel fuelled engine, and apart from its greatest power for weight ratio, the petrol engine has little to recommend it for small boat use for two reasons. The flash point of petrol is quite low, about minus 38° Celsius, and the vapour given off is highly explosive. This vapour can permeate a boat and cause a very potent fire risk. The second reason is that a petrol engine is dependent upon electricity for its operation. The petrol and air mix drawn into the cylinders from the carburettor is ignited by a spark from the ignition coil, which draws its power from the batteries. Only rarely these days are petrol engines found which use a magneto for the ignition spark, which avoids using the batteries (outboard motors are an example of engines that use magnetos). Electrics and small boats do not usually go too well together. Salt water and dampness which are permanent hazards in small boats, have a detrimental effect on electrical circuits and equipment.

If a petrol engine fails to start the fault usually lies with the fuel supply or the electrics. To check the electrics, remove one of the spark plugs, lay it on the engine, and work the starter. If a spark is seen across the points of the plug, then the electrics are probably all right. If no spark occurs, check the distributor, and clean the points and the rotor arm head, and try again. To improve the spark on a plug, rub the contact points with a lead pencil. If there is still no spark, the trouble could be a loose connection, a broken capacitor in the distributor, or the ignition coil has failed. If it is either of the latter, you are going to need spare parts, and you might as well get in a mechanic to check the engine over.

It is possible to get a petrol engine to run, provided it can be hand wound, by putting eight ordinary 1½ volt torch batteries in series and connecting them to the ignition coil.

To check the fuel supply, disconnect a spark plug and turn the engine. A mist of petrol should be expelled. If it is not, check that petrol is getting to the carburettor by disconnecting the supply pipe and switching on the ignition to operate the fuel pump. If petrol is not flowing through, check that there is fuel in the tank and that the filters are clean. If it is getting through then the trouble is in the carburettor, which should be stripped down and cleaned, paying particular attention to the jets. In two-stroke engines, the failure to start can often be due to the wrong oil to petrol mix.

Diesel engines A diesel engine uses fuel oil (gas oil which has a much higher flash point, 66° Celsius), and is therefore far less of a fire risk in a boat. A diesel engine depends upon the compression of the oil and air mix to ignite the mix and create the power. No electrically supplied spark is necessary. Provided fuel is still being pumped to the injectors, a diesel engine will usually continue to function. Thus, once a diesel engine has started it requires nothing but fuel to keep it going. It runs better when loaded, and if run for long periods without a load, it will soot up and the injectors will have to be cleaned.

Diesel fuel system If a diesel fails to start, or stops when running, the cause is usually the failure of fuel to get to the injectors. The way to check this is to unbolt the high pressure pipe, which runs from the fuel pump to the injectors, at the injector end. Then run the starter motor and fuel should come out of the pipe under very high pressure (approx 1500 psi). If no fuel comes out then the most likely cause is air in the fuel system. Air, which is compressible, will act as a spring in the fuel pump, with the result that the pump just compresses the air instead of pushing fuel through to the injectors. The air can be drawn into the system from any of the joints on the fuel system. To rid the system of air, the whole system must be bled

Diesel Fuel System Line

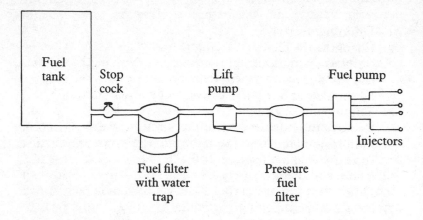

through, but start by bleeding the fuel pump in case the leak is there. There is a small bleed screw on the fuel pump. Slacken this screw and work the lift pump until clean fuel comes through. If the fuel bubbles out, there is still air in the system. If the engine has no hand lift pump, work the starter motor instead until clean, unbubbled fuel comes out. Then tighten up the bleed screw. The engine will restart after a few turns if the air was in the fuel pump. If air continues to stop the engine, then it may be coming from elsewhere, and the whole system, starting from the first fuel filter, must be bled.

Bleeding a fuel system is very much easier if the fuel tank is higher than the engine in the boat. Apart from allowing the fuel to run gravitationally to the engine, it means that there is a little pressure on the fuel system at all times which makes it harder for air to get into the system.

Care of the engine and inhibition   Engines are usually placed in an awkward part of the boat, where nothing else can be put. Most often this is close to the stern, where the hull is narrowing and gives little access.

The difficulties of access means that engines do not get the attention and routine maintenance that they would be given if, say, they were fitted to a car. Just as a car engine should be given a weekly check, so the boat's engine should be checked each time the boat is going out.

If the engine is to be left for some time without use, it should be inhibited. This means:

1. Draining the sump.
2. Changing the filters.
3. Re-filling with inhibiting oil; if inhibiting is not available, use the normal recommended lubricating oil. (Inhibiting oil should not be used when running the engine.)
4. Turn engine to circulate oil.
5. Remove injectors or spark plugs, and put a few squirts of inhibiting oil into the cylinders. Turn the engine by hand to spread the oil in the cylinders
6. Replace plugs or injectors.
7. Drain all water systems, switch off seacocks, and place a bung in the exhaust.
8. Remove all rubber impellers.
9. Liberally spray all electrics with protective liquid.
10. Disconnect the batteries and grease the terminals.

In cold areas, where frost is likely, the fresh water side of the cooling system should have anti-freeze added if the engine is being left undrained. If the engine is not inhibited, then it should be run at least every week to circulate the lubricating oil, and prevent condensation inside the engine. Where possible an electric heater, the greenhouse type is ideal, should be left in the engine room when cold weather comes along as it will keep the compartment dry.

Engine cooling Most boat engines are water cooled. The usual system is a closed circuit fresh water system, which circulates through the engine block and at some point passes through a heat exchanger, which is the equivalent of the radiator on a car, only instead of being cooled by the air rushing through the radiator, the water is cooled by contact with metal which is kept cool by sea water pumped through the other side of the heat exchanger. This cooling sea water is pumped from a seacock low down in the boat, through the heat exchanger, and then overside into the sea once more. Frequently the sea water is pumped overside via the exhaust pipe. To prevent the water running back into the engine down the exhaust pipe, the water joins the exhaust pipe after a water trap, or an inverted U pipe which extends well above the waterline.

The sea water inlet should be fitted with a weed strainer to prevent foreign bodies being drawn up the system and causing a blockage. A weed trap is a brass cylinder with a filter of gauze, or a simple strainer, through which the water must pass. If it becomes blocked the engine temperature will rise. To check the strainer simply switch off the seacock, open the top of the tube, remove the gauze and clean it, and then replace it back in its tube, close it up and open the seacock once more. Do not run the engine knowingly with a blocked strainer, as the lack of water passing through the system will wear out the impeller on the cooling water pump.

In boats with a hydraulic gear box, the oil in the gear box is circulated through a separate heat exchanger. This exchanger is connected to the engine sea water cooling system. Make regular checks of the oil in the gear box to ensure that the heat exchanger has not leaked water into it. If the engine is air cooled it is important to ensure that air can ventilate freely from the engine room to outside.

Lining up an engine   Although the engine in a boat has usually been lined up properly with the tail shaft, it is sometimes necessary to do this without professional assistance. If the

Lining Up the Engine with the Tail Shaft

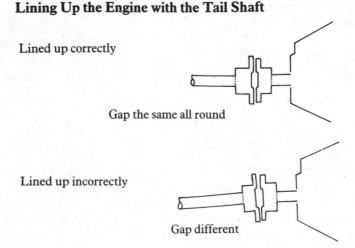

Lined up correctly

Gap the same all round

Lined up incorrectly

Gap different

engine and tail shaft are not lined up properly, wear will occur on both the gear box bearing and the stern tube, and apart from causing vibration, the bearings will start to leak.

Undo all the bolts in the coupling between the tail shaft and the gear box, and push the couplings apart so that they are not in contact with each other. Then gently push them together until they are just touching. Insert a feeler gauge between the two halves of the coupling at various points around the circumference. If the couplings are together and the gap is the same, then the shaft and engine are in line. If the gaps are different, they are not in line, and the engine's position must be adjusted until the couplings fit exactly.

When the engine is first fitted, its mountings, that is, the brackets that are bolted down to the engine bearers in the boat, are moved up or down individually until the two halves of the coupling fit exactly together. To do this, small thin, flat pieces of metal, called shims, are inserted beneath the mounting legs until the engine is in the correct position.

In some cases, where an engine has been coupled up in a boat at the factory or before the boat is launched, its relationship to the tail shaft can change once the boat has been put into the water, and the strains on the hull are more even. This can lead to wear on the bearings or vibration. Engines should therefore be coupled up *after* the boat has been launched.

Ventilation   Engines require a source of air, to mix with the fuel to create combustion, and good ventilation to the engine compartment is essential for this purpose. Good ventilation will also help to prolong the life of the engine. The engine compartment will get very hot when the engine is running. The heated air will absorb water vapour, and this will condense very quickly once the engine compartment starts to cool. If fresh air is drawn into the engine compartment, this will replace the warm moist air and reduce condensation. If the engine room is fitted with a fan, this fan should be kept running after the engine has stopped, until it cools.

PAINT AND PAINTING

Most boat owners use modern composite paints, but there are still places where these are unobtainable, and this section therefore includes the old oil-based paints and how to mix them if necessary.

The principal reasons for applying paint to any surface are preservation and decoration, and the only way to achieve these objectives is to prepare the surface to be painted properly by ensuring that it is dry and clean and has been made as smooth as possible by means of scrapers, pumice stone, sandpaper and filler.

New surfaces should always be primed before the undercoat and topcoat are applied. In the case of wood, a 'lead' or pink primer is used. For steel, red lead paint or special metal primers are applied. For galvanised surfaces, unless an etch primer or zinc yellow chromate is available, it is best to leave the surface to weather for six months or so before applying paint. Aluminium can be painted with either yellow chromate or an etch primer. GRP has to be painted with an etch primer or mechanically abraded as other paints will not adhere properly to smooth gelcoat. Concrete is best covered with epoxy paints.

When applying an undercoat, carefully follow the manufacturer's instructions regarding how soon to apply the topcoat as, if some undercoats are left too long, they can become damp and not allow the topcoat to adhere properly.

Covering power   Different makes of paint will cover different areas of surface. Usually an approximate covering area per pint or litre is given on the tin, but this will vary depending upon whether a brush or roller is used, and upon the skill of the painter.

As a rough guide, the table below gives the approximate areas to be covered by different types of paint.

Metallic primer	11 sq metres/litre	60 sq yds/gal
GRP primer	18 ,, ,,	100 ,, ,,
Undercoats	10 ,, ,,	55 ,, ,,
Topcoat enamel	10 ,, ,,	55 ,, ,,
Polyurethane	11 ,, ,,	60 ,, ,,

Varnish	13 sq metres/litres	70 sq yds/gal
Deck paint	8 ,, ,,	40 ,, ,,
Non-slip deck paint	7 ,, ,,	35 ,, ,,
Normal anti-fouling	10 ,, ,,	55 ,, ,,
Thick anti-fouling	7 ,, ,,	35 ,, ,,

To calculate the amount of paint required to cover different areas of the boat, use the following guide:

Topsides   (Overall length + beam) × twice mean freeboard.
Decks   Overall length × beam × 0.75.
Anti-fouling   Waterline length × (beam + draft).

Composition of paint   There are four essentials to a good paint: the pigments, the binder, the thinner and the drying agent.

The pigments   The principal pigments are white lead, zinc oxide and red lead. White lead is the most common as it has good covering power and improves with age; it has less body than red lead but is more durable and retains its pure colour better. White lead and zinc oxide are provided in oil, but red lead comes in powder form and when mixed dries quickly and forms a good tough coat. Other colour pigments are provided for giving a specific colour to a paint, but they serve no purpose other than as colouring agents.

Binder   Oil is used to bind a pigment down to a surface. The most common is boiled linseed oil, although a variety of vegetable oils may be used. Linseed oil is made from a nitrogenous oil contained in the seed of the flax plant. Boiling linseed oil takes about five hours and whilst it is boiling, drier is added in the proportion of 5lbs of drier to a ton of oil. On very fine work 'Gold Size' is used as a binder. It is made from very pure gelatine.

Thinner   A thinner is usually added to paint to make it easier to apply by making it more fluid. Turpentine, which is the product of distilling the resin of certain coniferous trees, is the best thinner, but substitutes such as 'white spirit', a petroleum derivative, are very often used. Thinners should always be water white and free from solid matter.

Drier Added to paint to accelerate the drying process. It acts on the oil, but not the pigment, and has no protective or decorative value. There are many types of drier most of which contain compounds of lead or types of manganese. Terebene is a common drier made from raw linseed oil, gum capal and litharge, and monoxide of lead. Too much drier reduces the life of a paint.

Mixing paint It is very rare these days to have to mix paint from scratch. Good paints come ready for use from the manufacturers, but a knowledge of how paint is made up is often useful.

White paint 7lbs of white lead or zinc oxide, ½ gallon of raw linseed oil (boiled oil makes a paint dry and creamy coloured), ¼ pint of turps and 2 ozs of driers. White paint improves with standing so mix it 2–3 weeks before it is required and give it a stir every so often. It is better to leave adding the driers until the paint is required as otherwise a skin forms very quickly and the paint would have to be strained before use. A good practice is to mix a very small amount of blue into white paint as it gives a 'bleached' effect.

Red lead To make up one gallon mix 20 lbs of red lead powder, 6 pints of linseed oil, 2 gills of turpentine. To prevent the lead settling too much, it pays to damp the lead powder with boiled oil and let it stand for half an hour before mixing. The lead pigment has such good natural drying qualities that driers need not be added.

Flatting Mix up white zinc and turpentine to the required thickness. Add a small quantity of gold size to act as a binder.

Polyurethane paint There are two types of polyurethane paint, one-pot and two-pot. One-pot polyurethane paint has a slightly different chemical mix, and comes ready for use. Two-pot polyurethane paint comes with two separate components, a saturated polyester resin which will be pigmented, and a hardener, a chemical substance called isocyanate. The two components are mixed well together, and then left to stand for 10 minutes or so before being used. The polyurethane paint cures in rather the same way as a resin laminate, and the makers mixing instructions should be slavishly followed if a good finish is to result. The paint cures (dries) in about 2–3 hours in two ways; the solvent evaporates and there is the chemical reaction between the two components. If a second coat is required it should be applied between 6 and 24 hours after the first, as the first coat will not have hardened properly and a chemical bond can take place between the two coats which provides good adhesion. If the second coat is left longer, the first coat should be rubbed down to provide good adhesion. Polyurethane paints and varnishes give a good hard surface which, if applied properly, will outlast normal paint. Because of the strong solvents used to dissolve the resin in polyurethane paint, this paint will not always stick to a previous coat of ordinary paint, and it is best to start from a bare surface.

Epoxy coatings Epoxy paints are very hard and water resistant and again consist of two components, the resin and the hardener. The resin is formed by condensing epichlorhydrin and diphenylopropane in a caustic environment. The hardener is generally an organic diamine or polyamide. Epoxy resins will only mix with certain solvents which include alcohol, so good ventilation is required when using them. Epoxy paints will not adhere on any other paint and have to be applied on a bare, well prepared, surface.

The two components should be well mixed and left to stand for 10 minutes before use. Discard paint that has not been used after 3–4 hours. Each coat should be rubbed down before the next coat is applied. Once the final coat has hardened, it can be burnished with very fine wet and dry sandpaper, followed by rubbing down paste and car polish.

VARNISH AND VARNISH WORK

There is nothing more attractive on a boat than smart varnish work, or bright work, as it is called, and opinions vary as to whether it is best to use the traditional oil varnishes, or the more recent one or two-pot polyurethane varnishes.

The major difference between oil and polyurethane varnishes is that polyurethane varnish gives a hard, almost brittle finish, which seals the wood. It is more resistant to knocks, but once the surface starts to split, the whole surface has to be taken back to the bare wood, and built up again. Oil varnishes are less hard, and need to be rubbed down and re-coated annually. However, if the surface is grazed, it just needs rubbing down and touching up.

Varnish should always be applied in thin coats and uniformly, five to seven coats for oil varnish, three coats for polyurethane. Like enamel, varnish will form into ridges if put on too thickly. It will lose its gloss quickly if applied too sparingly. Varnish applied in damp conditions or to a damp surface will 'bloom' or turn creamy. Ideally, varnish should be applied to a smooth dry surface on a warm dry sunny day. When varnish becomes thick, it can be made suitable for application by heating either on a stove, by placing its pot in a pail of hot water or by mixing in thinners.

There are five types of varnish: natural varnish, oil varnish, spirit varnish, water varnish and polyurethane varnish. Varnish should only be applied to a clean, smooth surface. All grease or mineral oil should be removed, and the surface should be rubbed down with fine sandpaper before application. All old varnish should be removed and, if the wood has become stained, it can be cleaned, and its natural colour restored, by being scrubbed with oxalic acid. Most wood benefits from the application of linseed oil, as it helps to replace the natural moisture in the timber which evaporates over the years. If an oil varnish is to be used, a couple of slightly thinned coats of linseed oil can be applied first, but let it soak well into the wood before applying the first coat of varnish. Turpentine should be used as thinners. To bring up the grain in the timber, use thinned boiled linseed oil instead of raw oil. If a polyurethane varnish is to be used, allow longer for the oil to dry before applying the varnish.

Always use a clean, paint free, springy brush for varnish. Varnish brushes should be kept separate from paint brushes, and in a pot or jar with a mix of linseed oil and turpentine.

Mixing varnishes
Best white varnish   1 gallon rectified spirits of wine, 2½ lbs

gum sandorac, ½ lb gum mastic, 2 lb gum anima. Shake well before using.

Spar varnish   4 lbs raw linseed oil, ½ lb crushed rosin, stir until dissolved and then add ½ lb turpentine.

Coloured varnish   Sealing wax dissolved with spirits of wine.

Oak varnish   1¾ lb pale clear rosin and ½ gallon turpentine.

Copal varnish   1 quart spirit of wine, 1 oz gum copal, ½ oz shellac.

Spirit varnish   Resin dissolved in methylated spirits, turpentine or other volatile spirit. Add a little oil to make it more durable and elastic. Spirit varnish is also known as knotting.

Black varnish   Asphalt and bitumen mixed with linseed oil and driers consisting of red lead, litharge and manganese dioxide. The mixture is heated to a high temperature and when it has cooled, turpentine is added to bring the mixture to the right consistency. Coachbuilder's black Japan is the best of the many grades of black varnish.

ANTI-FOULING

Before looking at anti-fouling paints, it is useful to look at the various types of fouling that the paint must resist. Fouling is the name given to anything which hinders the boat's movement – weed or crustacea on the hull is known as bottom fouling; a rope caught around the propeller or rudder is said to have fouled the propeller or rudder; a halyard caught up the mast is said to be fouled.

Bottom fouling   The name given to any form of vegetable or marine life that grows on or in a vessel's bottom. That which grows on the outside of the hull causes an increase in friction and loss of speed, that which grows in a hull, borers, slowly eat away a hull.

The surface waters of the sea are full of microscopic animal and plant life such as the larval forms of barnacles and mussel and spores of sea weeds. This 'soup' is densest in harbours and estuaries which have only a small fresh-water supply, and thinnest in the open sea. 'Green' water contains a lot of plankton, 'blue' water contains very little. These spores and larvae settle on boats' hulls and grow into fouling.

Weed fouling (grass fouling) There are three main groups of seaweeds, the green, the brown and the red. Green weed requires more light than brown, and brown more than red; so green weed is found nearest the surface and red nearest the bottom.

Seaweeds multiply by releasing very small spores that swim around heading towards moderate light, but avoiding intense light. As they near their time to settle they tend to avoid light and thus if they come into contact with a hull below the surface they will settle and grow.

Muddy waters do not encourage weed growth as there is insufficient light below the surface, but yachts may become fouled with enteromorpha, green ribbon grass, on their waterlines. The slime frequently found on the hull of a boat is a vegetable moss which will grow into a tangled mass of small threads if not removed.

There are a number of animals that resemble weeds and are thus classified with them as grass foulings. The most important are hydroids which are related to the sea anenome, and polyzoa which are related to marine worms. They feed by means of minute tentacles that trap small forms of plankton. The polyzoa has one form that instead of growing out from the hull, spreads thinly over the hull. The form provides a firm base for other, more obstructive, forms of fouling.

Shell fouling There are a number of forms but the most common is the barnacle which attaches itself directly to the hull. The gooseneck barnacle has a shell head attached to the hull by a long flexible stalk.

Barnacles begin life as microscopic eggs. These hatch into the nauplius larva which grows, moulting its skin as it does so, before changing into the cypris larva. It is the cypris larva which attaches itself to the hull by secreting a cement, and then the larva changes into the adult barnacle. Whilst growing, barnacles exert considerable force on their bases which will easily penetrate paint.

Jelly bag fouling The jelly bags often found attached to the hull of a boat are a very low form of animal life known as ascidians or tunicates. In larval form this animal behaves much as the barnacle, but once it has attached itself to a boat it fails to grow the lime shell.

Ship worms The best known is the teredo of which there are three species in British waters, but there are other forms of ship worm, all related. The teredo larva swims around for the first month of its life until it finds a suitable resting place. It then becomes a mollusc and drills into the hull, the hole being as small as a pin head. Once inside the wood, it becomes a worm, with shells at one end for cutting. It cuts straight into the wood for a short distance and then turns at right angles and eats its way along the grain of the wood. The burrow rarely breaks the surface and is lined with a shelly secretion. Teredos vary in size, being up to six feet long in the Tropics, but rarely more than eight inches in British waters. They are found nearly everywhere, even in the littoral, and can live in wood out of water for more than three weeks. They are much less affected than most weeds by fresh water, and moving a boat into fresh water does not always kill them. The existence of teredo is difficult to detect once it is in the wood.

Martesia This is another mollusc which bores into the hull of a boat. It does not dig a tunnel like the teredo, but excavates a hole slightly larger than itself which may be up to two inches long and half an inch wide. It is found in the same waters as teredo and frequently attacks in large numbers which are capable of destroying up to an inch of wood within six months.

Gribble or limnoria A timber-destroying crustacean similar to a wood louse but smaller. They are free swimming and bore into a piece of wood to a depth of an inch and then return to the surface and bore in again. In a short space of time they can eat away a large area of timber and they have been known to live up to two weeks out of the water.

Anti-fouling paint Nearly all forms of fouling start as free swimming larvae or spores that settle upon a hull before commencing to dig into it or grow over it. The purpose of anti-fouling compositions is to kill the spores of the larvae before they have adhered to the hull, by means of a steady release of toxic substances into the water around the hull, called a bioxide. The bioxide is released continuously in a controlled manner (this is known as leaching) but once all the bioxide in the paint has been released there is no further protection and fouling will commence. Anti-fouling paint should be applied at regular intervals depending upon the area in which the boat is kept. Generally coats of anti-fouling will need to be applied more frequently in warm climates than in colder.

There are a number of different bioxides suitable for use in anti-foulings; the most common are:

1. Cuprous oxide and metallic copper
2. Organo-mercury compounds
3. Organo-arsenic compounds
4. Organo-tin compounds
5. Organo compounds such as TMT and DDT. Compounds of arsenic, mercury and DDT are less used now for environmental reasons.

Applying anti-fouling Before putting on new anti-fouling, scrub off the bottom to remove all weed or loose paint, and wash down with fresh water. Always read the manufacturer's instructions carefully before application. Some anti-fouling is best applied just before a boat is re-launched as if the paint hardens it will not leach out properly. Hard racing anti-foulings have generally less anti-fouling properties than softer finish paint, and are designed to give a smooth hard finish which is better for racing. If an anti-fouling of different manufacture to the previous coating is to be applied, check whether the new and old paints are compatible, as different manufacturers use different chemical mixtures and some will react with each other. If the paints are not compatible; a barrier primer will have to be put on before the new paint is applied.

When applying anti-fouling on a grid and using an undercoat, make sure that the topcoat can be put on during the same tide or the bond between undercoat and anti-fouling will not be a good one. If the boat is too large for there to be sufficient time, paint one side on one tide and stay on the grid another tide to do the other side. Anti-fouling should not normally be thinned; although it is often hard work, the paint should be applied as it comes in its tins.

PAINT BRUSHES

The most commonly used brushes at sea are flat brushes, and the most useful are between 1 and 2½ inches width for all general work. The only other brushes that are likely to be required are pencil brushes for name painting and scroll work. Never use a larger brush than can be conveniently handled, and for a fine finish use a medium size brush that has been well worked in.

A good quality paint brush will last longer, and give a better finish than a cheap brush, but no brush will perform well if it is not looked after properly. New brushes seldom 'stroke off' neatly, and to break them in they should be used on a rough surface for their first few days. When the bristles are nicely tapered, the brush is ready for any work that requires a good finish.

After use, the brushes should be cleaned out with white spirit or turpentine and then washed with soap. Brushes used for polyurethane paints will not clean out with white spirit or turpentine, and special solvents have to be used before using soap and water. Manufacturers usually show the type of solvent recommended on the paint tin. However well the brushes are washed, never confuse brushes used for anti-fouling with those used for normal paint as some anti-foulings contain bitumastic compounds which are almost impossible to completely wash out and will discolour other paints.

Brushes should be stored by standing them in water. However, if left for a long time, the bristles will be bent, so they should be suspended so that the bristles are clear of the bottom of the tin. Brushes set in metal will last longer if they are placed in linseed oil, or a mixture of oil and turpentine or white spirit. Varnish brushes should always be left in oil or an oil and turpentine mixture, as water in a varnish brush will turn varnish creamy.

Before use, all the water should be shaken out of the brush and then it should be dipped into the paint pot and rubbed around the side of the pot to let the paint find its way right into the bristles.

Rollers should be treated the same way as brushes. Lambswool rollers wash out best, if after being cleaned with white spirit, they are washed with soft soap. Sponge rollers are harder to clean. If a brush or roller is to be used for the same paint within a day or so, unless they have been used for polyurethane paints, they can be left in water without being properly cleaned off, but all the water must be shaken off before the brush is re-used.

12 SHIP AND BOAT IDENTIFICATION

The numbers and types of vessels to be found at sea show an almost infinite variety. However, the seaman should be able to recognise the basic types to be aware of their probable activity, speed and manoeuvrability, so that the right avoiding action can be taken in good time if necessary. The position and course of a ship sighted at sea can be a useful confirmation of one's position, and enables that ship to be called up more positively in an emergency. The call 'All ships' is not as effective as 'Norwegian tanker in position _____ steering a course of _____'.

Most merchant ships stick to a steady course and speed, and, close to coasts, they will usually stick to the shipping lanes. They do not normally make unpredictable alterations of course. Warships, particularly when exercising, can make substantial alterations to both course and speed, and should be given plenty of searoom.

MERCHANT SHIPS

The simplest way to recognise a merchant ship is by the size and type of her deck structure, and the variety of colours of her hull and superstructure. At a distance it is often difficult to pick out the national flag, but most shipping companies have identifiable colour schemes, particularly on their funnels.

Passenger ships There are few regular trans-oceanic passenger routes operating these days, and apart from ferries operating close to coasts, most large passenger ships are usually on cruises. The most distinctive features of modern passenger ships are their stylish hull lines and high superstructures, and one or two streamlined funnels. Although many are capable of speeds in excess of 20 knots, fuel economics mean that most travel at between 15 and 20 knots.

Ferry

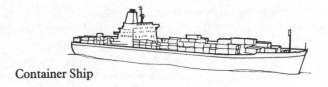

Container Ship

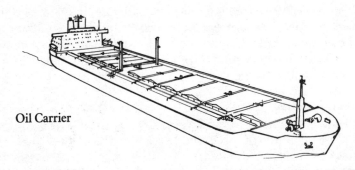

Cargo Ship (ro-ro)

Oil Carrier

not to scale

Ferries do not differ greatly in shape from ocean-going passenger ships, except that they are probably more boxy. If their route takes them across shipping lanes, they will alter course frequently and at high speeds.

At night, both passenger ships and ferries can be distinguished by the large number of accommodation lights, but their ordinary navigation lights should be clearly visible.

Container ships During the last twenty years, container ships have replaced many of the general cargo ships that used to dominate the world's shipping lanes. The cargo is pre-packed in boxes, the standard size being 40 × 8 × 8 feet, and the boxes are loaded onto the ship, instead of the cargo itself being individually stowed within a general cargo ship. This has led to much quicker turn-arounds by container ships, some of which now exceed 30,000 tons, and are capable of speeds up to 27 knots although they usually travel at a slower, more economic speed.

The most distinctive feature of a container ship is the high box shape, which is caused by up to five layers of containers stacked on deck. From a distance they can look similar to a ferry. When they are loaded with containers, the Officer of the Watch does not always have good visibility, especially close to and in front of the ship.

General cargo ships Once the most common type of vessel on the world's oceans, the numbers have decreased in recent years as more cargoes have been either containerised or carried in bulk. The standard type has accommodation and funnel in the middle of the vessel, with masts or samson posts fore and aft. On many, the traditional derricks have been replaced by cranes. Cranes and derricks on deck are what distinguish general cargo ships from the other types, even if the accommodation and engine room are aft, as in tankers. Most general cargo ships travel at between 15 and 20 knots, with a few capable of higher speeds.

Heavy-lift ships The distinguishing features of heavy-lift ships, and usually the only difference between them and general cargo ships, are the very substantial masts, sometimes in pairs, which provide the support for the heavy-lift derricks. Some are capable of lifts in excess of 350 tons.

Tankers These vessels, used for carrying liquids in bulk, but particularly oil, vary in size from the small coastal variety of 1000 tons or less, to monsters of 500,000 tons. In all cases the engines are aft, but the bridge may be aft or amidships. The decks are clear of derricks or cranes, but there is usually a catwalk along the deck, connecting the fo'c'sle with the bridge or accommodation aft. The average speed of tankers varies between 12 and 18 knots, but they often have very limited stern power, and are not always very manoeuvrable. They can take up to 6 or 8 miles to stop, and should be given a wide berth. On large tankers, with the bridge aft, the officer of the watch may be 600 feet or more from the fo'c'sle, and his visibility can be very restricted, particularly close under the bows.

Bulk carriers From a distance, bulk carriers are not dissimilar to tankers in silhouette, as they usually have their bridge and accommodation right aft, and a long flat deck forward to the fo'c'sle. One obvious difference is the large hatches, evenly spaced along the deck, but these are not always visible at a distance. Their size can vary from 1000 to 100,000 tons, and they do not usually go much faster than 14 to 18 knots. Their cargoes can vary from iron ore, coal, grain, scrap metal, in fact anything that can be carried in bulk. The same restrictions apply to the visibility and manoeuvrability of bulk carriers as do to tankers.

FISHING VESSELS

The types of fishing vessel to be found around the world are as numerous as the different methods used to catch fish. There are four basic types: trawlers, drifters, seine netters, and longliners or trollers.

Trawlers Most modern trawlers bring their nets in through a ramp at the stern, and thus have no need of the low freeboard that used to be a feature of this type. Their shape is rather stubby, and they will have a large gallows at the stern. When trawling, they drag a large open net along the bottom of the sea, and this can extend a good distance astern so they should be given a clear berth. Trawlers have a disconcerting practice of altering course without warning, and being in the middle of a fleet of trawlers is rather like being an unwilling partner in a disorganised maritime square dance.

By day, a trawler, when trawling, shows two black cones with their apexes together. By night it can be distinguished by the usual side and stern lights, but instead of the white masthead lights, it will show two all-round lights on the mast, the upper green, and the lower white. Small trawlers, of less than 20 metres, may show a basket by day instead of the two cones.

Drifters   The traditional drifter specialised in catching herring. They fish by shooting out nets, weighted at the bottom with floats at the top, which lie just below the surface of the sea, and then lie downwind and attached to these nets, which can extend for as much as a mile. These vessels also show two cones with their apexes together by day, and if their nets extend more than 150 metres from the vessel, they will show another cone, apex uppermost, in the direction from the first two cones in which the nets are lying. By night, drifters will show two all-round masthead lights, the upper being red, and another all-round white light in the direction of the nets. If underway, they will also show side and stern lights.

Seine netters   These vessels make their catches by dropping a net all round a shoal of fish, and then tightening up the purse strings at the bottom to trap the fish inside. They steam in circles whilst shooting their nets, and then lie stationary as the nets are hauled on board. They show the same lights and shapes as a drifter.

Long-liners   The fish are caught on hooks attached to lines that are towed slowly through the water, an action known as trolling. The number of lines varies, and their length can extend up to a mile. Long-liners show the same lights as drifters.

TUGS

Modern ocean-going tugs can reach sizes of 5000 tons. Tugs have a high freeboard forward, and a long low aft deck. They have a large bridge structure at the aft end of the fo'c'sle, with a funnel and mast immediately behind. A deep sea towline is usually a very heavy wire, attached to the anchor cable of the towed vessel. Because of its weight, it will sink beneath the surface and not be visible to another vessel except when it springs taut from time to time. Therefore whenever any tug is sighted, always check to see whether there is another vessel keeping the same distance astern at the same speed. If the length of tow exceeds 200 metres the tug will show a diamond shape by day, and by night if the length of tow is less than 200 metres it will show an extra masthead light, and if it exceeds 200 metres, it will show two additional masthead lights. The towed vessel shows, by day, a diamond shape, and by night side and stern lights.

SURFACE SKIMMING CRAFT

These fall into two main categories, hovercraft and hydrofoils. Hovercraft rely upon a cushion of air held beneath the hull by a skirt, to keep them clear of the water and reduce their friction. There are two methods of propulsion used, either aircraft engines driving propellers mounted on top of the craft, or long shafts from ordinary engines within the craft that drive high speed propellers in the water. The former are extremely noisy, and sound like a low flying aeroplane, the latter are no more noisy than a normal fast powerboat. Hovercraft, particularly those driven by air propellers, tend to glide over the surface of the sea, and do not alter course quickly.

Hydrofoils look like normal sleek power craft when at rest or at slow speeds. As the speed builds up, the boat lifts up on foils that stick down beneath it, and the boat tends to 'fly' over the surface, at speeds of up to 60 knots.

Both types are mainly used for short passenger or military

services, and the only difference between them and normal vessels, apart from their speed, is that they show a quick-flashing orange light at night in addition to the normal navigation lights.

WARSHIPS

Warships are almost uniformly various shades of grey in colour, regardless of nationality. They are usually long and sleek in shape, and can be recognised at a distance by their large radar and aerial assemblies above the superstructure. Although it is possible with experience, to identify the nationality of a warship at a distance by its style of build, if the national flag cannot be seen, most warships have a pennant number written in large letters on the hull.

Aircraft carriers This is the largest size of warship, the biggest in the world being the USS *Enterprise* of 89,600 tons which is 1102 feet long. Their box-like shape is distinctive, with a long flat deck extending the full length, and a small island superstructure set over on the starboard side of the deck. They are capable of speeds in excess of 30 knots, and some of the larger ones are nuclear-powered. A smaller, very similar looking vessel is used for operating helicopters, and the British Invincible Class (19,500 tons) have a distinctive ramp at the bows used to launch 'jump jets'. Aircraft carriers will turn into the wind when launching or landing fixed-wing aircraft, and often build up to high speeds to create a strong wind over the deck to assist the aircraft. They rarely travel without a surface escort of frigates or destroyers, and supply ships.

Battleships Once the ultimate weapon of sea power, and designed to deliver and absorb punishment from very heavy shells, battleships lost their dominance with the advent of aircraft carriers. There are now only four left in existence, the American New Jersey Class, of 58,000 tons, all built at the end of World War II. These are now being brought out of retirement, and fitted with missiles in addition to their nine 16-inch

Aircraft carrier

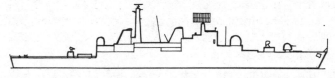

Destroyer

Frigate

Landing craft

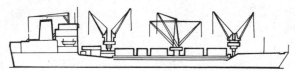

Fleet service vessel

not to scale

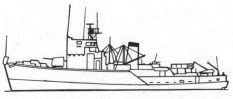

Minesweeper

guns which are capable of throwing one-ton shells over twenty miles. This class of ship is capable of 33 knots.

Cruisers   A few of the old cruisers are still in service, but most have been withdrawn or modernised as missile vessels. The traditional cruiser bridged the gap between battleships and destroyers, at about 10,000 tons, and were designed to have a long range for commerce protection. The modern vessels of this size are difficult to distinguish from large missile frigates except for their greater size.

Destroyers and frigates   These are the most versatile surface warships and the most numerous of the ocean-going types. Originally destroyers were larger and faster, but the difference between the two types has narrowed so much that it is hard to differentiate between the two. The only positive identification is 'F' or 'D' in front of the pennant number painted on the side. They vary in size from 1000 to 9000 tons, and can be picked out at a distance by the continuous superstructure over the middle section of the boat. Many nowadays have a helicopter hangar and landing platform at the stern.

Mine counter-measure vessels   There are now two main methods of clearing mines; by sweeping with wires, magnetic cables or acoustic apparatus, or by mine hunting. Mine hunters usually move at about 8 knots when using a high definition sonar to search the bottom for ground mines. Mine sweepers tow large wire assemblies astern of them, which can be identified by the floats. Minesweepers often work in pairs or larger formations, and should not be approached closer than 500 metres on each side, and 1000 metres astern. Most can make speeds of about 16 knots but operate at about 8 knots. When operating, a minesweeper will show three black ball shapes, one from the masthead, and one from each yardarm. By night these balls are replaced by all-round green lights, in addition to the usual navigation lights. If a magnetic sweep is being towed, a red flag will be hoisted from the mast, and if an acoustic sweep is in use, a black flag will be shown from the same position. When a minehunter is operating, it shows the 'Not under Command' signals.

Submarines   Many modern submarines are nuclear-powered, and will not be seen on the surface except when close to their bases. The conventional, or diesel-electric type, have to surface or use their snort masts to recharge their batteries. The most distinctive features of a submarine are its long low shape and conning tower or 'sail'. They are almost always painted black. Most submarines are highly manoeuvrable, and many are capable of speeds up to 30 knots, but will usually only do this sort of speed when submerged. The usual surface speed is about 16 knots. Because submarines do not have masts, their navigation lights are on the conning towers, and not visible from small boats at great distances.

Patrol vessels   These are small, fast, coastal vessels, used for protection and inspections within territorial waters, from fishery protection to anti-drug-running and smuggling patrols. Most are operated by navies, but some bodies, such as the US Coast Guard, operate very similar vessels. The silhouette varies, but, as a general rule, they can be recognised by their sleek shape and central superstructure. They carry standard navigation lights, but the brightness, for the size of vessel, usually gives them away at night.

Fleet auxiliaries   Most navies operate a fleet train of support vessels, which carry fuel, ammunition and other supplies. Most are undistinguishable from normal merchant ships apart from their grey colour, and the large hangar and helicopter pad on deck at the stern of the larger ones. They have the same characteristics as normal merchant ships of their type.

SAILING SHIPS

By day, the sails of a sailing ship make it easily recognisable and, with the wind direction known, it is usually possible to get a good estimate of the course being steered. Sailing ships, of whatever size, used to carry only port and starboard sidelights and a white stern light, but in recent years they have been allowed/required to carry a masthead light to make them more visible.

The ship A three- or more masted sailing vessel, square-rigged on all masts. Very few are left in existence and these are now used as sail training ships. Seen at sea, with all sail set, they are a glorious sight and every effort should be made to go and see one if possible. The scale of the masts, and the complexity of the rigging, represented man's most efficient use of the forces of nature before the great dams were built.

Barque A three- or more masted vessel, square-rigged on all masts except the aftermost. Barques were the maids of all work at sea in the nineteenth and early twentieth century, because they were more economic in crew than the ship. Very few remain, and these are mainly used for training.

Brig A two-masted vessel, square-rigged on both masts. Extremely rare today, the only one built recently being the British training vessel *Royalist*.

Topsail schooner A vessel with two or more masts, the after mast being the tallest. It is distinctive because it is fore-and-aft

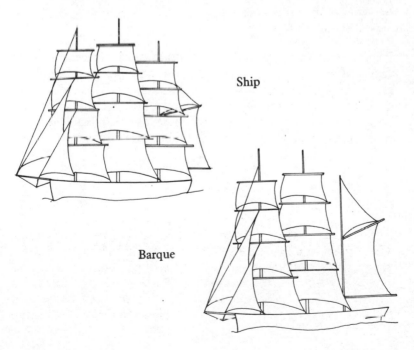

Ship

Barque

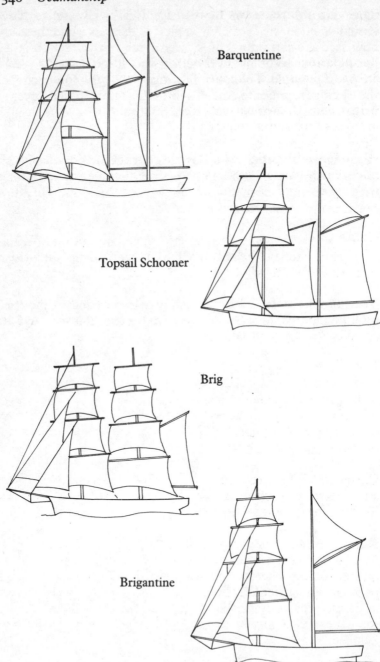

Barquentine

Topsail Schooner

Brig

Brigantine

rigged on all masts, but has two or so square topsails on the foremast.

Barquentine A vessel of three or more masts, square-rigged on the foremast and fore-and-aft on the other masts.

Brigantine A two-masted vessel, square-rigged on the fore-mast and fore-and-aft on the aft mast.

Hermaphrodite brig Half-way between a brig and a brigan-tine. A two-masted vessel, square-rigged on the foremast and with square topsails on the aft mast.

MODERN YACHTS

Bermudian sloop The most popular yacht rig because of its economy and efficiency. It has one headsail, the jib or genoa, and a triangular mainsail.

Gaff sloop The only difference from the bermudian sloop is that the mainsail is quadrilateral, and has a gaff yard held by tackles to the mast which supports the head of the sail. As a rig, it is much older than the bermudian, and has the disadvantage of more spars and weight aloft, but it is still seen in quite large numbers.

Cutter Can be either bermudian or gaff-rigged. The difference between a cutter and a sloop is that a cutter sets two headsails as its normal rig.

Ketch A two-masted rig, either bermudian or gaff. The main mast is forward of the mizzen mast which is less tall. The mizzen mast in a ketch is placed forward of the rudder. This is a popular rig, particularly for cruising, as it gives a comparatively large sail area with shorter masts, and the sails, being smaller than those of a similar sized sloop, are easier to handle and balance.

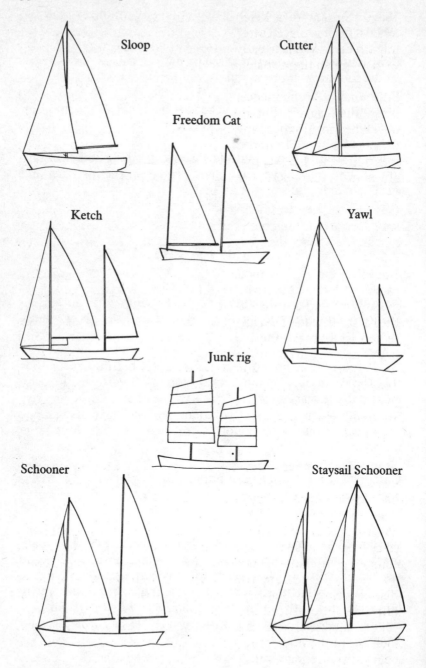

Sloop

Cutter

Freedom Cat

Ketch

Yawl

Junk rig

Schooner

Staysail Schooner

Yawl Similar to a ketch, but with the difference that the mizzen mast is placed astern of the rudder post. In practice, the mizzen on a yawl is usually smaller than a ketch, and this helps to distinguish them at a distance.

Schooner A schooner can be two- or more masted, and gaff or bermudian-rigged, but the tallest mast is aft. The rig really developed in America, and it is still quite popular, particularly for boats with more underbody aft. A yacht with two or more masts of equal height, provided they are only rigged fore-and-aft, is still a schooner.

Cat rig A very simple single mast rig, with the mast placed well forward in the boat. The rig may be either bermudian or gaff, but no headsails are set.

Freedom cat rig A modern development of the bermudian cat rig with one or more masts, and using a wishbone instead of a boom to hold out the clew of the sail. The sail wraps around the mast, instead of having its luff in a groove or on slides, and is reefed by rotating the mast. Its advantage lies in its ease of handling. The masts are unstayed.

Junk rig Introduced in the 1950s as a simple, easily reefed sail for yachts, on one or two masts. The square shape of the sail, and numerous horizontal battens are distinctive. The masts are unstayed.

Staysail schooner Usually two-masted, with a bermudian mainsail and a staysail set between the masts. An easy rig to handle but not seen very often.

Motor yachts Modern motor yachts come in all shapes and sizes from 20 or so feet with a small cabin, to vessels that would shame a cruise liner. It is reasonable to assume that most above 30 feet in length are twin screw, and therefore capable of manoeuvring easily. Speeds vary from 6 knots up to 30 knots, but a mean top speed is in the region of 10–20 knots. Motor yachts capable of over 30 knots usually have a racy streamlined look about them. There are numerous shapes of hull, from the heavy displacement hull, to the light planing hull.

The Principal Spars and Sails in Square Rig

1 Lower fore mast
2 Fore topmast
3 Fore topgallant mast
4 Mainmast
5 Main topmast
6 Main topgallant mast
7 Lower mizen mast
8 Mizen topmast
9 Mizen topgallant mast
10 Jigger mast
11 Jigger topmast
12 Bowsprit
13 Jibboom
14 Lower yard
15 Crojack yard
16 Lower topsail yard
17 Upper topsail yard
18 Lower topgallant yard
19 Upper topgallant yard
20 Tops
21 Crosstrees

If there were further yards above the upper topgallants, they would be called the royals.

A Outer jib
B Inner jib
C Topmast staysail
D Staysail
E Course
F Crojack
G Spanker
H Lower topsail
I Upper topsail
J Lower topgallant sail
K Upper topgallant sail

With the exception of the crojack, the courses and all other sails are distinguished by prefixing the name of the mast on which they are set.

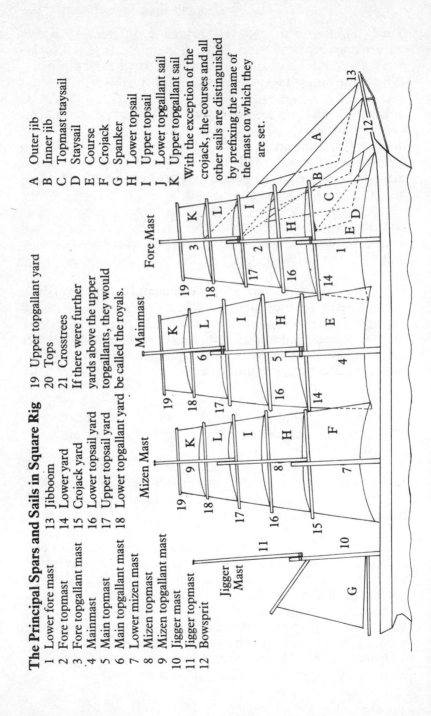

SQUARE RIG

There is a simple logic to the naming of the yards and sails in square rig. It is based upon two principles. The first is that the masts are built up in sections, lower mast, topmast, top-gallant mast, royal mast, and, in some cases, a skysail mast above the royal. The second is that all the sails, with the exception of those on the lower masts, take their names from the section of mast to which their yards are attached. So, a square sail set on the main topmast will be known as the main topsail, and one set on the fore royal mast is known as the fore royal. The sails on the lower masts are known collectively as the courses, with the foremast's course being known as the foresail, the mainmast's course being known as the mainsail, and that of the mizzen as the cross jack or crojack.

Up until about the 1860s when crews began to be reduced to help compete with steamers, all ships were rigged with single topsails. As crews became smaller, these sails were too large for them to handle, and were divided into two, the upper and lower topsails. In the 1870s, as crews became even smaller, the top-gallants were similarly divided.

APPENDIX 1 SAFETY EQUIPMENT

The following is the minimum requirement to be carried by yachts as recommended by the Offshore Racing Council.

2 Fire extinguishers. Accessible, and in different places.
2 Manually-operated bilge pumps. Not discharging into the cockpit, and with handles attached by a lanyard.
2 Buckets. Of strong construction, and fitted with lanyards.
2 Anchors and cables.
2 Flashlights. Water resistant, and one capable of being used for signalling. With spare bulbs and batteries.
1 First Aid kit and manual.
1 Foghorn.
1 Radar reflector.
1 Set International Code Flags and Code book.
1 Set emergency navigation lights and power source.
1 Storm trysail.
1 Storm jib.
1 Emergency tiller.
1 Tool kit. Including adequate means of severing the standing rigging in an emergency.
1 Marine radio transmitter and receiver. With emergency antenna if the main antenna depends upon the mast.
1 Radio receiver capable of receiving weather forecasts.
Lifejackets sufficient for the entire crew, which must each have a light and whistle attached.
Safety harnesses with safety lines sufficient for the entire crew.
1 Liferaft. Capable of carrying the entire crew, and not exceeding 40 kgs in weight. If a large crew is carried this may entail carrying more than one liferaft. The liferaft shall be stowed so that it can be carried to the rail within 15 seconds. The liferaft must have:
  Two separate buoyancy compartments.
  Canopy to cover the occupants.
  Valid annual test certificate.
  Sea anchor or drogue.
  Bellows or pump to maintain air in chambers.
  A signalling light.
  3 Hand flares.
  Baler.

Repair Kit.
2 Paddles.
Knife.
Provision of emergency water and rations.

2 Life rings. Both fitted with drogues and self-igniting lights. One must also be fitted with a whistle, dye marker, pole, which will fly a flag at least 6 feet (1.8 m) above the water, and be permanently attached to the lifering by 25 feet (8 m) of floating line.

1 Set of distress signals. In a waterproof container, and including:

12 Red parachute flares.

4 Red hand flares.

4 White hand flares.

2 Orange smoke day signals.

1 Buoyant heaving line. At least 50 feet (16 m) in length.

APPENDIX 2   RADAR REFLECTORS

The increased use of and reliance upon radar at sea has meant that it is now stupid to set out on a voyage without a radar reflector.

The principle of radar is that a radio wave is transmitted by a radar set via its scanner or aerial, and when this radio wave strikes an object, some of it is reflected back and picked up by the scanner, and appears on the screen as a blip. The strength of the blip, and therefore the chances of it being seen, depend upon the strength of the returning radio wave. The larger the target, or the better its reflectiveness, the more radio waves are going to be returned. Large metal ships have a large reflective capability, but small boats do not. Although radar waves bend slightly around the surface of the earth, the radar horizon is normally only about 117 per cent of the visible horizon. Thus, if a small boat wants to be seen in plenty of time by a ship equipped with radar, it needs to be able to provide a good reflective surface as high up as possible.

For years, the standard radar reflector has been the octahedral reflector which is basically three metal plates slotted together at right angles to each other. This reflector creates eight corners, known as re-entrant trihedrals, which will return a very high proportion of a radar wave which strikes them on their centre-line. The strength of the reflected wave decreases away from the centre-line. Thus a standard octahedral reflector, which has been properly hoisted in the 'catchwater' position, provides six good reflection sectors, with diminished performance in between. It is also a nuisance in the rigging of a boat, as it can catch the sails and halyards with its sharp edges.

A far more efficient type of reflector has been developed, which consists of many more re-entrant trihedrals and therefore a more consistent return of radar waves around the horizon. As these metal reflectors are encased in a watertight plastic container, they have less wind resistance, and do less damage aloft, in addition to giving a much better performance.

Radar Reflectors

Standard octahedral in correct position

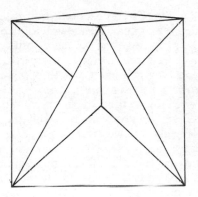

More efficient type of reflector

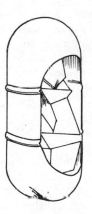

APPENDIX 3   COMPASS CORRECTION

Normally, a boat's compass will be magnetic and not a gyro. This means that the compass needle will line up with the magnetic lines of force passing through the binnacle position. These lines of force will normally be a combination of the earth's and the ship's magnetic fields, and they will exert an effect which will cause the compass needle to be deflected to the east or west of true north.

The deflection caused by the earth's magnetic field is known as variation, and is given on most charts. The effect of the ship's magnetic field is known as deviation, and this is reduced or compensated for by applying small magnets close to the compass to provide an equal and opposite effect. This operation is usually done by a specialised compass adjuster who will 'swing' the compass by turning the boat through 360 degrees whilst the boat is on a known transit ashore.

By noting the compass bearing of the transit when the boat's head by the compass is on north, north-east, east, south-east and so on, and then adding or subtracting the variation depending upon whether the variation is east or west, the deviation on each of these headings can be calculated. The adjuster will then place the boat on the east and then west heading, and add fore and aft magnets until the deviation on these headings is eliminated. Next, the boat will be put on the north and south heading, and athwart magnets added until the deviation is eliminated. Finally it will be checked again on east and west, and then swung completely. In an ideal world, the compass error should now be equal to the earth's variation on all headings, but in practice a small error usually remains and the adjuster will supply a deviation card which will show these errors. The deviation curve should be a sine curve.

On larger craft, the compass may be fitted with two spheres, one on each side athwart the compass. These are to correct the effect of the earth's lines of force on the structure of a boat, and will normally be found only on steel boats, or boats with steel wheelhouses. This induced magnetic effect will change as the boat alters her heading, and therefore the angle which the lines of force make to the structure. To find this error, the boat is headed on the inter-cardinal points of the compass (north-east, south-east, south-west, and north-west) and the spheres moved in and out on their brackets until the deviation is removed. This correction will be made roughly at the beginning of the adjustment, and re-checked after the cardinal corrections have been made.

Only on large boats, with the wheelhouse forward of amidships, will a Flinders Bar be found. It is used to correct induced magnetic fields in the fore-and-aft plane, such as are caused by a funnel just abaft the wheelhouse. The compass adjuster will estimate the amount of correction required from experience, and place soft metal inside the Flinders Bar to suit. The correction metal in the Flinders Bar should never be tampered with as, if it is inaccurate, it will vary its effect with magnetic latitude.

As a rule, the correcting magnets on the compass should be left alone. If, however, the boat has been left for a prolonged period tied up, the earth's magnetic lines of force will induce magnetic fields into the metal parts of the boat, which can have a permanent effect bearing in mind that one way of magnetising metal is to leave it lying for a long period in the same position in a magnetic field. The seaman should check the compass by swinging the boat through 360 degrees and see what sort of errors there are. Apply the variation to establish the deviation. If the deviation is small, say up to 7 or 8 degrees, leave well alone, and use this deviation until a qualified compass adjuster can be found. If the resulting deviation is large, or the deviation curve is not close to a sine curve, have the compass checked at once, and before putting out to sea. Only if there is no adjuster available should the seaman adjust the compass himself.

The only adjustments that should need to be made are to the fore and aft and athwart magnets, and the simple procedure is as follows:

1. Swing the boat through 360 degrees on a known transit, noting the bearings of the transit on the cardinal and inter-cardinal points.
2. Apply the variation to give the compass error.
3. Place the boat on an east or west heading, and adjust the fore and aft magnets to eliminate the error.
4. Place the boat on a north or south heading, and adjust the athwart magnets to remove the error.
5. Go back onto an east or west heading and remove half of any error found by adjusting the fore and aft magnets again.
6. Go back on the north or south heading and remove half of any error found by adjusting the athwart magnets again.
7. Swing the compass again, checking it on all cardinal and inter-cardinal points, noting the bearings, and then draw up a deviation card.

Important points to remember are as follows:

a) The correct bearing of the transit will be the true bearing adjusted for variation; this is known as the magnetic bearing.
b) If the deviation curve is offset to one side or another, then the compass is not in line with the fore-and-aft line of the boat.

c) Take regular checks of the compass by means of transits, sun, moon or star azimuths and log the results as a record, in case the error changes.
d) Have the compass swung properly by an adjuster at the earliest opportunity.

APPENDIX 4 WATER

Before embarking on a long voyage or at the beginning of the season, the water tanks should be cleaned. It is not always necessary to physically wipe out the tanks, and on some tanks it is not even possible to do this because no opening of sufficient size has been put in (although it should have been). Once the tank has been pumped, re-fill it with fresh water and add some potassium permanganate to the water. Alternatively you can use chloride of lime, or chlorinated lime. If the exact measurement is not shown on the tin, use 1 grain per 1½ gallons water. (Chloride of lime is known as calx chlorinata in the USA and chlorure de chaux in France.) These are double the usual mixtures and should be left in the tank for a few days. It will not matter if you leave them in longer, and I have often put the mixture into the tank when laying up and left it there all winter. The chemicals kill off anything that has grown in the tank. When the chemicals have completed their job, pump the tank completely, re-fill with plain fresh water, and pump it out again. This flushes out the tank and cleans it ready to take the new supply.

Drinking water should be clear, almost colourless, and should bubble freely when shaken. However, even water that corresponds to these requirements can contain germs or disease, and always ask about the quality of the water if in doubt. If still worried use a purifying agent.

Chloride of lime is a cheap and effective agent and easily available, but there are plenty of other proprietary purifiers from most chemists. It is worth putting some in the tank, just as a precaution whenever taking on water. One simple method if nothing else is available is to use vinegar or old wine, about one bottle per 15 gallons of water. It will kill most foreign bodies and is not known to harm humans.

The quality of fresh water varies from place to place. An excellent guide is the British Admiralty Pilot, and even if the Pilot is out of date, the basic source of water will not have changed too much. Some places are renowned for their bad water, either due to the taste or because it contains impurities. Try to avoid taking water in these places and if you have no choice, always boil it before use even if you have added purifying tablets. Always make sure that the delivery hose is clean and does not taint the water.

Bottled water is much more readily available these days and is excellent for a long voyage. If you are unhappy about the water supply, soft carbonated drinks which are available nearly everywhere make a good substitute for all purposes bar cooking.

When calculating the minimum quantity of water in gallons required for a voyage, multiply the number of crew by the number of days you expect to be at sea (plus a safety margin) and divide by two. This gives half a gallon per person per day for all purposes. It is not a lavish ration, and if you can take more, it is always worth doing so. The minimum allowance should be a quart (two pints) a day.

Always ensure that there is a container of water in addition to the tank supply. This is the reserve in case the tank becomes tainted, or the crew have to take to the life-raft.

Water can be obtained from rainfall, and it is usually good to drink. The best way of catching it is in the sails, and if the boom is topped up the water will run down to the gooseneck making it easier to collect. New Terylene sails will give the rain water an unpleasant taste, but the water is otherwise perfectly drinkable. It is always worth allowing the first minute or two of rain to run away to wash off the sail.

Rain at sea is generally more likely in unsettled areas such as the Doldrums and Westerly Trades in the North Atlantic, and in the Roaring Forties where there are a succession of depressions. It is much less likely in the North-East and South-East Trade wind belts. It is quite possible to obtain all fresh water requirements from rain, as long as it can be stored for use in the 'dry' belts. I managed 8½ months at sea like this.

In emergency, a survival ration of one glass of water per day will sustain life and the ability to work. Do not allow anyone to drink sea water – it will cause a raging thirst.

APPENDIX 5 FOOD

On a long ocean voyage, the disciplines of tidiness, cleanliness, preservation and conservation of gear, food, water and equipment are imperative. The crew must have impressed upon them that nothing can be replaced until the destination is reached, and profligate consumption of stores in the early part of the voyage can lead to shortages and even distress before the voyage is completed. If supplies run short, institute rationing early rather than at the last moment. It is always possible to increase rations if the situation improves, but never possible to invent more food. If rationing becomes necessary, ensure that the food is evenly distributed, and that no-one steals. Nothing upsets a crew more that the feeling that someone is cheating or receiving favoured treatment. Any normal person can manage quite adequately without food for a day, and one day without food tends to reduce the appetite. If there is plenty of water, or it can be caught from rain squalls, then the diet can be supplemented by fresh fish. Do not eat raw fish unless there is a plentiful supply of fresh water. Fish is protein rich, and too much protein is damaging. Water is needed to wash the surplus protein out of the system.

As a last resort, one can try and attract the attention of a passing ship for supplies, but this should only be attempted when it is obvious that the voyage cannot be completed with the existing stocks. Merchant ships, when cruising, take quite a long time to switch to manoeuvring on their engines, particularly diesel-engined ships, as they use a heavier oil for cruising which can only be used for manoeuvring in emergencies. You should not get too close to the ship as its wash can cause the boat to slew wildly. If conditions permit, row across to collect stores. This is how I collected stores in mid-Atlantic, and we boarded by means of a pilot ladder. If the sea conditions do not permit launching a boat, ask the merchant ship to throw half-filled containers of water into the sea as these will float and can be picked up. Similarly, food in plastic bags which have plenty of air enclosed will float.

Feeding on a boat is often treated rather haphazardly, which is a serious mistake. The provision of good wholesome meals is as important as good sails to the successful and safe prosecution of the voyage. The crew will have more muscular exercise than they would usually expect ashore, and they need the fuel from food as energy to put into sailing the boat. An underfed crew tire more quickly, feel the cold more easily, and are more susceptible to depression and complaints. Apart from their essential nutritional value, meals give a break from the normal sailing of the boat, and good varied meals provide something to anticipate which is good for morale.

The basic essentials are cereals, vegetables and fruit; the body will function indefinitely on these. It cannot do the same on meat alone, so meat must be balanced with the other food for a good diet. Ideally meals should combine all four.

It helps to have meals at about the same time each day. It is also a very pleasant custom to brew a hot drink for the oncoming watch, particularly at night as not only does it cheer them as they come on deck, it also means that they are more likely to arrive on watch punctually!

Whenever possible, live off fresh food, and always take the opportunity to re-stock with fresh provisions in port. Be selective about the fresh food you purchase, as apart from the smell of decomposing food, bad food can cause severe stomach upsets, and affect other provisions.

Meat It is always good to start the voyage with fresh meat but, particularly in hot climates, it needs to be purchased carefully and then cooked and consumed immediately. If you are lucky enough to carry a deep-freeze on board, then of course there is no problem. A sealed container of dry ice can help to keep meat fresh for a reasonable time, particularly in cooler climates. If in any doubt with fresh meat, always discard it at once. Tinned meat is the usual standby for voyages of more than a day or so where there are no refrigeration facilities available, although in certain countries the choice is, sadly, very limited.

Fish Usually the smell tells you whether the fish is fresh, but fish should be firm to the touch, and the skin and eyes bright and glistening. All tainted fish is dangerous to eat, so if fresh fish is brought on board, or caught, eat it quickly. Most pelagic fishes are edible and dorado dolphin and members of the tunny family are particularly good to eat. Flying fish can be very tasty, and it is always worth checking the decks in the morning to see if any are available when sailing in the areas where they are found. Shark can be eaten; it is a little coarse, and needs to be soaked in salt water for about 24 hours to remove the ammonia from the flesh. It is usually possible, with a little luck, to catch something in whatever waters you are sailing.

Eggs Eggs will last a few weeks in their normal state, but if they need to be kept for longer they should be coated with beeswax, lard, grease, or stored in a preservative such as waterglass. Always check egg containers for bugs, particularly when the eggs are bought in hot countries. Eggs should be given cool and dry storage. If the eggs are doubtful, break them individually into a separate container.

Canned food If canned food is to remain on board for more than a month, each can should be marked with paint so that its contents can be recognised when the label is removed. Can labels do not last for long in a boat and clog the bilges, so remove them once the cans are marked. The cans should be treated with some form of protective coating before being stowed, a thorough coat of varnish being as good as anything.

In order to check whether the contents of a tin are still in good condition, start by examining the ends. If they are concave all is probably well, but if convex, some pressure has pushed out the ends and it is usually gases caused by decomposition. In this case throw away the can. If in doubt, immerse the tin in water and pierce it, if gas comes out the contents are bad. If the contents have a disagreeable smell when the tin is opened, it is safest to throw the contents away.

In hot weather, the contents of some cans, particularly meats with fat, will liquefy. This does not mean the contents are bad, but check the smell.

Vegetables Vegetables must be kept dry and aired. Greens such as lettuce and cabbage have a limited life, whereas roots such as carrots, potatoes and onions, will last a considerable time if well stowed. Netting hung from a bulkhead or deckhead is an excellent method of storing vegetables. Some vegetables, onions for instance, can often be purchased in open net sacks which allow good ventilation, and the sack has only to be turned daily to ensure this. New potatoes do not keep for as long as old.

Vegetables should be inspected regularly, and any that look as if they are going bad should be thrown away, as once rotting starts, it will quickly spread to good produce.

Always wash vegetables bought from a dirty market with fresh water containing a few grains of potassium permanganate, then wash in clean fresh water and leave to dry before stowing. In warm dry conditions at sea, it is well worth bringing the vegetables on deck for a good dry airing. It is always interesting in foreign ports to sample new exotic vegetables and fruit, but wash well if you are eating them raw.

Bread Bread should be kept well aired. It will last up to ten days if properly stored, and even then, if the mildew is cut off, the bread can be toasted. It is possible to obtain specially baked long-lasting bread, but if this is not available, make sure that there is a plentiful supply of biscuits on board.

Butter, fats, etc These need cool dry stowage. If left in a hot place, they will melt and go rancid. Butter and margarine can be purchased in tins which will keep indefinitely if stowed in a cool spot. It is usually better to buy cooking oil than lard.

Milk Fresh milk only lasts a day or two, so when possible buy long life. Also carry a good supply in powdered or canned form.